LEABHARLANNA CHONTAE FHINE GALL
FINGAL COUNTY LIBRARIES

Items should be returned on or before the last date shown below. Items may be renewed by personal application, writing, telephone or by accessing the online Catalogue Service on Fingal Libraries' website. To renew give date due, borrower ticket number and PIN number if using online catalogue. Fines are charged on overdue items and will include postage incurred in recovery. Damage to, or loss of items will be charged to the borrower.

Date Due	Date Due	Date Due
29/07/R	Blanchardstown Library Ph: 8905563	
14 Dec		

The Author

A Senior Lecturer at the School of Sociology and Philosophy, University College Cork, one of Niamh Hourigan's areas of specialisation is mapping the sociological impact of debt and austerity on the Irish middle class. A frequent commentator on national media on these subjects, she has written for *The Irish Independent, The Irish Times* and *The Irish Examiner* and contributes to 'Prime Time', 'Tonight with Vincent Browne' and 'Morning Ireland', among others.

Praise for *Rule-breakers*

'Niamh Hourigan's probing, perceptive and highly readable exploration of the Irish value system that led to the collapse of the Celtic Tiger should be required reading for anyone seeking to fully understand the roots of the catastrophe.'
J.J. Lee, New York University

'Lucid, engaging and persuasive, Niamh Hourigan's *Rule-breakers* digs out the cultural and historical roots of the Irish banking, economic and political crises that the country has been mired in since 2008. She traces these crises to a centuries-old aversion to rules in Irish culture and a deep-seated cultural bias that prioritises relationships. From Cromwell to corruption, from Parnell to penalty points, she teases out how a unique and delicate balance between rules and relationships evolved in Irish culture, and how that balance disintegrated in recent decades. Every politician should read this – and so should every voter.'
Colin Murphy, writer of *The Guarantee*

'Compulsively readable and teases out the €60 billion question, debated furiously wherever thinking Irish people are gathered. Did our own value system ultimately sweep us to economic disaster? Did the culture of "being there" versus "being fair" finally catch up with us? We may not like the answer, but in a work that takes us all the way from colonialism to Michael Lowry, we can begin to understand ourselves.'
Kathy Sheridan, *The Irish Times*

RULE-BREAKERS

Why 'Being There' Trumps 'Being Fair'
in Ireland

NIAMH HOURIGAN

Gill & Macmillan

Gill & Macmillan
Hume Avenue, Park West, Dublin 12
www.gillmacmillanbooks.ie

© Niamh Hourigan 2015
978 07171 6620 6

Index compiled by Eileen O'Neill
Typography design by Make Communication
Print origination by Síofra Murphy
Printed and bound by CPI Group (UK) Ltd, CR0 4YY

This book is typeset in Minion 12/15.5 pt.

The paper used in this book comes from the wood pulp of managed forests. For every tree felled, at least one tree is planted, thereby renewing natural resources.

A CIP catalogue record for this book is available from the British Library.

5 4 3 2 1

CONTENTS

ACKNOWLEDGMENTS

This book emerged from the ashes of several abandoned research projects which made me feel that my own research was heading the same way as the Irish economy at the time of the banking crisis. The fact that the book finally made it to publication is due to the support of many people. First, I would like to thank all the team at Gill & Macmillan, including Conor Nagle, Deborah Marsh, Teresa Daly, Deirdre Rennison Kunz and copy-editor Jane Rogers. My colleagues at UCC must also be thanked, especially Dr Kieran Keohane and Prof. Patrick O'Donovan. Support in different forms was also provided by Prof. Sinisa Malesevic (UCD), Prof. Luke Gibbons (NUI Maynooth), Prof. Martin Mac an Ghaill (Birmingham), Prof. Eoin O'Sullivan (TCD), Dr Geraldine Moane (UCD) and Prof. Des McCafferty (Mary Immaculate College, Limerick). I am especially grateful to Helen O'Sullivan and Ciara Breathnach, who read drafts of individual chapters, and Deirdre O'Riordain, who assisted with the first stage of interview research.

My colleagues in the Irish media gave me lots of opportunities to road-test my ideas as well as the chance to debate them with those who profoundly disagreed with me, so I would like to thank them. My family, especially my parents, Michael and Patricia, and my siblings, Conor, Sinead, Neasa, Brian and Kate, must be thanked for listening to me worry about this book at one point or another. My partner, Seamus, provided unwavering support and continued to have faith in me and the project even when I lost heart. Finally, the book is dedicated to my own two little rule-breakers, my children, Curtis and Isabel, who every day teach me more and more about 'being fair', 'being there' and 'being good'.

NH

| INTRODUCTION

Ireland's Crisis and Social Bonds

Will everything be okay? I've been waking up with that question on my mind, going to sleep with it, ignoring it, remembering it, trying to forget. The question reminds me of problems I have yet to solve. Mistakes I have made. Uncertainties. Fears. Missed opportunities. Stupid me. Stupidity. The question brings me to my knees, back to childhood, to that desperate innocent craving for certainty and security that never comes. Will everything be okay?[1]

I t seemed in early 2011 that everyone in the country was feeling the same sense of panic that Róisín Ingle wrote about in her *Irish Times* diary. In November 2010, under the threat of impending financial collapse, the Irish government accepted a bailout of the Irish banking system which involved handing over economic sovereignty to an international Troika made up of the European Central Bank (ECB), International Monetary Fund (IMF) and European Union (EU). In exchange for the bailout, the state had to agree to a programme of public service cutbacks and new taxes which would hit almost all sectors of Irish society hard.[2]

Ordinary people's financial circumstances were already declining dramatically. Newspaper headlines from the period give a flavour of the situation: 'Repossessions at all-time high and crisis expected to get worse';[3] 'GAA losing 250 players a month to emigration';[4] 'Suicides now rampant in rural areas, warns coroner.'[5] It was a rapid and frightening descent from the Celtic Tiger high, which had seen Ireland become one of the 'richest nations in the world'.[6]

While the Irish economic crash turned out to be just one piece in an international jigsaw of financial crisis,[7] the quote at the beginning of this chapter conveys two themes that appeared again and again in research interviews I was conducting at the time. First, interviewees believed that the crisis had revealed something deeply wrong in Irish society. Second, many sensed that the behaviour and values of ordinary Irish citizens had, in some way they couldn't quite define, contributed to the crisis. Although the anger towards individual politicians was palpable, it was always accompanied by phrases like, 'We lost the run of ourselves' and 'How could we not see it coming?'

At the time of the crash, a number of financial commentators published books demonstrating that relationships between small groups of powerful people in politics, banking, business and construction were at the heart of the disastrous financial decision-making which underpinned the crisis.[8] In *Ship of Fools*, Fintan O'Toole notes that 'an atmosphere of insider intimacy in which cronyism thrived continued to hang over boom-time Ireland' and he traces how this intimacy contributed to the property bubble that was central to the collapse of the Irish economy.[9] In Ireland's over-heating property market, ordinary people were lent large amounts of money at very low interest rates to buy houses and apartments sold at inflated prices. These transactions, which were facilitated by the Irish banks, benefited property developers, builders and the politicians who drew on their support. The inter-elite relationships underpinning this bubble were copper-fastened in places like the Fianna Fáil hospitality tent at the Galway races, where 'insider intimacy' was deliberately cultivated.[10]

At the same time the Irish government commissioned a series of expert reports on the causes of the crisis. These experts – Klaus Regling and Max Watson (2010), Patrick Honohan (2010) and Peter Nyberg (2011) – agreed that weak rules and poor regulation by institutions such as the Central Bank, the Office of the Financial Regulator and the Department of Finance had contributed to the collapse of the economy.[11] Describing what he called 'boom-time Ireland', Peter Nyberg observes, 'adhering to either formal or traditional, often voluntary rules, constraints and limits on banking and finance, does not seem to have been greatly valued in Ireland during the period.'[12] This indifference to rules was coupled with 'very specific and serious breaches of basic governance principles' which had not been challenged by regulators of corporate governance in the Irish state.[13] The same politicians who pressed the flesh at the Galway races had a prominent role in constructing and maintaining these weak rules, which largely benefited individuals and groups in their own circles. Consequently, by the end of 2011 there was already a consensus that weak rules and strong relationships had played a causal role in the Irish financial crisis.

Both the expert reports and the books tended to focus exclusively on the behaviour of political and financial elites. Unsurprisingly, the elites themselves were unwilling to accept all the blame. They suggested that the behaviour of ordinary Irish people had contributed to the crash, tapping into an anxiety evident in Ingle's piece. In a robust interview on RTÉ's *Prime Time* in 2010, the late Minister for Finance Brian Lenihan said, 'Let's be fair about it, we all partied.' The implication was that everyone had enjoyed the benefits of the Celtic Tiger boom and now they had to pay the price.[14]

After the general election of February 2011, the new Taoiseach, Enda Kenny, insisted in his pre-budget address, 'Let me say this to you all. You are not responsible for the crisis.' However, by early 2012, he appeared to have changed his mind, telling the World Economic Forum in Davos, 'What happened in our country was that people simply went mad borrowing.'[15]

Of course, both Lenihan and Kenny were right – up to a point. Many ordinary Irish people had invested heavily in property and spent a lot of money on consumer goods during the Celtic Tiger boom.[16] But it was the precarious balance between weak rules and strong relationships amongst Ireland's most powerful interest groups that allowed the property boom and consumer spending to spiral out of control.[17]

In examining the question of how much responsibility ordinary Irish people bear for the financial crisis, this book focuses on a deeper question. How much is the 'weak rules/strong relationships' balance a reflection of the value system of ordinary Irish people? And has this balance changed in response to the pain inflicted on so many Irish people by the austerity process?

RULES AND RELATIONSHIPS

Rules (principles governing conduct) and relationships (ties between two or more people) are found in all societies.[18] Human beings are social; they need each other to survive. Prehistoric people recognised that it was safer to live in groups and that methods of growing food that couldn't be achieved alone were possible with other people.[19] People who live in groups have a range of different ways of being tied to each other, from formal legal contracts to sexual relationships.[20]

When St Patrick came to Ireland in the early fifth century, he encountered communities where relationships were, by and large, more important than rules. People lived together in family-based groups or clans and a person's position in the hierarchy depended on their relationship to the clan leader.[21] This clan-based social structure was mirrored throughout Europe. Rules were few and, because administrative government had not developed to a great extent, they were difficult to enforce. As bureaucratic structures developed from the Middle Ages onwards, rules became much more important in the lives of ordinary Europeans.[22] Two of the founding fathers of sociology, Max Weber and Émile Durkheim, have written about this transition from relationship-oriented to rule-oriented societies, noting that as societies develop, rules tend to dominate over relationships.[23]

Durkheim also argued that relationship-dominated societies define good and bad behaviour in a different way from rule-dominated societies.[24] In relationship-dominated societies, a good person is the person who keeps faith with their obligations to other members of their social group. The good person is the one who is 'there' for other people. The bad person is the one who ignores these kinds of obligations. In rule-dominated societies, rules are generally enforced by institutions which are supposed to apply them in the same way to everyone. This approach creates systems that are fair. In this type of society, a good person obeys the rules not only because they want to conform but also because obeying the rules upholds this fairness.[25] A person who breaks the rules is seen as bad not only because their actions are wrong but also because they are undermining the fairness of rule-based systems.[26]

Historical experiences – wars and colonialism, for example – and cultural factors, such as religion, help to determine whether rules or relationships dominate in shaping how a society defines good and bad behaviour. This means that the way rules and relationships are interwoven is different in every society, and this creates a unique pattern, rather like a fingerprint. This book aims to map this fingerprint in Irish culture and to explore how it contributed to the Irish financial crisis and the subsequent period of austerity. Identifying this pattern is a complex task. A starting point was provided for me by an elderly lady, Sadie,[27] whom I interviewed in County Cork. She told me the following story about her brother, John Joe, in the 1970s.

> John Joe would have been a real leader in the local community and he was working for the Department [of Agriculture] running some experiment for the EEC. A group of local farmers had to get up at five and feed their calves this particular grain. I think at the end of it, some of them would get a special grant. Anyway, he found out that one local farmer was fiddling the scheme by giving the animals drugs. John Joe was in an awful state about it. If he reported this farmer, everyone would know it was him that did it. But if he didn't report him, then he had to live with the fact that the results of this experiment would be totally wrong and all his neighbours were getting up at cockcrow for nothing. In the end, John Joe decided to tell the Department. He just couldn't look at his neighbours being made fools of. The funny thing was after that, John Joe was sort of boycotted in the local community. Nobody would chat to him after Mass and he stopped going to the pub. I think they felt that he'd betrayed one of his own to outsiders.

At the heart of John Joe's dilemma were two competing visions of how to be good. A relationship-based vision of good behaviour demands that the individual is there for others in their community and that 'being there' takes precedence over the rules. A rule-based vision of good behaviour dictates that keeping the rules is more important than keeping faith with local relationships. In the end, John Joe chose the rule-based vision of good behaviour and reported the farmer to the Department. However, his neighbours didn't support his decision and ostracised him. John Joe's choice didn't tally with their value system, which prioritised relationships. This is ironic given that part of his rationale for reporting the wrongdoing was his guilt about his neighbours 'being made fools of', which shows that he valued relationships as well as rules.

This story illustrates the delicate tension between rules and relationships in Ireland that will be explored in this book. The first chapter examines the historical experiences that have shaped the balance between these rules and relationships in Irish culture. The way in which colonialism generated a distrust of rules and a leaning towards relationships is contrasted with the close adherence to rules promoted by the Roman Catholic Church and the Irish democratic nationalist movements of the nineteenth century. After the foundation of the Irish state in 1922, relationships remained an important feature of Irish culture. Chapter 2 shows how, under the pressure of modernisation in the 1960s and beyond, the relationships that bound Irish citizens together began to loosen, and top-down ruling systems began to take their place. Despite these changes, a relationship-based vision of good behaviour has continued to be an important part of the Irish value system. This vision is particularly evident in the widespread popular use of the term 'our own' to describe relationship-based groups to which Irish people have obligations, and this is explored in Chapter 3. Chapter 4 argues that rules and relationships not only shape a sense of belonging to 'our own' but generate two different understandings of reality. These distinct understandings of reality generate contrasting approaches to trust, communication and conflict as well as different visions of good and bad behaviour.

Chapter 5 considers how these two understandings shape the way ordinary Irish citizens engage with politicians and examines how constituency work helps build relationships between politicians and voters. Chapter 6 traces the emergence of elite-level relationships between business leaders and politicians since the 1960s and argues that it is a parasitic offshoot of these same behaviours and understandings that governs intimacy between politicians and ordinary voters. Chapter 7 explores whether Irish attitudes to rules and relationships have changed since the bailout. Research conducted during the 2011–2013 period demonstrates that austerity has, in fact, reinforced a range of negative attitudes to rules that centre on their perceived unfairness. This resentment of unfair rules persists, despite popular anger at the corruption of bankers and politicians that provoked the financial crisis.

The book concludes by arguing that the everyday culture of 'pull' and 'favours' has created a blind spot in this Irish value system, a blind spot that elites have exploited for their own benefit. This blind spot, which prioritises 'being there' over 'being fair', was generated as a result of colonialism, but has failed to adapt to the reality of Ireland's economic modernisation. The first generation of Irish political leaders had a very negative view of corruption,[28] but they created a political culture in which relationships were incredibly important.[29] After modernisation in the 1960s, a generation of entrepreneurs used this emphasis on intimacy to build relationships with the political elite which supported their own interests but not necessarily the interests of all Irish citizens.[30] Because their actions were embedded in a value system that views meeting obligations in relationships as good, the Irish state and ordinary Irish people have been slow to create rules to restrain and balance these relationships.

STUDYING SOCIAL BONDS IN IRELAND

While plenty of sociological research has been carried out on family and community in Ireland over the last seventy years,[31] few studies have examined how the value placed on relationships in Irish culture has shaped visions of good and bad behaviour.[32] Research for this book took more than six years and was carried out in three stages. Between

February and July 2008 – before the bailout – 36 lower middle-class and middle-class Irish citizens in Cork, Dublin and Limerick were interviewed about their attitudes to immigrants.[33] I subsequently spoke with 25 working immigrants about their experiences of living in Ireland.[34] Although rules and relationships were not originally the major themes of the research, they were discussed so frequently by both groups that I began to consider making this tension the major focus of my study.

The second stage of the research was carried out in very different circumstances. In October 2010, I held four focus groups with recently unemployed Irish middle-class people, a group the Irish media were beginning to call the 'squeezed middle' or the 'coping classes'.[35] I also revisited 11 of the immigrants I had interviewed two years earlier.[36] I found a heightened sense of 'them and us' and a new defensiveness towards immigrants who were seen as taking *our* jobs. Participants expressed increasing panic about the deteriorating state of the Irish economy and concerns about how the crisis was being managed by politicians and senior government officials.

At the time of the bailout in November and December 2010, the anger towards political and financial elites became palpable. With an election looming in February 2011, I decided to broaden my research to include an investigation of rules and relationships in Irish politics. I added North Tipperary and Laois as research locations. North Tipperary offered the opportunity to study the case of Michael Lowry TD who, despite being publicly castigated in the report of a Tribunal of Inquiry, continued to be re-elected by voters in this constituency.[37] County Laois's estimated 18 ghost estates, the most visible physical legacy of the Irish property bubble, offered the opportunity to study the impact of austerity more closely.[38] These unfinished housing projects were largely populated by middle- and lower middle-class families headed by individuals aged between 35 and 45, the demographic group most affected by austerity.[39] Many of these families were struggling with all the major problems associated with the recession, including mortgage arrears and unemployment.[40] In total, 35 interviews were conducted during this stage of the research. I also began attending meetings of new political movements such as Democracy Now, the National Forum and the United Left Alliance in order to map how Irish political culture was being transformed by the crisis.[41]

The final and longest stage of the research was carried out between July 2012 and December 2013. By this time, the anger and panic of the earlier austerity period had subsided into a resigned cynicism that seemed immune to the early signs of economic recovery. This stage focused primarily on Irish attitudes towards rules and explored the sense of injustice that many people in the Irish middle classes expressed about the way the austerity process had been managed. I began by organising five focus groups on the theme of 'Rules and Austerity' and then conducted 41 individual interviews with ordinary citizens on the same theme. I also interviewed 13 politicians at local, national and European level, as well as five experts in debt management.[42] A key objective of this part of the research was to assess whether austerity had changed the delicate balance between rules and relationships in Irish culture.[43] In total, 166 interviews and nine focus groups were conducted over the six-year period of research for this book.

CONCLUSION

The Irish political culture that led to the property bubble and the bank guarantee was a product of the weak rules/strong relationships tension that operates not only at the highest levels of Irish society but also at its most ordinary levels. This tension has a profound impact on how people behave and how they judge the behaviour of others.

In investigating the link between the value system of ordinary Irish people and the corruption that preceded the bailout, I am not blaming Irish citizens for the financial crisis or the austerity process that followed. The expert reports and journalistic accounts of this period have given us clear evidence of where the blame for the crisis lies. It is possible that whatever policies the Irish government pursued during the 2002–2007 period, Ireland would still have experienced a period of recession after the 2008 global banking crisis. But the strategies of government and financial elites during this period resulted in Irish austerity being more traumatic and painful than it might have been if the rules had been stronger and the intimacy more restrained. These disastrous financial decisions were taken in a democratic society in which ordinary people had a role in selecting the political leaders who made them. These voters selected politicians who perpetuated this system of intimacy in face of sustained evidence of the damage it was doing to the Irish economy, *evidence which was available prior to the bailout.*[44]

Why did this evidence not produce a sustained demand for regulatory reform and more restrained intimacy? In answering this question, this book suggests that we must look to the value system of ordinary Irish people. This system contains two competing visions of good and bad behaviour, one based on rules and the other on relationships. Irish people are inclined to view rules as inherently unfair and operating in favour of elites, a view that has been reinforced by the deep inequity that characterised the framing of rules during the austerity process. As a consequence, an intimacy- or relationship-based vision of good behaviour which stresses the importance of 'being there' for others in circles of intimacy (groups often described as 'our own') has dominated. What this model fails to recognise is that since Ireland's integration into global capitalism, 'our own' has changed. At the top of 'our own' is a group whose wealth is based on the capacity to extract resources from everyone else. This group has used intimacy to enable its wealth-gathering activities, and this strategy has not been challenged effectively because it is embedded in an everyday Irish value system which prizes relationships. This intimacy lies at the heart of the celebrated warmth and friendliness of Irish culture. It also lies at the core of every corruption scandal that has bedevilled the Irish economy since the 1960s, corruption which eventually brought it crashing to its knees in 2010. Without any understanding of how this corruption has developed as a parasitic growth on everyday intimacy in Irish society, there is little chance of developing any sustained and widely supported response to the problem. 'If you always do what you've always done, you always get what you've always got.'[45] This book is an attempt to understand and break this cycle.

Chapter 1

A HISTORY OF RULES AND RELATIONSHIPS IN IRELAND

*Forgiving does not erase the bitter past. A healed memory is
not a deleted memory.*[1]

Louis B. Smedes

O ne of the few bright spots in the rather grim year of 2011 was the
visit to Ireland by Queen Elizabeth II in May. The visit, which
was both a popular and a political success, seemed to promise
that even if Ireland was in a dire financial mess, at least something
was going well. The peace process in Northern Ireland remained on
track, and the Queen's visit to the Republic provided a moment, many
thought, for healing Ireland's bitter colonial history. However, as the
pastor Louis B. Smedes succinctly notes, a history healed is not a history
deleted. Even as the Queen visited the Garden of Remembrance, some
commentators were wondering how far the roots of the financial crisis
could be traced to Ireland's colonial past. In his contribution to the
website 'Ireland after NAMA', Cian O'Callaghan commented:

> The legacy of colonialism played a key role in Celtic Tiger Ireland
> and its catastrophic aftermath. Nowhere is this more apparent than
> in the IMF/ECB bailout. Here Ireland draws closer to its spiritual
> neighbours in the post-colony than perhaps ever before … as the
> Queen visits these shores, rather than drawing divisions between
> those who have 'moved on' and those 'living in the past', perhaps
> we should be asking what this past really means for our present.[2]

Certainly, the memory of Ireland's painful colonial past appeared to have been actively shaping how both public figures and ordinary citizens responded to the crisis. When the Troika team arrived in Dublin to negotiate the terms of the bailout agreement, the 2FM DJ Hector Ó hEochagáin played the rebel song 'The Foggy Dew', especially, he said, for team leader A.J. Chopra. The implied message to the Troika contained in the song's lyrics, which describe Irish resistance to British colonialism, was not lost on Ó hEochagáin's audience even if the IMF official did not hear the programme.

This post-colonial perspective on the crisis was also evident in a political spat the following week. During a Dáil debate on the national recovery plan, Fianna Fáil TD Mattie McGrath accused his own party leader, Taoiseach Brian Cowen, of being 'worse than Cromwell'. Martin Mansergh, one of Cowen's ministers, rushed to his defence. In response, a national newspaper pointed out that Mansergh's own ancestor, Bryan Mansergh, had benefited from the Cromwellian invasion, having been given a castle by Cromwell's forces.[3] After the change of government in 2011, McGrath, who had left Fianna Fáil, continued to draw comparisons between austerity and colonialism. In a radio debate on the introduction of septic tank charges as part of the austerity programme, he commented, 'God, we got rid of the Black and Tans and Cromwell, not a bother. I don't want to wake up some morning and see two or three gentlemen in my back yard, peeping into my septic tank like the Peep O'Day boys out doing searches.'[4]

As the new taxes inflicted under austerity increased in 2012, politicians on the left of the Irish political spectrum also invoked Ireland's colonial past to justify protests. In January of that year, Clare Daly TD commented that the household charge issue 'may be the one that changes the view of the Irish from one of passive compliance with any amount of austerity thrown our way, to a reawakening of the traditions of a nation that coined the term "boycott" in the first place.'[5] Launching a campaign against austerity, socialist republican Dublin councillor Louise Minihan characterised the bailout process as a form of neo-colonialism: '[T]he goal of those who are pushing this treaty[6] is to force the further erosion of our national and economic sovereignty.

Their aim is to remove our hard fought economic rights. Ireland is now in a position of total colonial occupation. We are a colony.'[7] Although this perspective might be considered extreme, popular historian Tim Pat Coogan also saw the public response to austerity in neo-colonial terms. In his blog, he commented, 'In the case of the Famine and in today's Ireland, people are either accepting whatever burdens have been placed upon them with varying degrees of despair or they are getting out.'[8] Publicly at least, Irish government officials seemed to resist these neo-colonial parallels, but behind the scenes, the legacy of colonialism also seemed to influence their perspective. Journalist Pat Leahy of the *Sunday Business Post* described a senior government official musing in early 2013 about his ideal bailout exit scenario: 'My plan is to get the jeep that Michael Collins arrived in to Dublin Castle to accept the handover from the British in 1922. We'll put Enda and Eamonn in the back!'[9]

As the mortgage arrears crisis worsened in 2013, the fear of banks repossessing homes raised the spectre of evictions, a common feature of the colonial period. Describing legislation passed to facilitate bank repossession, Liam MacNally wrote in the *Mayo News*, 'For those of us, outside the well-paid loop and mindset of politicians and bankers, the legislation reminds us of colonialism. It transports us back on the plains of the pale ghost of history where eviction was the order of the day, Irish families ousted by the foreigner, aided and abetted by Irishmen.'[10] The Land League also cast a long shadow in County Meath, where in 2013 Jimmy McEntee, the brother of a deceased Fine Gael politician, launched a movement he described as a new 'Land League' to resist bank repossessions.[11]

International commentators on the Irish crisis also saw parallels between the austerity process and colonialism. In the *Huffington Post*, for instance, Ellen Brown commented:

The Irish have a long history of being tyrannized, exploited and oppressed – from the forced conversion to Christianity in the Dark Ages, to slave trading of the native in the 15th and 16th centuries, to the mid-nineteenth century 'potato famine' that was really a holocaust. The British got Ireland's food exports, while at least one million Irish died from starvation and related diseases, and another million or more emigrated. Today, Ireland is under a different form of tyranny, one imposed by the banks and the Troika – the EU, ECB and IMF. The oppressors have demanded austerity and more austerity, forcing the public to pick up the tab for bills incurred by profligate private bankers.[12]

Given the parallels between colonialism and the loss of economic sovereignty, it is not surprising that Ireland's bitter past came alive again during this period. Memories of the colonial period were much less evident between 2003 and 2007, although it is arguable that historical conflicts over land may have contributed to the public appetite for owning property, which in turn fuelled the spending bubble that led to Ireland's economic implosion. Official and media analyses of the causes of the crisis tended to shy away from references to the Irish colonial experience, focusing instead on the immediate failure of regulating systems and the dominance of insider intimacy linked to the weak rules/strong relationships balance. However, the repeated references to Ireland's colonial past in public discussion of the crisis suggest that colonialism may have had a particularly profound role in shaping this balance. The goal of this chapter is to search for historical evidence of this process.

COLONIALISM, RULES AND TRAUMA

At the very least, one would expect that colonisation would inform a popular distrust of rules in Irish society. In colonised societies, the rules that govern society are designed to promote the political, military and economic interests of the coloniser. In his research on British colonialism and the law, Nasser Hussain highlights that 'rules' were central to the British model of colonialism in the eighteenth and nineteenth centuries. He says: 'Government by rules became the basis for conceptualisation of the "moral legitimacy" of British colonial rule. The applicability of rules to all was understood as the distinguishing feature of British rule and counterpoint to "personal discretion".'[13]

However, British colonisers were fairly clear that it was *their* rules that mattered. Hussain quotes James Fitzjames Stephen, a legal member of the Indian Colonial Council in the 1870s, who exemplified this perspective when he stated that establishing the 'British' rule of law:

> ... constitutes in itself, a moral conquest more striking, more durable and far more solid than the physical conquest which renders it possible.... *Our* law is in fact the sum and substance of what we have to teach them. It is, so to speak, the gospel of the English and it is a compulsory gospel which admits of no dissent and no disobedience.[14]

The majority Catholic population in nineteenth-century Ireland had several problems with this viewpoint. First, many of the rules established under British colonial rule, particularly after the Act of Union in 1801, were viewed as unfair. These rules included legislation that entirely excluded Catholics from voting until 1829. They also deeply resented rules on tithing, which forced them to pay a proportion of their income for the upkeep of the Protestant Church of Ireland.[15] Arbitrary rent increases imposed by absentee landlords, and state support for evicting tenants who could not pay these rents, did little to reinforce popular confidence in the fairness of the rules.[16]

Aside from the perception that the rules were unfair, there was a widespread view that British colonial administrators were operating the rules in a corrupt fashion. Donnchadh Ó Corráin notes that the Act of Union itself was only passed because:

> Peerages, jobs and pensions were liberally promised. In Ireland, members of the Parliament were returned by boroughs which were mostly corrupt and by counties where results were almost always determined by the landlords.... Castlereagh set out to win every possible vote by promises, threats, and bribes. Support for the Union was made a pre-condition for any Government office or favour. As Castlereagh put it, his job was 'to buy out, and secure to the Crown forever', the fee simple of Irish corruption.[17]

Popular Irish resentment of unfair rules and corruption became increasingly evident towards the end of the nineteenth century, when members of the Irish Parliamentary Party were openly criticised for accepting patronage from British governments, a perception which was to contribute to the Party's downfall during the 1914–1916 period.[18]

While a popular distrust of rules is an unsurprising outcome of colonialism, the wounds of colonial oppression played a much deeper role in shaping the balance between rules and relationships in Ireland. As Hussain highlights, the process of establishing colonial rules only happens after indigenous populations have been suppressed by force. This suggests that colonialism operates, first and foremost, as a violent and abusive process of oppression. In the 1990s, historians began to draw on theories of trauma which outline the impact of abuse on individuals to understand how whole societies respond to traumatic and abusive processes such as colonisation. Historian David Lloyd comments:

> Trauma entails violent intrusion and a sense of utter objectification that annihilates the person as subject or agent. This is no less apt as a description of the effects and mechanism of colonization.... It would seem that we can map the psychological effects of trauma on to the cultures that undergo colonization. By the same token, the after-effects of colonization for a culture could be held to be identical with those for the traumatized individual.[19]

By applying this model to Irish history, we can identify a range of elements that can be considered part of the cultural trauma of colonialism which may have shaped the balance between rules and relationships in Ireland.

First, the physical violence experienced by Irish Catholics during British colonial rule, particularly during the Cromwellian era, remains a feature of Irish post-colonial memory – as evinced by Mattie McGrath's comments in late 2010. During the Cromwellian invasion in the middle of the seventeenth century, half a million Catholics died or emigrated from Ireland; and many of those who remained were dispersed to the less fertile land in the western half of the country. In Cromwell's conquest of Drogheda, four thousand people – including women and children – were killed, while two thousand were killed in Wexford. An English visitor to Ireland provided a stark image of the scale of devastation generated by this violence in the *London Chronicle* in 1652. He said, 'you may ride 20 miles and scarce discern anything or fix your eye upon any object, but dead men hanging on trees and gibbets.'[20] While scholarly debate rages as to whether the Cromwellian violence was 'unexceptional by contemporary standards',[21] or genocide,[22] Irish popular memory of this period is far less ambiguous. For instance, in his 1965 autobiography, Brendan Behan says of Cromwell:

> His actions in Drogheda and Wexford were those of a Heydrich and Himmler combined. In the town of Wexford, he massacred 200 women grouped round the Cross of the Redeemer and delighted his soldiers with the slow process of individual murder, stabbing one after another. When his soldiers were running their pikes through little babies, in between psalms, they would shout 'kill the nits and there will be no lice'.[23]

This hatred for the abuses perpetrated by Cromwellian soldiers runs right through to contemporary internet debates on Irish history typified by the thread on Politics.ie in 2007, entitled 'Oliver Cromwell was a Pimp and a Child Sex Trafficker'.[24]

But it is the memory of the Irish Famine that has been the strongest impetus for analysing British colonialism in Ireland as a form of cultural trauma. During the 2008–2013 period, there was a striking increase in popular and scholarly interest in the Famine. The *Atlas of the Great Irish Famine* provided minute regional detail on the number of deaths and highlighted horrific local accounts of starvation.[25] Alongside this scholarly work were a number of popular history books on the subject and an RTÉ radio series, *Blighted Nation*.[26] While scholarly historians debated whether the Famine was genocide, popular commentators focused more on how the legacy of the Irish Famine might be shaping responses to the contemporary trauma of the bailout. This link was clearly evident in Tim Pat Coogan's mind in 2013 when he said:

> I've been pondering the implication of a discovery I made while researching my book on the Famine, namely that one of its principal legacies to Ireland was what the psychiatrists called 'learned helplessness'. The beliefs that no matter how one tried there was nothing to do in the face of catastrophe save succumb to it or emigrate. There was no possibility of getting back at those who brought about the disaster … if one looks at the plight of modern Ireland and comments in astonishment 'and nobody is going to jail', one can be certain that the automatic knee jerk reaction will be: 'No. And nobody will go.'[27]

The parallels between Irish colonialism and the trauma of child sexual abuse are particularly strong and have been highlighted by several commentators, including singer Sinéad O'Connor and literary critic Richard Haslam.[28] Victims of both processes are either encouraged to be silent or told that the abuse is for their own good. Trauma expert Judith Herman notes:

> If secrecy fails, the perpetrator attacks the credibility of his victim.… To this end, he marshals an impressive array of arguments, from the most blatant denial to the most sophisticated and elegant rationalisation.… The more powerful the perpetrator, the greater is his prerogative to name and define reality, and the more completely his arguments prevail.[29]

Evidence of both silencing and discrediting can be identified in the Irish context. Irish language experts have shown that many of the victims of the Famine who were Irish speakers were effectively silenced in the short term through death and emigration. In the long term, the fragmentation of their language community provided few spaces to discuss their Famine trauma in the language in which it was experienced.[30]

For those who couldn't be silenced, there were some members of the colonising elite ready to convince Irish Catholics that the processes of colonisation, including the Famine, were ultimately for their own good, that their criticisms of colonialism were neither credible nor justified. In his book *The Realities of Irish Life*, published in 1868, land agent William Steuart Trench published a list of the good things that had come from the Famine, including the fact that it 'hurried free trade and hastened the arterial drainage of the rivers of Ireland'.[31] In the same year, R.M. Heron wrote:

> What was the condition of Ireland when the conquest was affected in the reign of Henry II? The people were without history or organisation. The society as compared with that of contemporary states, was of the rudest most primitive character ... From the loose way in which wrongs are imputed to England by national prejudice and foreign sympathy, one would be inclined to infer that the conclusion was that the conquest of Strong-bow had destroyed Irish civilisation. It would be much nearer the truth to say that this very conquest of Ireland was the first step in its acquaintance with modern civilisation.[32]

In similar vein, the Duke of Argyll's 1893 pamphlet, *Irish Nationalism: An Appeal to History*, quotes Edmund Burke, who said:

> What grievance has Ireland, to complain of with regard to Great Britain; unless the protection of the most powerful country upon earth – giving all her privileges, without exception, in common to Ireland, and reserving to herself only the painful pre-eminence of tenfold burdens, be a matter of complaint.[33]

The tendency to silence victims, or to convince them that abuse is for their own good, provides a strong rationale for using the cultural trauma model to understand colonialism. However, I believe that the insights gained from this model have been limited because of the way it has been applied.

Following the lead of early abuse experts, cultural trauma theorists have tended to focus on how traumatic events are forgotten. They argue that it is essential that the traumatic event is remembered in order for healing to take place.[34] However, individual trauma therapy has moved far beyond this model in understanding the long-term impact of traumatic experiences. It recognises that remembering is only the starting point for understanding the legacy of abuse and that remembering alone rarely brings healing or recovery.

This deeper analysis of trauma has focused on the process of disassociation. During the traumatic experience, it is common for the psyche of the individual experiencing the trauma to split. One part of their consciousness becomes focused on coping with the realities of the abusive situation; they may try to negotiate and bargain with the abuser, or they may try to minimise their pain by seeming to go along with the abuse. The other part of the psyche separates out from the experience itself and becomes the repository of the person's true feelings about the experience and about their abuser.[35] Abuse survivors Bass and Davis note that through disassociation,

> We disconnect from what is happening to us. Our capacity to feel – both physically and emotionally – shuts down and we distance ourselves from the pain and terror we would ordinarily experience. Disassociation is an extremely effective survival mechanism shielding us from the full impact of traumatic events.[36]

However, if the wounds to the psyche that are created by the traumatic events are not healed, the person's consciousness remains split. The abuse survivor tends to disassociate in everyday non-traumatic situations and their behaviour and perceptions of reality become distorted. Much contemporary therapeutic work focuses on getting survivors to recognise how this split impacts on their behaviour in order to reintegrate their consciousness.

If we accept the application of the trauma model to colonialism and assume that simply remembering traumatic events will not lead to healing, can we identify a similar split operating at the level of entire societies? In an article published in 1985, psychologist Vincent Kenny argued that colonialism had indeed created such a split in the Irish consciousness. He asserted that the superficial compliance, or pseudo-compliance, subsequently highlighted by Clare Daly and Tim Pat Coogan might be linked to a split in consciousness developed to cope with the realities of colonialism. He said:

> In order to survive in the face of hated authority one must appear to be at least superficially compliant. Open rebelliousness tends to meet with immediately harsh measures. It is important to create an external image which reassures the oppressor that the status quo is being maintained.... This is the beginning of a splitting process, between self and other.[37]

It is possible to argue that in Ireland rules and relationships fell on either side of this split. Rules were imposed by the coloniser; and even though many ordinary citizens thought the rules were unfair, they had to appear compliant in order to survive. Their real feelings about the abusive process of colonialism were only expressed through relationships in safe circles of intimacy, among family, community and friends – groups often described as 'our own'. In this space, feelings of resentment and anger were shared. This sharing was an important way of binding the group together. Most important, the everyday morality of the society, its vision of good behaviour, emerged from this split. Because the rules of the coloniser were seen as unfair, conforming to rules wasn't viewed as an important form of 'being good'. Instead, 'being good' to members of circles of intimacy – 'looking after our own' – became the key measure of virtue.

Ireland is not the only post-colonial society where this split has been observed. Exploring corruption in Nigeria, Peter Ekeh has made a number of observations about how this split impacts on public life in a colonised society. He notes that in societies that have not experienced colonialism, private and public life are generally divided into separate realms, one dominated by relationships and the other by rules. Each realm has its own morality and these moralities exist in tension with each other. However, he argues, public life in a colonised society has a second split, a split generated by the trauma of colonialism. In a colonised society, some public activity is linked to the colonised people's own families and communities. Ordinary citizens and community leaders who engage in public activity on behalf of these relationship-based groups are regarded as morally good. The rest of public activity is associated with the political, military and civil structures established by the coloniser. In order to survive, citizens in a colonised society must engage with these rules-based systems. But because the rules of the coloniser are viewed as unfair, conformity to rules is not seen as morally important.[38] Citizens of these societies have, in fact, two different moral approaches to public life. In public activities linked to intimacy-based groups, the colonised people behave in a moral fashion. However, when they engage with the rule-based systems of the coloniser, a dishonest approach is regarded as morally excusable because these systems are not really sites of moral behaviour.[39]

Ekeh argues that this split continued to be evident in the behaviour of his fellow Nigerians even after colonialism ended. He notes that Nigeria's civic authorities have 'a sad record of muddle, corruption and strife'. Paradoxically, the ethnic unions that are closely linked to circles of intimacy within families and communities in Nigerian society 'are handling sums of money comparable to those of many local authorities; … they are spending it constructively and … they are handling it *honestly*.'[40] In their study of corruption in Africa in the 1960s, Wraith and Simpkins also noted this split public morality. They write, 'to put your fingers in the till of the local authority will not unduly burden your conscience and people may well think you a smart fellow and envy you your opportunities. To steal the funds of the union would offend the public conscience and ostracise you from society.'[41]

Therefore, a split in public life resulting from the cultural trauma of colonialism generates a dual morality which shapes the balance between rules and relationships in the society. The effects of this split can be identified in Irish attitudes to rules-based systems and the dominant position of intimacy-based groups in Irish economic and social life from the nineteenth century onwards.

RELATIONSHIPS AND INTIMACY GROUPS IN NINETEENTH-CENTURY IRELAND

One of the most effective ways for Irish Catholics to cope with the unfair rules of colonialism was to retreat as far as possible into the family. Families are small units with high levels of trust, so it is almost impossible for external colonising forces to monitor them. Judith Herman explains why close-knit groups are so important in developing responses to oppression and trauma: 'To hold traumatic reality in consciousness requires a social context that affirms and protects the victim and that joins the victim and witness in a common alliance.'[42] Frantz Fanon has argued that colonisers often stigmatise family life precisely because families provide spaces where anti-colonist understandings of reality can be affirmed and validated in colonised societies.[43]

The structure of Irish society in the nineteenth century is striking in that family was not only the place where children were reared but also an important sphere of economic activity. Ireland's industrial revolution was largely centred on Belfast, although food processing provided some industrial employment in southern cities such as Cork, Dublin and Limerick. Outside these cities, most people worked on family farms. Sean Connolly provides a good indication of the sheer numbers of Irish people involved in family farm activity during the nineteenth century:

> One recent analysis suggests that the farming population can be roughly divided into about 50,000 wealthy farmers with an average of 80 acres per family, 100,000 strong farmers with an average of 100 acres, and 200,000 family farmers with an average of 20 acres. Below them came 250,000 smallholders, with an average of 5 acres per household and one million labourers, who worked on other men's land either for a cash wage or as 'cottiers' in exchange for a plot of ground on which to grow food for themselves and their families.[44]

Even in factories and retail businesses, most people worked in family contexts. Writing about industrial development, J.J. Lee says, 'The family firm had much the same ethos as the family farm … clienteles often consisted of a web of favours rather than efficiency. And even the industrial sector did not foster widely different mentalities.'[45]

Family farms and family businesses had historically dominated much Western European economic activity, but as the nineteenth century progressed, the process of earning money moved, for many Europeans, to impersonal industrial locations such as factories. These sites were governed by rules rather than family relationships. Where the rules were unfair, workers could engage in protests to improve pay and conditions.[46] However, in nineteenth-century Ireland, most Irish Catholics continued to work in contexts where family relationships rather than rules dominated. This pattern of economic activity may have contributed significantly to the dominance of relationships over rules in Irish society. A young man or woman working in a family farm or business would find it extremely difficult to use the industrial relations model to negotiate pay and working hours with their parents. As late as the 1930s, Arensberg and Kimball noted, 'there is an absolute co-incidence of "social" and "economic" factors within single relationships. In the case of the farmer and his son, there is only one relationship; to separate their social from their economic activities is meaningless. They are one, in fact and as far as the peasants are concerned, they are one in name.'[47]

The main rule-governed economic structure of the nineteenth century was the formal tie to the landlord. As the activities of the Land League intensified in the second half of the century, it became clear exactly how unjust Irish Catholic farmers regarded the formal rules governing these relationships. James Fintan Lalor of the Land League disputed the claims of landlords to ownership of any land, stating:

> The absolute ownership of the lands of Ireland is vested of right in the people of Ireland – that they, and none but they, are the first landowners and lords paramount as well as the lawmakers of this island – that all titles to land are invalid not conferred or confirmed by them – that no man has a right to hold one foot of Irish soil otherwise than by grant of tenancy and fee from them.[48]

The effect of the tenant farmer/landlord system appears to have been to position relationships over and above rules in moral terms, and to reinforce the link between relationships and economic activity.

The circles of intimacy created by families and communities were also the starting point for resistance to the day-to-day injustices of colonialism. Secret societies such as the Whiteboys, the Ribbonmen, the Rockites and the Moonlighters emerged as a response to evictions, tithes and the unjust actions of larger tenant farmers. Because the peasantry viewed both parliament and the criminal justice system as unfair, they felt that they would not get a just, rule-based response to their grievances from these institutions. Christianson comments:

> Unable to obtain redress for their grievance either through the Irish judicial system or the Parliament at Westminster, peasants increasingly took the law into their own hands by resorting to coercion and violence to bring about the desired resolution of their longstanding problems.[49]

The secret societies had no public leadership or even a publicly advertised agenda. They operated at night and usually in deep secrecy. Pat Feeley describes the activities of the Ribbonmen:

> The men conspired at the fair, in the pubs and in the shebeens, at the very heart of the community. After an outrage, they went back to the safety and anonymity of the community. There were no charismatic leaders. They were not needed. Nor are there many songs or ballads written about them, except where they happened to clash spectacularly with the police or military. The routine of their lives was too familiar to allow it to be romanticized by the people.[50]

Located in the sphere of intimacy where secrets could be conveyed with a nod or a look, the secret societies exercised a severe discipline on the local community. Anybody who broke the code of silence and gave witness testimony could expect little mercy from their members.

Victims of the secret societies included not only landlords and clergy but also tenants who had taken up residence in cottages and farms after evictions. As an indication of the strength of intimacy in Ireland, Charles Whitworth, Ireland's Lord Lieutenant, described how difficult it was to get victims of atrocities to testify against members of secret societies: 'It frequently happened that the sufferers of atrocities ... would depose only generally to the fact of their having been perpetrated, and not denying their knowledge of offenders, would yet steadfastly refuse to disclose their names or describe their persons.'[51] The sheer scale of secret society activity in Ireland during this period shows the extent to which these societies might have promoted the dominance of relationships over rules. Patrick Buckland writes: 'to some contemporaries the Irish countryside seemed to be one of the most disturbed and violent areas in Europe in the first half of the nineteenth century.'[52] Pat Feeley notes that only Russia had more secret societies than Ireland.[53]

The injustice and inequality at the heart of colonial structures meant that a relationship-based response to flawed rules was inevitable. The secret societies were effective in stalling the closure of commonage and some forms of rack-renting. Christianson concludes: 'the only way peasants could have been persuaded to abandon the anti-social tactics employed by secret societies would be for the government supported by the gentry to seek rational solutions to the numerous economic and social problems plaguing the countryside.'[54] Therefore, it was the very absence of fairness at the heart of political, legal and economic rules that led to this intimacy-based response to colonialism.

RULES IN NINETEENTH-CENTURY IRELAND

Although the experience of colonialism in Ireland during the nineteenth century provoked much distrust of rules *per se*, Irish Catholics also engaged in open campaigns to demand fair and equitable rules. The tradition of democratic political activity in Ireland pre-dates the 1801 Act of Union and became powerfully evident when Daniel O'Connell established the Catholic Association in 1823. The campaign for Catholic emancipation in Ireland demonstrated a clear belief that:

(1) the 'rules' of government and law were important; (2) the rules could be changed through orthodox political activity; (3) ordinary Irish people could play a significant role in openly demanding changes to these rules. Richard English argues that the Catholic Association 'has some right to be considered the first truly popular, mass-democratic organization in the modern world'.[55] The penny-a-month schemes, the public meetings and the 'monster meetings' of the 1830s and 1840s laid a pattern for democratic political participation in Ireland which demonstrated a clear understanding of the fairness that *should* be at the heart of rule systems. The success of the campaign in 1829, which was largely achieved through non-violent means, showed that you could achieve political goals without resorting to the secret, violent culture more typical of intimacy-based groups. A commitment to the rules – law, government and the political process – lay at the heart of O'Connell's belief system. Richard English notes:

> Though frequently deploying martial imagery in his speeches, O'Connell was sharply opposed to the practice of rebellious, insurrectionary or communal violence in practice. As a lawyer, he revered the law and wanted it obeyed and adhered to: illegal violence was the enemy of the kind of ordered Irish democracy whose creation he so keenly sought.[56]

This reverence for the law was most evident in 1843 when he cancelled a monster meeting in Clontarf in response to a ban by the British Prime Minister, Robert Peel.

Charles Stewart Parnell, the other major democratic nationalist leader of the period, also did much to generate a pull towards rules in Irish culture. Throughout his campaign for land reform, he highlighted the need to change unjust rules. He was also prepared to obstruct the operation of rules-based institutions, such as parliament, to draw attention to his cause. By encouraging mass participation in parliamentary politics, Parnell's campaign laid the foundation for a non-violent political culture which remains the bedrock of Irish politics today. Parnell's Irish Parliamentary Party provided a profound example of how rules-based parliamentary politics could be used to attain political goals. English concludes, 'The notion of parliament and of organized party politics, of bargaining centrally through parliamentary means, came to define much – if not most – modern nationalist practice in Ireland.'[57]

The strategies of O'Connell and Parnell had mixed success. They did not succeed in repealing the Act of Union or achieving Home Rule, although their movements did make very significant political gains in terms of Catholic emancipation and land reform. These concessions were wrung from a rule-based system that still overwhelmingly favoured the interests of the coloniser.

After the Famine, however, Irish Catholics increasingly turned to an alternative system which provided rules which they believed had far more legitimacy.

Catholicism

Into post-Famine Ireland came Cardinal Paul Cullen, who in 1850 called the first National Synod of the Irish Catholic Church to be held since the Reformation. The explicit purpose of the synod was to reintroduce Irish Catholics to the 'rules' of their faith. Before the Famine, Catholic practices in Ireland had been characterised by low levels of mass attendance, devotion to local Irish saints and visits to sacred sites such as holy wells. These practices reflected both the legacy of the Penal Laws and continuing links with pagan forms of Celtic mysticism.

Cullen's 'devotional revolution' had three elements. First, he wanted more contact between the clergy and Irish Catholics; and members of the clergy were to be deeply immersed in the 'rules' of the Catholic Church. Second, he sought a corresponding increase in attendance at mass, confession and other religious sacraments so that Catholics would be better informed about the 'rules' and their conformity to the 'rules' could be monitored. Finally, through mass, parish missions and novenas, he sought to place Catholicism at the heart of intimacy-based communal life in Ireland.[58] This devotional revolution brought a new rules-based discipline to the practice of Catholicism in Ireland

and its success impacted significantly on the tension between rules and relationships.

First, it established Catholicism as the most legitimate, popular and widely accepted rules-based system among the Irish middle and small farmer class. This was partly done by characterising the life of English cities, which produced the rules-based systems that governed Irish society, as polluted, dirty and corrupt. For instance, Tom Garvin notes that in his autobiography, *Mo Scéal Féin*, Fr Peter O'Leary describes an 'evil city versus virtuous village polarity, tied up with an identification of England and English modes with the former and Ireland and Irish language traditions with the latter'.[59] In this characterisation, Catholic clergy were particularly keen to celebrate the virtue of the small farmer and his family. In 1871, Bishop Nulty of Meath claimed that 'the purest, the holiest and the most innocent of society in this country, at least, certainly belong to the class of small farmers.'[60]

Hoppen argues that the Irish middle and small farmer classes had their own reasons for embracing these rules, particularly those relating to the suppression of sexuality. With the decimation of the cottier class during the Famine, the practices of early marriage and land division between inheriting siblings came to an end. The larger tenant farmers, whose position was consolidated after the Famine, now chose a single heir who could be married to a girl with a dowry. Under this system, the chance of marriage for the remaining children was limited and only strict control of sexual behaviour kept this approach to land inheritance functioning. Hoppen comments:

> All the consequent denunciations of immodest dances, company keeping and fleshy sins in general, however restrictive for particular individuals, involved in the end, a kind of invited repression. Before the Famine, the clergy's attempts to demolish the extravagance of folk religion had been only very partially successful because then the church had in fact been kicking against the pricks. Thereafter, the priesthood was moving with the grain of social and economic development and laying siege to fortresses already under energetic demolition from within.[61]

Placing clergy at the centre of communal life – through mass attendance and other religious celebrations – meant that priests were able to direct their flock how to deal with the rule-based systems of the state. According to Richard English, 'from 1881 onwards the Catholic Church was crucially and integrally part of the Parnellite advance. This had organizational implications and it also counted heavily in terms of local clerical guidance as to how the flock should vote.'[62] Although there were sharp divisions among the clergy about the nationalist struggle, priests not only gave advice on voting but also provided public leadership during the protests of the Land League.

One of the most important ways in which the Catholic Church influenced Irish attitudes to rules was its role in expanding formal education systems in the late nineteenth century. Ireland's primary education system had been established in the 1830s with the aim of providing basic literacy and numeracy skills. Tom Garvin argued that it was essentially part of the British colonial project to produce 'literate subalterns for a subordinate role in running a great empire'.[63] After the Famine, however, the Catholic Church became a key provider of education. The Irish Catholic population found that education provided a crucial safety valve in a system of land succession that provided limited opportunities for surplus children. The expansion of education in Ireland was based on the idea that by mastering, for example, Latin or mathematics and by demonstrating this mastery in exams, upward mobility could be achieved. At the core of second-level education was a state exams system (first introduced by the Intermediate Education Act 1878) that operated as a strong pull towards rules-based systems. Desmond Keenan describes how important passing exams was to the Irish religious who ran schools:

> The Irish Christian Brothers had a reputation as crammers, but their lower middle class pupils had to pass exams, and pass them well if they were to enter a whole range of occupations. The parents who sent their children to the 'Brothers' relied on them to beat knowledge into them and get them through their exams.[64]

This system established the idea of the state exam as a benchmark of knowledge that existed outside the realm of relationships in Irish society. Lower middle-class students were under pressure to achieve in exams because results were seen as a fair assessment of their abilities. The exam system was itself viewed as a legitimate and 'fair' measure of ability for those lucky enough to have access to education.

School exams also enabled students to take university and civil service entrance exams, so success in exams could have a profound impact on the life chances of the individual. It provided a route into work in the professions or the public sector, which was expanding rapidly in Ireland during this period. Lynch and Hill note:

> Local government, the police force and the civil service provided ever-increasing employment. The well-educated could gain access to these jobs through competitive examinations and selection. The role of the civil servant in many aspects of life became increasingly more important as Government expanded as the nineteenth century progressed. Overall between 1881 and 1901, there was a 17% increase in the number of persons employed in Government in Ireland. By 1901, there were 34,281 Government employees in total, one for every 104 inhabitants of Ireland (excluding the armed forces).[65]

For a class who still had vivid memories of mass starvation during the Famine era, the lure of a well-paid, secure job in the public sector was considerable. However, enabling a rules-based system which was still viewed as fundamentally unfair posed a considerable psychological challenge for Irish Catholics. In managing this psychological challenge, the psyche split between rules and relationships, which Ekeh noted in Nigeria, became more evident.[66] Ekeh argues that for African civil servants – as for Irish civil servants during British colonialism – it was essential to present an outward image of conformity and submission to colonial culture. For instance, in describing the image management issues for the Irish civil servant in late nineteenth-century Ireland, Caitriona Clear notes the importance of conforming to the expectations of the colonising class in dress, behaviour, speech and so on:

> A clerk in a government department, local authority or business had to speak politely and have a clean white shirt or blouse; a policeman, warden, workhouse master or mistress, or asylum attendant had to be both authoritative in bearing and deferential to superiors. National school teachers were forbidden to, among other things, lodge in public houses and attend political meetings.... These white collar, professional workers were only one generation away from the uncertain existence of small farms, businesses and trades: the prospect of losing the security of their jobs constrained their freedom of expression considerably.[67]

To be successful in a public sector job you had, to some degree, to suppress your native identity; but presenting an outward image of conformity came at a considerable psychological cost. First, the individual had to appear to conform to rules they may not have viewed as legitimate. Second, this process threatened their connection to their 'own', their intimacy-based group, creating a potential fear among family and community members that the civil servant had left them behind. Ekeh notes that in the African case, 'New men with non-literate parents and brothers and sisters – from non-chiefly families ungrounded in the ethics and weight of authority – are emerging to occupy high places. Behind the serenity and elegance of deportment that come with education and high office lies waves of psychic turbulence.'[68]

Maintaining links to intimacy-based groups through favours and strokes became an important way of showing continued attachment and loyalty to 'our own' even when the individual occupied a position as a civil servant in the rules-based institution of the coloniser. J.J. Lee notes that officials in Irish local government in the late nineteenth century 'dutifully attended to the three F's of popular politics – family, friends and favours'.[69]

Examining the same process in Nigeria, Ekeh says that as the country's middle class became more confident in its demands for independence, it increasingly engaged in non-conformity to rules, taking the view that those rules were no longer legitimate. He notes that in Nigeria:

> [T]he struggle entailed a necessary but destructive strategy: sabotage of the administrative efforts of the colonizers.... The African who evaded his tax was a hero ... such strategy, one must repeat, was a necessary sabotage against alien personnel whom the African bourgeois class wanted to replace.... The irony of it all, however is that the ordinary African took the principles involved in such activities quite seriously.[70]

As Ireland moved closer towards independence, non-co-operation with the rules of the British colonial administration became increasingly evident. After 1916, journalist Robert Lynd wrote, 'So far as the mass of people are concerned, the policy of the day is not an active but a passive policy. Their policy is not so much to attack the Government as to ignore it and to build up a new government by its side.'[71] After the general election of 1918, this policy of 'ignoring government' became fully fledged. In 1919, the Dáil sanctioned a policy of ostracising members of the Royal Irish Constabulary (RIC), which meant that local police lacked co-operation from many communities. There were strikes by organised workers throughout the period, most notably in Limerick city. In April 1920, four hundred abandoned RIC barracks were burned to the ground so that they could not be used again and, significantly, almost a hundred income tax offices were burned.[72]

The Inland Revenue ceased to operate in most parts of Ireland and the Dáil government began collecting its own contributions. Rates were still being paid to local councils, but since nine out of eleven councils were controlled by Sinn Féin, the money was retained rather than sent to London. Finally, as the introduction of martial law in 1921 signalled the total breakdown of colonial rule in Ireland, the IRA attacked and burned the Custom House, the centre of local government in Ireland. This attack was one of the most bloody and costly of the entire IRA campaign, yet the Custom House was regarded as a critical symbol of

British rule in Ireland. Thus, by the time independence was achieved in 1922, Irish nationalists had successfully de-linked a sizeable proportion of the island of Ireland from the British Empire. This achievement was only gained at the cost of undermining the already compromised moral basis of rules-based systems in Ireland. Although the institutions themselves would be reinstated with relative ease, the tension between rules and relationships in Irish society would continue to be unsteady in some respects for the next ninety years.

CONCLUSION

The combination of weak rules and insider intimacy which contributed significantly to the Irish economic crisis in 2010 prompted some commentators to ask how much the legacy of colonialism might have contributed to Ireland's financial collapse. This chapter has explored the role of colonialism in shaping the balance between weak rules and strong relationships. The distrust of rules-based systems generated by the British colonial state is evident throughout the nineteenth century. The activities of a succession of nationalist movements suggest that Irish Catholics believed that the rules governing their society were neither fair nor legitimate. This belief in the unfairness of the rules was exacerbated by the cultural trauma generated by the more violent aspects of British colonialism. The response of many Irish Catholics was to retreat into intimacy-based groups. Families became not only the site of child-rearing but also of economic activity. Effective local resistance to some of the harshest and most unjust elements of colonialism emerged from secret societies embedded within communities. These intimacy-based responses were effective in sustaining resistance and ensuring the survival of the Catholic middle and lower middle classes.

However, Irish Catholics also made open demands for fairer rules through peaceful democratic protest. These campaigns were most successful in delivering Catholic emancipation and land reform, but they did not achieve the ultimate goal of Home Rule. After the Famine, Catholicism became increasingly viewed as a more legitimate rule-based system and a familiarity with the rules of Catholicism was actively promoted by the Catholic Church. The Church, in partnership with the Catholic middle class, espoused rules focusing on the need for sexual repression, which helped the middle class to shore up its system of land inheritance. The link between the Church and the middle classes was copper-fastened by the significant increase in participation in formal education in the late nineteenth century, which provided the upwardly mobile Irish middle classes with new routes into lucrative public sector jobs.

Taking up these jobs came at a considerable psychological cost. Ekeh's examination of a similar situation in Nigeria suggests that the split in public life which occurs as a result of the cultural trauma of colonialism generates psychological challenges for the civil servant who comes from the indigenous population. For them, public activity on behalf of their own families and communities is viewed as moral. However, public activity linked to the rule-based systems of the coloniser is viewed as less moral. This weak moral base produces a culture of favours, strokes and other ways of showing loyalty to relationship-based groups. This split poses a significant challenge to post-colonial political elites who, after independence, have to establish rule-based structures which are viewed as legitimate sites of moral activity. As Chapter 2 will show, this was a tough challenge in post-independence twentieth-century Ireland.

Chapter 2 ∽

CHANGE AND THE TIES THAT BIND

The Provisional Government was simply eight young men in the City Hall standing amidst the ruins of one administration, with the foundations of another not yet laid.... No police force was functioning through the country, no system of justice was operating, the wheels of administration hung idle, battered out of recognition.[1]

Kevin O'Higgins

The pain expressed by citizens of the Republic of Ireland at the loss of economic sovereignty in late 2010 mystified many international commentators, particularly those in the German press.[2] The degree of distress was perhaps linked to the difficulty of achieving sovereignty in the first place. Irish nationalists were among the first twentieth-century revolutionaries to break free from the British Empire, an achievement all the more extraordinary given the close proximity between the two states. The final stages of the War of Independence and the Civil War were particularly traumatic. Many of the rules-based institutions of the British colonial state were dismantled, while tensions within the nationalist movement led to splits that divided Irish families and communities for generations. The scale of the task facing Ireland's revolutionary elite was clearly evident to Kevin O'Higgins, Minister for Justice in 1922, who recognised that achieving independence was no guarantee that legitimate rules could be established.

In this context the Provisional Government began the process of creating new rules-based institutions for the Irish state, a task further advanced by Fianna Fáil in the 1930s. The revolutionary generation had one striking advantage: the powerful unifying ideology of Catholicism. In contrast, post-independence Nigeria had no unifying ideology which could hold its disparate relationship-based groups together.[3] Catholicism was particularly important in Ireland: not only did the bulk of nationalists come from a Catholic background, but also the Irish variant of Catholicism strongly encouraged conformity to rules.[4] The rules of the Catholic Church challenged violence, and the Church's own rejection of violence played a significant role in removing the gun from Irish politics in the 1920s.[5] As the Civil War ended, the real task of state-building began. Both Church and State were to play an important part in shaping the balance between rules and relationships in independent Ireland.

INTIMACY AND THE RULES 1922–1960

Faced with the need to put in place a new public administration, the leaders of the new Irish state sought to revive much of the British colonial administration which had been in place. This task was relatively easy because before the War of Independence many senior positions in the Dublin Castle administration were held by Irish Catholics.[6] These individuals had competed in exams in order to achieve their position and the same emphasis on rule-based competition was carried into the new Civil Service Commission, established in 1924.[7] However, this generation of civil servants faced a number of challenges. There was still a popular distrust of the rules and a degree of affection for the rule-breaker – and O'Higgins himself recognised the potential dangers of a cultural rejection of rules, stating (somewhat ironically for an Irish nationalist), 'the ceasing of the bailiff to function is the first sign of a crumbling civilization.'[8] More important, civil servants – most of whom were from rural backgrounds – were still under pressure to demonstrate their loyalty to their families and home communities.[9] Despite the insistence in the 1920s that public sector positions should be above 'personal pressure',[10] by the 1940s the contours of the late nineteenth-century systems of patronage had returned. Tom Garvin writes that during the 1932–1948 period, connections to political elites were 'required for appointment to the police and many local government agencies. This was despite the Land Appointments Commission and the Civil Service Commission which were supposed to be non-partisan and meritocratic agencies. It is difficult not to suspect that in a society where everyone knew everyone else, everyone expected corruption and clientelism.'[11]

Despite this culture of patronage, the rules of democracy remained broadly robust. This adherence was strongly tested during the period when the Cumann na nGaedheal government lost the 1932 election to their Civil War opponents Fianna Fáil and when Fianna Fáil subsequently lost power in 1948. During each transition, the commitment to keeping the rules of democracy proved solid, underpinning a long-term democratic stability, unusual in post-colonial states.

Key to these successful power transfers was the early separation of political and security roles, a process enabled by the establishment of An Garda Síochána in 1922. Unlike the Royal Irish Constabulary (RIC), whose members were seen as agents of the colonial state, the Guardians of the Peace were an unarmed force dedicated to working with relationship-based groups such as families and communities. Diarmaid Ferriter writes, 'The Civic Guard was to be the servant of the people, not militaristic or coercive.'[12] The rules this new police force upheld largely converged with Catholic morality, focusing on protection of property and non-violence. The degree of popular acceptance and the support the new police force achieved in a relatively short time demonstrated that a strong pull towards rules had survived the turmoil of the revolutionary period in Irish culture.[13]

Despite the new state's success in establishing a civil service and popularly supported police service, there was a certain tentativeness in their approach to state-building that may have been linked to a post-colonial distrust of rules. J.J. Lee notes that while most post-colonial governments are 'committed to the view that the state should adopt a developmental role in their societies. The first Free State government was not. It broadly took the view that the state should do as little as possible.'[14] Instead, the state increasingly turned to the Catholic Church to provide services such as schools, hospitals and orphanages, expanding a Church–State alliance which had begun under the British colonial administration. However, the government of the new Irish state took this partnership further, using the imprimatur of Catholicism to add legitimacy to its own sovereignty. Richard English notes that the process was particularly marked during national celebrations such as St Patrick's Day, when 'all government ministers would attend Irish language Catholic mass in Dublin's Pro-Cathedral, nationalist gesture fusing here together with state, religion and cultural expression.'[15] The celebration of the centenary of Catholic Emancipation in 1929 and the Eucharistic Congress in 1932 further cemented this process of using the legitimacy of the Church to affirm the 'goodness' of the new state.

Despite the fact that Church, State and the police force were all rule-based institutions, there was a curious convergence in their vision of an ideal Irish society. This vision stressed that intimacy-based groups such as family and community represented the highest forms of social life. Since the nineteenth century, Catholic teaching had celebrated and protected its view of the married family. The Irish version of this Catholic idealism specifically stressed the virtues of rural family life. After independence, this emphasis on the rural family was complemented by a renewed focus on community. Church leaders strongly supported civic participation in community groups rather than trade unions, which, they felt, raised the spectre of anti-clerical socialism.[16]

This Arcadian vision of families and communities in rural Ireland was also shared by leading politicians of the 1930s and 1940s, most notably Éamon de Valera,[17] whose famous St Patrick's Day speech of 1943 set out his idealised vision of Ireland as a land 'whose countryside would be bright with cosy homesteads, whose fields and villages would be joyous with sounds of industry, the romping of sturdy children, the contests of athletic youth, the laughter of comely maidens, whose firesides would be the forums of the wisdom of serene old age'.[18] Even

An Garda Síochána was embedded in rural relationship-based idealism; 50 per cent of early recruits were young men from rural backgrounds – former farmers or land workers. Eoin O'Duffy, an early commissioner, publicly stated, 'the son of the peasant is the backbone of the force'.[19] As an unarmed police force, the Gardaí were heavily dependent on trust and good relationships forged within the community. Ciarán McCullagh argues that the Gardaí continued to view the family and community as the first point of response to crime until the latter half of the twentieth century.[20]

Although the attractions of this idealised vision of family and community were obvious, the state's approach to economic development did little to support these relationship-based groups. The laissez-faire approach to the economy adopted by the Cumann na nGaedheal government was followed in the 1930s by a unsuccessful attempt by Fianna Fáil to achieve economic self-sufficiency. The Second World War provided a new demand for Irish agricultural produce, but as European economies transformed during the post-war era, the Irish economy was left behind. The net result of this economic failure was emigration on a massive scale. The families and communities celebrated by the Church and State and protected by the Gardaí lost their young people, who left to find employment and opportunity in the UK, USA and elsewhere, and rarely returned. By the late 1950s, Denis Meehan, Professor of Ancient Classics at Maynooth, commented, 'In purely physical terms, the population cannot dwindle any further, the bottom of the curve must come somewhere, there is literally nowhere to fall from.'[21]

It was allegedly a cartoon of Ireland entitled 'Have I a Future?' in the *Dublin Opinion* magazine that prompted the Secretary of the Department of Finance, T.K. Whitaker, to consider how to transform Ireland's model of economic development in order to stem the tide of emigration. In the 1960s Whitaker, along with other civil servants and politicians, set in train a series of rapid changes to the Irish economy that would have significant implications for the balance between rules and relationships in Ireland.

TRANSITION AND NEW RULES

Although some historians have characterised 1958 as a turning point in Irish economic fortunes, the building blocks of economic transformation had been gradually assembling throughout the 1950s. Lemass and Whitaker's first Programme for Economic Expansion, inaugurated in 1958, did, however, achieve a remarkable economic transformation in a relatively short period of time. Tariffs on trade between Ireland and Britain were eliminated, strategies were developed to attract foreign direct investment and the tourism industry began to grow rapidly. Not surprisingly, given the close links between family and economic relationships in Ireland, the first signs that this approach was working came from emigration and marriage statistics. Ferriter notes that the emigration rate dropped from 14 per cent between 1951 and 1961 to less than 5 per cent between 1961 and 1971. According to J.J. Lee:

> Lemass prated little about the sanctity of the 'family'. But 4 per cent economic growth and a rise of about 50 per cent in material living standards during the 1960s at last made it feasible for the numbers of families to increase. The numbers of families as recorded by the census rose by 48,000 between 1961 and 1971, compared with a rise of only 11,000 in the preceding fifteen years.[22]

Family farms and family businesses were no longer the main source of employment, and a growing number of Irish citizens worked in multinational companies in the manufacturing sector. The new approach to economic development depended on attracting global corporations by setting low tax rates and emphasising the availability of a cheap English-speaking labour force. Once these companies arrived, a critical factor in their success or failure was the capacity of Irish workers to adapt to the rules-based scientific systems at the core of their production processes.[23] It was Seán Lemass's own conviction that Irish workers could adapt to these practices that drove his vision of economic change. During the election of 1957, he said: 'the assertion that this country can get out of its difficulties is based on the belief that Irish workers, given the same tools and leadership as workers elsewhere, can achieve equivalent productivity.[24] Multinational companies had more open promotional structures than older Irish industrial firms, most of which were, like farms, run by families.[25] By 1973, a third of people employed in manufacturing worked for these corporations. Therefore, the Programme for Economic Development had, in a relatively short period, a dramatic impact on work and social mobility in Ireland.

Along with Ireland's integration into global capitalism came a new relationship with global culture via the medium of television. Raidió Teilifís Éireann began broadcasting on New Year's Eve 1961. Ellen Hazelkorn says that television 'powerfully challenged traditional cultural forms and vented the aspiration of an emergent middle class, whose allegiances were increasingly attuned to continental Europe undermining the primacy of the countryside in national life'.[26] Dramas, comedies and serials imported from Britain and the USA gave Irish people images of a new consumer culture to which they could aspire, and introduced them to different cultural values and beliefs. More important, these imported programmes, as well as discussion programmes such as *The Late Late Show*, led to an increasing questioning of the existing 'rules' of Irish society.[27]

A further transformation came in 1966 with the introduction of free second-level education. Many of the younger generation could now gain the skills and confidence to engage with the rules at the heart of scientific production processes and global cultural knowledge systems. Along with changes to the second-level system came the establishment at third level of new institutes of technology and technical colleges, which focused on business, science and applied skills. Tom Garvin notes that these improvements in education led to further questioning of existing rules: 'the old peasant deference to clerical authority partly derived from the popular perception of priests as educated men'[28] was beginning to be eroded.

Amid this economic transformation, the structure of the Irish family began to change. Irish people were getting married in their early twenties and having fewer children, moving into line with the

European norm at the time.[29] The lack of availability of contraception was a considerable barrier to family planning,[30] and by 1971, members of the Irish Women's Liberation Movement were publicly challenging the Church–State rules on contraception. This activism kick-started a range of other challenges to rules governing sexuality and family life.[31] Irish feminists found themselves with an unexpected and surprisingly powerful ally – the European Economic Community (EEC), later the European Union (EU). Fintan O'Toole writes, 'The feminist movement was on the rise before Ireland joined the EEC, even if the need to conform with European legislation undoubtedly speeded up change…. But, without Europe, these changes surely would have been accompanied by a great deal more social conflict'.[32]

When Ireland joined the EEC in 1973, the government had to remove the bar on married women working in the civil service and to introduce maternity leave. Pressure from Europe also increased welfare state provisions, bringing changes to the qualifying age for the old age pension in the Social Welfare Act 1973, as well as provisions for deserted wives and unmarried mothers. But the scale of the new rules introduced by the EEC extended far beyond the family. Europeanisation involved a massive expansion of rules-based institutions regulating Irish society. Laffan and O'Mahony map the process:

> This process had begun with the creation of the Employment Equality Agency in 1977 and the Director of Consumer Affairs in 1978. The Health and Safety Authority in 1989, followed by the Pensions Board (1990), the Competition Authority (1992), the Environmental Protection Agency (1992), the Irish Aviation Authority (1994), the Food Safety Authority (1995) and the telecommunications regulator Comreg (1997) among others … these agencies became part of a network of European regulatory agencies.[33]

After the Single European Act was passed in 1985, local communities in Ireland became increasingly dominated by European rules on the management of waste and water, and the protection of natural habitats. While Irish farmers gained considerable benefits from the EU, they also had to deal with a vast array of new rules. Claiming payments, applying for schemes such as the Rural Environment Protection Scheme (REPS) and accessing entitlements pulled the farming sector of the Irish economy very strongly away from the intimacy of the family farm and towards rule-based systems.[34]

The degree of enthusiasm for the European project in Ireland during this period was surprising given that it involved a significant ceding of sovereignty, a sovereignty that had only recently been achieved. However, the rules of the EU were backed with European Structural Funds, which played an important role in building infrastructure and supporting industry and tourism. Therefore, the direct financial benefits of EU membership were visible.[35] It is also possible that the enduring legacy of colonialism led to a certain comfort with the remote power of both the EU and global corporations.

Relationships with both of these remote powers came under pressure after 2000. The dotcom/NASDAQ crash of 1999–2000 badly damaged the US-led IT manufacturing boom which had boosted much of the Irish economy in the 1990s.[36] The affluence of the boom also led to a shift in attitudes towards the EU. The first major stumble in this relationship occurred with the rejection of the Treaty of Nice in 2001. As the Irish economy moved into a construction-led boom after 2002, the relationship with the EU became increasingly uneasy. As monetary union tightened, anti-EU voices in Ireland became louder and more articulate. Irish voters were more and more hesitant to embrace new EU treaties, a hesitancy that by late 2010 had in some quarters become overt hostilty. This hostility may have been linked to the increasing intrusion of EU rules into Irish life. Yet despite this dramatic increase in the volume of rules in Ireland between 1958 and 2010, loyalty to relationship-based groups of the family, community and nation remained the key touchstone for 'goodness' in the Irish value system.

FAMILY, COMMUNITY AND 'BEING GOOD'
Arensberg and Kimball's study of West Clare in the 1930s highlighted the importance of extended families based around married couples with large numbers of children as the central unit of social life in

Ireland. These extended families, which included grandparents and single relations, played a key role in the economy, particularly through family farms and family businesses.[37] By 2011, Peter Lunn and Tony Fahey's study of family life in Ireland revealed just how much the structure of Irish families had changed as a result of modernisation. They found that 'One-in-three families in Ireland depart from the traditional model of a married couple both of whom are in their first marriage. One-in-four children under 21 years of age live in a family that does not conform to this model.'[38] They also noted a rise in cohabitation outside marriage and found an increasing number of single-parent, separated, divorced and same-sex families.

Though the structure of these families is dramatically different from de Valera's Arcadian vision of family life,[39] it is striking how much the concept of family has continued to serve as a touchstone for 'goodness' in the Irish value system. Before the banking crash, Irish spending on the family home and family celebrations outstripped that of other European countries. In their analysis of this spending, Keohane and Kuhling argued that in the Irish value system:

> Extravagant expenditure on the home and on children is legitimated as morally justifiable … it is not 'selfish' but contributes actively to … the traditional institutions of the home and family life. Extravagant expenditure on family groceries and home improvement materials are morally sanctioned.[40]

By spending money on family occasions and the family home, Irish parents were affirming themselves as 'good'. The reverse of this association between 'being good' and providing for the family was sharply evident in the research I conducted at the height of the austerity period between 2010 and 2012. In 2012, Jim, an unemployed builder, told me, 'Well, the worst thing that could happen to me right now would be that my daughter would come and tell me she's getting married. Sure what could I do for her? I've nothing to give her. It would be a nightmare.' Keohane and Kuhling conclude that Irish culture continues to celebrate 'Parents as "breadwinners and providers" taking care of children and providing for one another; and being seen by other families to be endeavouring to do so. Shopping therefore shores up and reinforces the collective representations of the traditional roles of the "good provider", the "good Irish mother" and the good of "traditional Irish family life".[41]

Tom Inglis argues that historically the Catholic Church played a significant role in creating this link between the family and 'goodness', a link which focused particularly on the role of mothers.[42] Because Catholic rules forbade contraception, 'good' Catholic mothers were very fertile, and having a large number of children was evidence of their 'goodness'. This positive view of large families continues to be evident in the Irish value system. Not only do Irish parents have more children than other Europeans, their ideal family size is also larger than other Europeans.[43] The link between having babies and 'goodness' persisted even in the face of the deep financial crisis of 2010–2011, when Ireland experienced a baby boom. In September 2011, the Central Statistics Office (CSO) released figures showing that the birth rate in Ireland in the first quarter of 2011 had increased by 7.6 per cent (19,950), the highest number of births registered in a quarter since the series began in 1960. Results from the 2011 census showed that the Irish population had reached record levels since the Famine and that the country had the highest birth rate in the EU. In the international context, this was a highly unusual response to an economic downturn. The USA was more typical: after the 2008 banking crash, the birth rate declined as parents delayed having second children in particular.[44]

Margaret Fine-Davis's research on family formation in Ireland, published in 2011, highlighted this continuing association in Irish culture between having children and 'goodness'. She found that a number of Irish parents wanted even more children than they had:

> The study showed discrepancies between people's ideal, expected and actual number of children. When asked how many children they would 'ideally' like to have, the average number was 2.73. However, when they were asked how many children they expected

to have in their lifetime, the mean was 2.41 children. Thus, people expect to have fewer children than they would ideally like to have. The actual number of children that each woman has when she completes her childbearing is currently approximately 2.[45]

She also interviewed a number of individuals who were single and childless and who revealed that they felt stigmatised in Irish society. Claire told her, 'I think there's still kind of a stigma attached to it. Poor Claire hasn't met someone yet. Will Claire ever meet anyone? People just don't accept the fact that you can be single and happy. It's the children thing.'[46]

The link between family and 'goodness' is so strong that business and sporting organisations frequently tap into this association to market their activities. The website for the GAA Club Championships sponsored by Allied Irish Banks is called 'Club is Family'. It claims that the individual's relationship to their local GAA club is 'part of their DNA',[47] stating 'you don't choose your club, you inherit it.'[48] Commercial organisations are also keen to make the association between family and goodness. A 2011 brochure for the Moran Hotel Group, a chain of hotels in Ireland and Britain, claimed that 'family is the foundation upon which the Moran Hotel Group has been built.' The brochure uses family relationships to explain the structure of the hotel group, describing two hotels in the chain as 'the eldest two in Dublin and Cork' and the Dublin pub, Red Cow Inn, as 'our first arrival'.[49] The concept of family is used in both these cases to create a positive image of the organisation and a link to the associated 'goodness' of the Irish family. This connection between goodness and relationship-based groups is also evident in Irish understandings of community.

Elaine Byrne argues that one of the long-term consequences of the 1801 Act of Union was a suspicion of the rules of the state and a deep trust in local communities based on networks of extended families.[50] After independence, Éamon de Valera put particular emphasis on the community in his vision of the 'goodness' of life in Irish society.[51] In de Valera's vision, what was good for the 'community' was automatically good for society, which was simply a group of communities on a larger scale. Paddy O'Carroll argues that the concept of community in Ireland was closely linked not only to family but also to place: 'many communities particularly in rural areas were locality descent groups where the same families have shared the area for generations.... The most important characteristic of these communities was the high proportion of people who were born there and who continued to live their whole lives in them.'[52] Therefore, the 'goodness' associated with community was based on its status as the place where lots of 'good' extended families lived.

The good behaviour associated with community is more outward-looking than the good behaviour associated with the family, which has an inward-looking focus on providing for other family members. During the 1930s, the Catholic Church developed a very strong emphasis on community as a morally approved site for political activism. Before the foundation of the state, the Catholic hierarchy had been suspicious of local co-operative movements because of the involvement of prominent Protestants such as Horace Plunkett. However, the 1930s saw the launch of Muintir na Tíre, a community movement supported by the Catholic Church. Sean L'Estrange argues that this movement did much to promote a link between community activism and 'being good' in Irish culture. It also encouraged participants to view many of the problems of society as problems which could be most successfully solved at community level.[53]

The Catholic Church not only provided a strong association between community and 'being good' but also a vital piece of local organisational infrastructure: the parish. Organisations that were based on the structure of the parish found they could tap into an association between community and goodness. Historian Mike Cronin argues that the GAA's decision to base its organisation on the parish was central to its rapid success:

> By choosing the parish as its structure, the Association openly allied itself with the Catholic Church, the single most important and powerful body at the time. It also gave the people an instantly recognisable framework around which they could establish clubs.

The parish focus allowed the players and followers of Gaelic games to forge instant ties with their home parish, and equally instant rivalries with the parishes down the road.[54]

This link between the structure of the Catholic Church and the GAA not only played a huge role in increasing identification with local communities, it also led to the characterisation of sporting achievements for the local community as a very significant form of 'being good'. In their history of the GAA, Duncan *et al.* note: 'this stress on the local proved a masterstroke.... This was vital to the success of the early GAA and to the roots it set down. It meant that when clubs took to the field, players were playing for more than personal glory – the reputation of their community was also at stake.'[55]

Despite the role of the Church and the GAA in reinforcing local identity, communities in Ireland experienced even more dramatic transformation than the family unit as a result of modernisation. New opportunities in manufacturing and industry meant that while many Irish citizens no longer had to emigrate, they did have to move to cities and towns where work was available. This wave of urbanisation created suburbs populated initially by families who had acquired their knowledge of how to '*do*' community in rural areas. One resident of the Dublin suburb of Leixlip told Corcoran *et al.* that in the 1970s:

Huge numbers of people were cleared out of rural Ireland and dumped on the outskirts of Dublin. What saved those communities was that people were rural – people were used to having to do for themselves: in Leixlip, people's backgrounds were rural. People would get [out] and mow the public greens, they would [do] the maintenance, taking pleasure in hacking down a bush. The residents' association reflected this rural and small-town ethos of mucking in and doing things.[56]

By the 1990s, many of these suburbs had become firmly established communities, but the construction-led boom of the post-2001 era led to a second major wave of urbanisation. Hundreds of new estates were built on the outskirts of small villages and towns throughout Ireland, particularly in counties neighbouring Dublin.[57] A significant proportion of residents on these new estates commute to cities and towns for work every day. In County Meath, for instance, the CSO noted that in 2011, 22,021 commuters were leaving the county for work in Dublin every day. Commuting has also become a significant feature of life in rural Ireland, with the rural ribbon development of stand-alone housing resulting in a pattern of commuting to nearby cities and towns for work.[58] The negative impact of commuting on communities is well established.[59] Robert Putnam says:

> The car and the commute ... are demonstrably bad for community life. In round numbers, the evidence suggests that each additional ten minutes of daily commuting time cuts involvement in community affairs by 10%. Fewer public meetings, fewer committees chaired, fewer petitions signed, fewer church services attended, less volunteering and so on.[60]

Corcoran *et al.* argue that because of these changes, residents of these new suburbs have quite a loose attachment to their community.[61] They describe one local activist, Martin, who 'has realized that most people [in his community] have neither the time nor the inclination to commit themselves to local affairs'.[62] Tom Inglis concludes that these changes mean that many Irish citizens no longer view their community as an important site of belonging and meaning.

> People are becoming more mobile. They have greater access to transport and systems of communication. They are no longer bound as much to place. Their family, friends, neighbours and workmates may not live in the same area. People move in and out of locations, to set up home, go to work, school, shopping, on holidays and to visit family. They are on the run.[63]

Despite these changes in communities, there continues to be a strong association between community and 'being good'. This is clear from the range of competitions and public initiatives aimed at getting communities to work together, such as the national Tidy Towns competition and the Community Games. Commercial organisations also tap into associations between communities and goodness. Esso Ireland's website states: 'wherever we do business, we put our energies into improving the quality of life of our neighbours and their communities.... Being a good citizen is about being a good neighbour and Esso values the relationship between the company and the local communities in which we operate.'[64] Diageo, Electric Ireland, Mace and a host of other businesses have sponsored grant schemes and initiatives that aim to support local communities.

The tendency to define national, society-wide problems as the problems of communities also continues to be evident. For instance, the Irish government's national plan to promote corporate social responsibility is entitled 'Good for Business – Good for the Community'.[65] Community is seen as being central to solving not only the problems of the corporate sector but also the problems of the marginalised in Irish society. In Dublin, the campaign group Canal Communities aims to tackle drug use and crime, and its mission 'embraces, encourages and practises the concepts and values of partnership, inclusion, participation, integration and equality'. This statement suggests that the community is the most appropriate space for this type of work.[66]

The belief that the 'goodness' of community could counteract society-wide problems continued to be evident during the austerity period, despite the international origins of the financial crisis. In 2012, RTÉ launched its Local Heroes initiative, which promoted positive community-based responses to the recession:

Across Ireland – towns and communities are struggling and unemployment remains stubbornly high. While it seems that much of our economic situation is beyond our control, every individual, business and community in Ireland has the power to make a difference to the wider economy.[67]

While the top-down association between 'goodness' and community is evident here, there have been more challenging bottom-up expressions of this link during the austerity period. Plans to build a series of wind farms across rural Ireland had to be revised in 2014 because of the rapid and effective mobilisation of residents to protect the 'good' of their communities.[68] The effectiveness of the wind farm protest demonstrated how quickly mobilisation to protect the 'good' of the community can still occur in Irish society.

The most sustained anti-austerity protest of the entire period has also occurred at community level. Since 2010, residents of the small village of Ballyhea, County Cork have met every Sunday to march in protest against the bank bailout as part of the 'Ballyhea Says No' campaign.[69] The effectiveness of the wind farm protest and the sustained commitment of the Ballyhea protesters is striking when compared to the sluggish level of public protest during the early austerity years at national level, a sluggishness that suggests that the association between goodness and the nation may be more problematic.

CONCLUSION

In Chapter 1, we looked at the role of colonialism in generating a perception that rules were unfair. In response, many Irish people retreated into the relationship-based groups of family and community, where they could express their real feelings about unfair rules. After independence, the Civil War generation of politicians had to establish the infrastructure of the new state within this tense balance between rules and relationships. As a consequence a number of strategies were used to bolster the stability of the Free State. The legitimacy of the rules of the state was shored up by a close alliance with the Catholic Church, which had a rule-based system the majority Catholic population really did believe in. The state's founding fathers also placed an idealised vision of family and community at the heart of the new state's ideology. While the state they established did achieve stability, it failed to deliver prosperity. The lacklustre performance of the Irish economy had, by the 1950s, resulted in levels of emigration which threatened the survival of the state's families and communities. Recognition of the scale of this crisis provoked a sharp shift in economic policy and changed attitudes to wealth and consumption.

These economic changes ushered in a wave of modernisation in which Irish families and communities were transformed by urbanisation, secularisation, new social movements and global culture. Despite these changes, it is astonishing how strongly communities and families still function as a 'touchstone' for goodness in the Irish value system. This is evident in attempts by commercial and state organisations to borrow the links to 'goodness' in their marketing campaigns. It has become even more pronounced since the financial crisis, when communities have become one of the few points of active public response to austerity. In a country where externally imposed rules became ever more oppressive between 2010 and 2013, the relationship-based groups of family and community became the focal point for the process of 'looking after our own', a process which is explored in Chapter 3.

Chapter 3

RULES, RELATIONSHIPS AND BELONGING

Giving and Taking from 'Our Own'

Rules and responsibilities, these are the ties that bind us. We do what we do because of who we are. If we did otherwise, we would not be ourselves.[1]

Neil Gaiman

In the normal run of daily life, we seldom think about the tension between rules and relationships in our culture. As Neil Gaiman notes, balancing rules and responsibilities to loved ones is viewed as simply part of being 'ourselves'. But a crisis – like the economic crisis that overwhelmed Ireland in recent years – can force us to question what being 'ourselves' means. Throughout the bailout, austerity and recovery period of 2008–2013, many people questioned whether attitudes to rules and relationships had contributed to Ireland's financial problems. While politicians and the media focused on the behaviour of elites, debates on internet forums, popular fiction and new political movements showed that ordinary people were engaging in deeper reflection on everyday Irish attitudes to rules and relationships.[2] How do Irish citizens experience rules and relationships in their everyday lives? How do rules and relationships shape their sense of belonging to Irish society?

This chapter will outline rule-based models of belonging that have evolved since the foundation of the state. These rule-based ties to the state are contrasted with relationship-based ties to the nation, which have also changed significantly since the modernisation of the 1960s. The way in which Irish people use the term 'our own' to describe relationship-based groups to which they have obligations is explored. The exclusion of outsiders from 'our own' is considered by examining how attitudes to immigrants have changed since the bailout and austerity period. Finally, the struggles of returned migrants to rejoin 'our own', struggles that signal a deeper tension between rule-based and relationship-based belonging in Ireland, are highlighted.

BEING AN 'IRISH' CITIZEN

The most important rule-based identity in Ireland is that of 'citizen'. After the foundation of the state in 1922, the Irish Free State defined its citizens as all those 'domiciled in the territory in the area of jurisdiction of the Irish Free State, at the time of coming into operation of this constitution'.[3] This early concept of Irish citizenship was based predominantly on residence in the territory of the Irish state. However, the 26-county state's claim to the six counties of Northern Ireland created a whole range of ambiguities about how this territory was defined. Family relationships became a more important part of Irish citizenship as the Irish state evolved. In 1956, the Irish Nationality and Citizenship Act made it easier for descendants of Irish emigrants to register for citizenship by proving their family ties to Ireland. At the time, Northern Ireland politician Terence O'Neill poured scorn on the legislation, describing it as 'an attempt by a small pastoral republic to create a vast empire of citizens'.[4] However, as Mary Daly succinctly notes, the key motivation for this reform was not empire-building but economic development. The state hoped to boost tourism by encouraging these new Irish citizens to visit their 'homeland'.[5] The legislation highlighted an increasingly close link between citizenship and money, a link that became even more pronounced during the 'passports for sale' schemes of the 1980s and 1990s, when wealthy individuals could obtain Irish passports – a key symbol of citizenship – in return for investment in the Irish state.[6]

For Irish people, there is also a clear link between citizenship of the state and access to material resources. For them, citizenship confers a right to public services and an entitlement to welfare payments, as well as obligations to pay tax and obey the law of the state. Laura, a 33-year-old mother of two in County Tipperary, says:

> No, I don't really think about what it means to be an Irish citizen but I think a lot about what I'm entitled to. That's means a lot to me. I pay more tax than I'd like to and if I could get away with paying less I would; but I still believe in paying some tax. I do vote but I suppose money is … the bit I think about most on a daily basis when I'm trying to make ends meet. What it means to be a citizen, that's not something I would think about much, really.

In the 1990s, debates about Irish citizenship occurred largely in the context of the Northern Ireland peace process. The abandonment of the Irish government's claim to the six counties of Northern Ireland indicated a continuing preoccupation with the rule of residence. From 2000 onwards, however, growing public controversy about 'citizenship tourism' (immigrant women having babies and claiming citizenship) resulted in a sharp shift in the constitutional definition of citizenship away from residence and towards blood relationships linked to family.[7]

As the media debates leading up to the 2004 citizenship referendum became more intense, even some naturalised citizens of Ireland who were not from Irish families felt that they did not truly 'belong' in Ireland. In a radio interview in 2002 Moosajee Bhamjee, Ireland's first Muslim TD, revealed this anxiety: 'I am an Irish citizen, of course – in one way, I will never be Irish.'[8] So is 'belonging' in Ireland more complex than simply becoming a citizen, paying tax and conforming to the rules of the state? 'Belonging' seems closely bound up with relationships, and during the Celtic Tiger era the Irish constitutional definitions of citizenship moved closer to this relationship-based form of belonging. Chapter 2 highlighted the strong links between family, community and goodness in the Irish value system. Does this same link apply to belonging to the nation in Ireland?

NATION AND BEING GOOD

The ties that bind Irish people to their nation are among their most important relationship-based bonds. The 2002/2003 International Social Survey Project (ISSP) found that over 90 per cent of Irish people reported feeling close to their country.[9] Benedict Anderson argues that in many countries there is a strong association between national identity and 'being good'. He says: 'Dying for one's country ... assumes a moral grandeur which dying for the Labour Party, the American Medical Association, or perhaps even Amnesty International cannot rival.'[10] National identities are powerful because they are built upwards from relationship-based bonds of family and community. Michael Herzfeld notes:

> Once created, national identity is both a moral fact and a collective representation ... It also subordinates smaller identities – kin, group, village, region – to the encompassing collective good. In displacing them, however, it must draw upon them for symbolic nourishment, for they provide the language that the people best understand.[11]

Perhaps the biggest obstacle since the foundation of the state to building a strong association between Irish national identity and 'being good' has been the disjuncture between the boundaries of the 26-county state and the 32-county concept of the 'Irish nation'. The anomalies generated by disjuncture were largely ignored during the first forty years of the state's existence. However, as Northern Ireland descended into deep sectarian violence in the late 1960s and early 1970s, it became increasingly problematic for Irish political leaders to publicly celebrate the 'goodness' of the Irish national group. Young members of the North's republican movement engaged in violent acts and claimed the mantle of Irish republican 'virtue'. They highlighted their commitment to a 32-county Irish nation as evidence of their 'true' nationalism, a vision still prominent in republicanism.[12]

As the 1970s progressed, there was increasing reliance on a bottom-up form of nationalism which used county-based identities as a way of locating each individual, family and community within the nation.[13] As we saw in Chapter 2, the structure of the GAA is rooted in the parish, and the best players from parish teams move through the club structure to play for their county. The GAA calendar in both hurling and football culminates in national All-Ireland finals held in Croke Park, Dublin, a stadium with a strong historic association with Irish nationalism. The annual ritual of the championships, therefore, reinforces the connections between family, community, county and the nation. In their study of nationalism in the border region of Ireland, Jennifer Todd *et al.* found that the GAA was vital in promoting county identities through which local people could understand and celebrate their place in the Irish nation. By locating themselves and their families in the nation via the county, they could set aside the rhetoric of republican nationalism – which they largely rejected.[14] However, Todd *et al.* also note that this county-based vision of the Irish nation in the competitive structure of the GAA is, ultimately, a 32-county rather than a 26-county vision, which does not acknowledge the existence of the border between the Republic and Northern Ireland. They conclude: 'this practice (institutionalized in the national sporting organization, the GAA) had the function of bypassing the significance of the border, avoiding the need to give legitimacy to it as a dividing line.'[15]

This denial of the border complicates the associations between the nation and 'being good'. At the height of the Troubles, a significant moment of national celebration in Southern Ireland occurred in 1970 when Dana (Rosemary Brown) won Ireland's first Eurovision Song Contest title. However, Dana herself was born in London and grew up in the Bogside in Derry City, so she was technically a British citizen. Despite his residence in the British state, County Tyrone football manager Mickey Harte clearly considered winning an All-Ireland title for the county as the pinnacle of 'being good'. His diary of this achievement is entitled *Kicking Down Heaven's Door*, where 'heaven' is winning the *All-Ireland* Football Championship, although he is also technically a resident of the British state.[16]

However, some Northern Irish sports stars find the contradictions between rules and relationship-based forms of belonging more difficult to reconcile. In 2012, golfing champion Rory McIlroy found himself enmeshed in controversy. As an amateur, he had been sponsored by the Golfing Union of Ireland, but having achieved considerable global success he publicly said that he was considering playing for the British team at the 2016 Rio Olympics. He said he had 'always felt more British than Irish'.[17] The deeply negative public reaction to his comments in the Republic of Ireland led him to acknowledge that he might not play in the Olympics at all as there was no way he could be perceived as good in the situation. He said 'This thing goes back hundreds and hundreds of years and there's war and battles of all sorts. It's a tricky situation to be in. If I was a bit more selfish, I think it would be easier.'[18] In the *New York Times* in 2013, Karen Crouse noted the significant cooling of public opinion towards McIlroy in the Republic of Ireland after these comments:

> The public opinion for Rory is not necessarily the way it once was. The public view of him in Ireland has definitely waned given the whole Olympic conversation. In pubs and cabs and on the Carton House course, McIlroy was variously described as 'a spoiled brat' and 'a snob' and hailed as being from 'a leafy loyalist suburb'.[19]

The response to the controversy by Patrick Finn, General Secretary of the Golfing Union of Ireland, is most revealing:

> The Ireland they played for as amateurs is not the Ireland represented by the tricolour ... When it comes to the Olympics, it's ... Rory's democratic right to be a British citizen or an Irish citizen. It is citizenship that governs who you can compete for in the Games. It has nothing to do with sport whatsoever.[20]

So in certain situations, the rules-based belonging of citizenship trumps relationship-based forms of belonging. Despite the technical accuracy of Finn's statement, the controversy continued and McIlroy responded by issuing an open letter in which he tried to explain his attitude to the matter. He said, 'As an international sportsman, I am very lucky to be supported by people all over the world, many of who treat me as *one of their own*, no matter what their nationality or indeed mine. This is the way sport should be.'[21] Although McIlroy subsequently declared that he would indeed represent Ireland in Rio,[22] his use of the term 'one of their own' is fascinating. Sixty-two per cent of Irish people interviewed for this study also used this term to describe groups to which they felt a strong relationship-based sense of belonging. McIlroy appeared to be saying that while his *rule-based* belonging might always be controversial, sport allowed him to access *relationship-based* belonging 'all over the world'. But is it really that simple? Every single individual interviewed for this study described not only the benefits but also the demands of relationship-based belonging – to family, community, nation and other groups they described as 'our own'. These obligations, while less formal than the demands of citizenship, were considerable. So understanding how obligations to 'our own' intertwine with rule-based citizenship is central to understanding the balance between rules and relationships in Irish society.

BELONGING TO 'OUR OWN'

During the course of interviews conducted for this book between 2008 and 2013, one of the most important ideas that emerged in the research was the concept of 'our own'. Interviewees used the term 'one of our own' to refer to their immediate and extended families, members of their local communities, friends and fellow members of the national group. The concept of 'our own' was also used to describe occupational groups such as the Gardaí and sporting organisations such as the GAA. Despite the widespread use of the term 'our own', there was little understanding of the boundaries and links between these various groups defined as 'our own'. From the way individuals used the term, it is clear that:

- The term 'our own' is commonly used to describe groups at the level of the family, community and nation, but it can exist in other contexts.

- 'Our own' in all these contexts has boundaries and can exclude individuals and groups.
- Being part of 'our own' involves moral obligations to other members of the group.
- Individuals can be part of a number of groups defined as 'our own' and have a different level of commitment to each group.
- The moral obligations to other group members weakens as the group gets larger and more remote from the individual.
- A 'good' person is the person who meets obligations to 'be there' for other members of 'our own'.
- 'Being there' for other members of 'our own' can take precedence over 'being fair' to individuals outside the group.

In his studies of rural China, Fei Xiaotong found a similar model of belonging. He says that ties within relationship-based groups in China are:

> ... like ripples formed from a stone thrown into a lake, each circle spreading out from the centre becomes more distant and at the same time more insignificant.... Everyone stands at the centre of circles produced by his or her own social influence. Everyone's circles are interrelated. One touches different circles at different times and places.[23]

Not everyone who lives in Irish society is firmly embedded in groups described as 'our own', but this form of belonging can be very powerful in the lives of people who do belong to these circles. It is particularly important in relation to their capacity to access 'favours', which are rooted in the system of moral obligations that is part of membership of these groups. Being one of 'our own' and being able to access favours from these groups has real material benefits. Within families, local communities and occupational groups, Irish interviewees described the favours that were exchanged by members of 'our own'. These favours included:

- getting a summer or part-time job for a family member during school or college holidays (71%)

- getting interviews for full-time jobs or specific educational courses (36%)

- getting their children into specific primary or secondary schools if they did not live in the immediate catchment area (23%)

- providing special treatment to friends or family members in service contexts such as restaurants, hotels, airports, hospitals, etc. (56%)

- getting a friend or family member a bed or a room in a hospital (12%)

- finding work for family members or friends in their own place of employment (23%).

The link between material resources and being part of 'our own' is clear in the exchange of favours at family and community level. However, the concept of 'our own' was also clearly linked to national identity and associated with access to material resources. At national level, the rule-based identities of citizen, taxpayer and social welfare recipient were viewed as being closely intertwined with membership of 'our own', with profound consequences for those located outside these groups.

MIGRANTS AND 'OUR OWN'

Between 1995 and 2007, Ireland changed from being a country of emigration to a country of immigration. According to the 2006 census, 10 per cent of the Irish population were of migrant origin.[24] Most newcomers to Irish society came from the Eastern European states of Poland, Latvia and Lithuania after these countries joined the EU in 2002. However, there were also significant numbers of African, Asian and South American migrants who arrived in Ireland, many of whom were able-bodied and seeking employment. Interviews conducted with immigrants during the 2008–2011 period revealed that they felt an increasing resentment from the Irish population. This impression was confirmed when a number of Irish citizens interviewed indicated that they believed that immigrants were taking jobs and welfare entitlements which rightfully belonged to Irish people, whom they described as 'our own'.

In June 2013, a report published by the ESRI showed a sharp spike in Irish opposition to immigration since the start of the recession. The number of people who were not in favour of immigrants of different ethnic backgrounds and from poorer non-European countries coming to Ireland rose from 5 per cent in 2002 to 20 per cent in 2010. There was a notable increase in the amount of racist graffiti, one family home in Dublin being daubed with the message, 'Out if you're not working.'[25] Immigrants described the difficulties they experienced when they attempted to challenge this prejudice. Julia is an African woman who complained to her manager about derogatory comments made by a co-worker.

> This manager kept me waiting for forty minutes and then said to me, 'Do you want to make an issue of this?' and I said, 'I don't really, I just don't want to work with this person any more.' Later I overheard him tell the supervisor that I was just trying to play the race card against *'one of our own'*. That was the exact term he used.

As the process of austerity deepened, attitudes towards migrant groups who were perceived as hard-working, such as the Polish community, changed considerably. These migrants came to be perceived as a threat to 'our own' because they were taking 'our jobs'. Eileen, who is in her 80s, says:

> I went to Dublin last week and all the shops round Henry Street had foreigners serving. I have no objection to that but I'm just saying where are *our own* girls? Are they aiming higher? You hear now that the unemployment register has gone up. And the same down town, when you go into an ordinary service shop, a lot of foreigners. I wouldn't have any objection if there were none of *our own* unemployed but I think if there are they should be employed ahead of foreigners.

Mikey, who is unemployed and looking for a job, says, 'I think if somebody has a job going, they should keep it for an Irish person. We have to look after *our own* first.' There is some evidence that employers share this view. Unemployment rates among immigrant groups were significantly higher than unemployment rates in the Irish population in 2012.[26]

By 2013, asylum applications had declined dramatically. Nevertheless, strong concerns were expressed about the welfare benefits being received by asylum seekers and the possibility that newly unemployed migrant workers would be receiving welfare payments. Maeve says:

> Well, I suppose I do feel entitled to things 'cause I'm an Irish citizen. It's not something I think about a lot. I just pay my taxes and get on with it, though in the last couple of years with the new taxes and bills I struggle with that more, but I feel that if I ever lost my job, then the system would be there for me. I could get Jobseekers or whatever. But I do really feel it should be kept for *our own* people. I'm not happy to bail out some Pole or Hungarian or some fat cat banker for that matter.

In her research on asylum seekers, Bríd Uí Chonaill found that they were particularly susceptible to being characterised as 'freeloaders' and 'spongers' who were taking from 'our own'.[27] Elaine Moriarty tracked the telling of a story in West Dublin about an African asylum-seeking woman who leaves her buggy at the bus stop because she believes she can get another from social welfare. Moriarty concludes:

> The story constructs the state through the 'health centre' as passive and possibly powerless with non-nationals casually taking and discarding resources which are not available to the perceived Irish population and also implying that the state should be *'looking after its own'*.[28]

Not all representatives of the state are quite so passive in expressing the idea that resources should be kept for 'our own'. In Limerick during

2013, there was significant local controversy when local councillor Kevin Sheahan called for an 'Irish first' social housing policy. Immigrants have to meet a range of additional criteria to apply for local authority housing in Ireland, and asylum seekers are excluded entirely from the process. Nevertheless, he claimed that immigrants who 'breezed in on a plane' were getting 'preferential treatment', while Irish citizens were being told to 'go home to mammy'. In the face of condemnation, Sheahan remained unapologetic, stating, 'we are borrowing money every day to keep the shop open.... At the same time, we are handing out money and resources to people who, in my view, we have no responsibility for.'[29]

The link between access to jobs, welfare benefits and membership of relationship-based groups defined as 'our own' became sharply evident during the austerity period in Ireland, but the exclusionary implications of being located outside 'our own' can also be seen in other contexts. In their study of immigrant candidates in local elections in Ireland, Fanning *et al.* quote one African candidate who described the response he received on the doorstep in Dundalk. He said 'Some say that they will vote for me before I say anything. Others will say that they are voting for *their own*.'[30] 'Their own' in this context appears to mean members of the local community, excluding not only recent immigrants but also others from outside the community.[31] Another migrant describes trying to access a service from a community organisation in Dundalk. He commented, 'There are some services in Dundalk that nobody outside Dundalk can tap into it, even an Irish, even from Drogheda [23 miles away]. I know, they will tell you, you know, white and black ... it's normally meant for Dundalk people.'[32] These comments reveal that the concept of 'our own' can lead to forms of exclusion that are not just confined to material resources. In addition, 'our own' can exclude at a range of levels; and this exclusion doesn't just affect immigrants but can impact on those outside the local community.

STRUGGLES WITH 'OUR OWN'
Research conducted with Irish emigrants who left Ireland in the 1980s and returned during the Celtic Tiger boom reveal that they also struggle

with belonging to 'our own'. Two major studies published by Corcoran (2003) and Ní Laoire (2008) indicated that many of these migrants returned because they believed that Irish culture places greater value on personal relationships than their host societies. For instance, a returner from New York comments:

> Family was a big issue. Neither of us had family in New York. We had friends but we didn't have family. You would come back on holidays and see that so much was happening. A feeling of belonging, to come back, and even though I had never lived in Dublin, to walk down Grafton Street and think, oh God, this feels right. It's Ireland, you go for a walk on the beach and it feels right.[33]

In seeking a cultural emphasis on relationships, returned emigrants were clearly aware of belonging to 'our own'. Claire, who returned from Britain, says:

> There is an understanding amongst your own nation, it's just an understanding that it's a recognised thing, of *'you're with your own'*, you know. That I can have a conversation with you and use terms or whatever and you know the nature of me because you know where I've come from so you already have an understanding of the kind of person I am because you're Irish yourself … I don't have to explain any of this or who I am or where I come from because it's an unsaid understanding.[34]

A number of participants in both studies revealed that they came back to Ireland because they wanted to live in a culture where relationships are important. One man commented, 'Our structure is different in that if someone belonging to you died you could take a few days off or a month off. It might piss your employer off but they would understand it. But over there, that wasn't the model at all. They just didn't understand it.'[35] Another interviewee, who came back from Silicon Valley, viewed the priority placed on relationships in Irish culture as a significant virtue. He said, 'The most important thing about Irish culture is the insistence – even in the most minute transaction such as getting a cup of coffee – on there being personal contact between the people involved. This is the healthiest part of Irish culture – nothing to do with saints and scholars.'[36]

The priority placed on relationship-based groups such as the family and community was part of a value system in Ireland which was particularly appreciated. One interviewee describes the greater emphasis on family in Irish culture compared to the emphasis on work in the United States:

> It's just the hours you worked. You felt like you were a working machine. Americans seem to accept that, not only accept it but espouse it as a way of life. Whereas, we weren't prepared to think like that. We were reared more on the mindset that you worked to enjoy life, and make the enjoyment of life possible, whereas their whole lives revolved around their careers and everything else – including *family* – was secondary as well.[37]

However, many of these returning migrants did not find the process of rejoining 'our own' that easy.[38] In both studies, migrants indicated that because they had been away, they were treated as if they no longer fully belonged to 'our own'. Tim, who had returned from Africa, told Ní Laoire, 'Coming back to Ireland, re-settling, was difficult in many ways because I thought it was going to be so easy to come back. You know the people, you know the places. But it's not that easy.'[39] In Corcoran's study, a returner from Vancouver comments:

> There is a sense of not being forgiven for being away and that when you come back who do you think you are coming back, trying to weave your way back into family and be there for all the roles that everybody has taken over in your absence. You were trying to reclaim some of your role in the family and it was deeply resented.

Another returner found it demanding to meet the obligations of relationship-based groups defined as 'our own'. He said 'You get roped into obligations that you never had before, like I was saying earlier, family and friends might be in your thoughts [over there] but suddenly you are obliged to go to every christening, or events, to remember birthdays. And it is a big time drag.'[40] Even if they meet these increased obligations, the returner may still feel that they are no longer part of 'our own'. Bill told Ní Laoire:

> I suppose there was a funny attitude in Ireland to emigrants. At one stage, it's phoney accents and everyone thinking 'oh God, here they come' and people trumpeting how wonderful where they are is, and nobody particularly wants to be one of those people ... and I suppose Irish people don't regard Irish abroad as one of us, so in that sense you're not really one of us any more, you're outside our circle now, you're not one of us now. When you leave, you're gone, you've left our tribe.[41]

It seems that relationships and belonging to 'our own' were the primary factors in migrants' decisions to return to Ireland. However, return to Ireland does not necessarily mean that the migrant automatically rejoins 'our own'. Migrants find that they are indeed 'outside the circle now' and have to work very hard to get back in. They do this by adjusting their accent and not talking about their experiences abroad. One returner from New York concludes, 'Irish people can be tough on emigrants. I found it so and now I am one of the people who makes it tough for emigrants. Irish emigrants talk about Irish people as a separate category, there is a "them and us" thing going on.'[42] Anne says, 'You really need to fit in, or else they treat you differently ... there's no leeway.' These quotes reveal that it is not just immigrants who can feel excluded from 'our own'. Relationship-based belonging in Ireland can cause a range of struggles and tensions even for those who have a relatively sophisticated understanding of Irish culture and its value system.

CONCLUSION

Rule-based belonging is very important in the lives of Irish citizens because it is linked to rights and entitlements to material resources. Since the 1960s, the number of rules that govern Irish citizens has increased significantly. Through the welfare system, these rules have become closely intertwined with ideas about belonging in Ireland. The structure of groups such as the family, community and the nation also changed significantly during the twentieth century. Despite these changes, there is still a strong association between 'goodness' and relationships in the Irish value system. One of the most striking features of this tendency is the frequent use of the term 'our own' to describe a range of relationship-based groups to which individuals have obligations. Not everyone in Ireland is located within 'our own', but being a member of 'our own' can have a profound impact on the individual's ability to access favours. These favours are part of the system of moral obligations that generate real material benefits for those who belong to 'our own'.

The consequences of being excluded from 'our own' can be serious and have become increasingly evident to immigrants since 2008. They are confronted by a relationship-based perspective in the Irish value system that insists that jobs should be kept for 'our own'. If they claim benefits they are resented because of a belief that welfare benefits from the national resource base should be kept for 'our own'. While the struggles generated by the concept of 'our own' are most evident in the experience of immigrants, returned emigrants to Ireland also find that rejoining 'our own' provokes a range of challenges linked to belonging, trust and communication as well as models of 'being good'. We shall explore these deeper conflicts in Chapter 4.

Chapter 4

THE PARALLEL WORLDS OF RULES AND RELATIONSHIPS IN IRELAND

Can you feel it?
Things are changing
Can you see it?
Watch as the worlds
Collide ...

'End of the Beginning' (30 Seconds to Mars)

T he balance between rules and relationships in each society is unique – rather like a fingerprint. Colonialism, wars, religious traditions and culture all contribute to this delicate balance. We can trace the historical roots of this balance in Ireland, but it is equally important to explore how ordinary Irish people experience it in their daily lives. This chapter draws on 148 interviews (112 Irish citizens and 36 migrants) and the findings of nine focus groups to map this rules/relationship fingerprint in everyday life in Ireland. The chapter will argue that rules and relationships are not only important in themselves; they are also the starting point for two parallel worlds, two distinct understandings of reality. These parallel worlds differ in terms of how rules and relationships provide information, create belonging, inspire trust and promote methods of communicating. The parallel worlds of rules and relationships also generate two different visions of 'being good'. The world of relationships celebrates a form of goodness which emphasises 'being there' for others in circles of intimacy (described in Chapter 3 as 'our own'). The world of rules promotes a vision of goodness which stresses that conforming to rules creates a consistency that promotes fairness. This chapter explores how the competing demands to 'be fair' and 'be there' can create tensions in the lives of ordinary Irish citizens.

The parallel worlds of rules and relationships shape how Irish people interact with each other within families, workplaces and local communities. The views of recent immigrants to Ireland provided particular insight into the balance between these parallel worlds as they are located outside the dense networks of relationships which form 'our own'. It is clear from this research that the parallel worlds of rules and relationships often co-exist harmoniously, but sometimes these worlds collide. It is arguable that the Irish banking crash resulted from a collision between the two worlds. In Chapter 5 we'll look at how the different ways of knowing, trusting, communicating, belonging and 'being good' that characterise these two worlds shape Irish citizens' dealings with politicians at local constituency level. Chapter 6 will use the same factors to consider how these two parallel worlds inform how Irish politicians have engaged with business elites since the 1960s.

The aim of these three chapters is to map how the weak rules/ strong relationships balance which caused the banking crash is linked to the interplay between these two parallel worlds, which operate in tension with each other throughout Irish society. The chapters also demonstrate the differences in how this balance operates at each level of Irish society, from the everyday life of the middle class through to the golden circles of Irish elites.

KNOWING, TRUSTING, COMMUNICATING

In describing the balance between rules and relationships in their own lives, almost a third of middle-class research participants said that rule-based knowledge (such as legal and scientific systems) had become a more important part of their work during the last thirty years. Colm, who has worked in a marketing firm in Dublin since the 1980s, describes how the world of rules had changed his job:

When I started in this game, people would rely a lot on their gut instinct when thinking about how to sell something. But it's totally changed now. Now it's all based on market research. We can tell how many people need a product say like baby wipes. We can find out what colours they like, when they eat breakfast, dinner and tea so we know the best time to place ads. All these decisions are based on research [rules-based knowledge]. If you went into an account meeting talking about your gut instinct, you'd be laughed out of it.

Noreen works in a human resources department in the public sector and has also found that rules-based knowledge has become central to her work.

Well, you know, HR has become a litigation minefield in the last few years, particularly in the public sector. Twenty years ago when I started, you'd just get a selection committee together and they picked who they liked. Now all the applicants have to be asked exactly the same questions, and marked on each area. The marks get added and they get feedback on each area. The bottom line is that if the person is not appointed you have to be able to give them a sound explanation why and the same procedure must be applied to everyone. You can't just go with who you like.

However, not all interviewees found this commitment to rules-based knowledge in the Irish workplace very convincing. Danny, an African migrant, says:

Before I came to Ireland, my background was in HR.... When I got my job, I studied the Induction Booklet very carefully and I know my rights. So if I want to ask for holidays, I don't beg. They really can't argue because I tell them I know but that doesn't really go down well with them and creates trouble down the line. They are not really happy if you insist they stick to the rules. If I keep quiet and be a kind of Uncle Tom, they prefer that better.

When Danny invokes his rights under the rule-based system, he meets with a hostile response from his Irish managers, which suggests to him a weak commitment to the world of rules in the Irish value system.

A key feature in the modernisation of the Irish workplace since the 1960s has been the introduction of rule-based performance evaluation systems. Some participants argued that these systems are fairer because performance is considered on the basis of specific criteria rather than personal relationships. Senan, who works in the public sector, comments, 'These performance evaluations have come in our place and to be honest, it can be better. At least, you can point to things and say "I've done that" or "I meet that requirement". I've worked in places where it's purely down to licking the boss's arse and that's soul-destroying.' Rule-based evaluations are used not only at the individual level but also for entire institutions – in the form of quality reviews, etc. Some participants criticised these evaluations because they felt that there wasn't a genuine commitment to the world of rules in these processes. Connor, a primary school teacher, described his experience of a whole school evaluation (WSE), the major auditing process in the Irish primary school sector:

> Our principal, Máiread, is a cute hoor. She nominated a class for the evaluation who were bloody angels, not like the monsters in some of the other classes. Senior teachers were recorded as doing work which was actually being done by junior teachers on much less pay. Policies were invented overnight. The whole thing was a farce really and to be honest, I think the evaluators know exactly what was going on.

The ability of managers to manipulate the rules of performance evaluations was raised by nineteen individuals in the interview series. A number of participants said that they saw the process of auditing an institution as simply a 'performance' of conformity to rules. Connor continued:

The day after the WSE was completed I had to go to Máiread about an issue that she had actually invented a policy about overnight for the evaluation. I was thinking this is great, now we actually have a policy about this and we can deal with it. So I told Máiread about the problem and she just looked at me and said, 'What do you expect me to do?' and I said, 'What about the new policy?' and she just looked at me and laughed.

While rules have become increasingly important in the Irish workplace, the experiences of Connor and Danny suggest that managers don't always have a strong moral commitment to this world beyond displaying conformity to rules.

Despite the increasing volume of rules at work, the continuing importance of relationship-based knowledge was a theme that appeared in over half of the interviews with Irish citizens. So what is relationship-based knowledge? When we meet people, we don't just listen to what they say; we react to their physical appearance, their body language and facial expressions. As we get to know someone better, we become more adept at reading their non-verbal signals, and this helps us to 'know' things about them. Colette, a housewife in County Tipperary, describes how relationship-based knowledge provided her with important information during the summer of 2011:

It was Liam's birthday last summer so I'd invited friends round for the evening, just cold meats and salads and a few drinks. It was mostly his golf buddies and their wives. All through the night I knew something was wrong with him. He put on a great show and made sure everyone had a great time, but I could see the expression on his face at times and I didn't like it. The minute the last couple left the house, I said, 'What in God's name has happened?' Turned out he'd been made redundant that day and couldn't face telling me. The poor man, he should have known that I'd know by taking one look at him.

Liam's friends may have thought he was having a great time that night, but Colette 'knew' that something was wrong – but if you asked her to define exactly *how* she 'knew' she might find it hard to explain.

While we commonly use relationship-based knowledge in families, a number of participants described how they drew on this form of knowledge (by reading facial expressions and body language) in their professional lives. Their understanding of emotion and their ability to read non-verbal signals became part of the skill set they used at work. Gerry, a garda in County Cork, described how he used this type of knowledge in dealing with one challenging professional situation.

> If you only used your head in my job, you'd be goosed. You have to have some compassion for people, for how they are feeling. For instance, I had to call to a family and tell them that their son had caused a car crash which had killed two people. Now he was the guilty party because he was drunk-driving but he wasn't going to walk again and the poor mother was so upset. She was devastated. I could see it in her face. You'd need a heart of stone not to feel for her.[1]

Gerry's sensitive approach to dealing with this situation draws on relationship-based knowledge which he delicately balances with his commitment to the world of rules. He contrasts his approach to the more zealous attitude to rules displayed by a young guard assigned to his station:

> The main thing you have to learn about being a guard in a small community is to use your discretion. Knowing when to assert yourself and when to hold back. I'll give you an example. I'd a young guard come down here after his stint in Templemore and he was mad for action. Of course, this is a quiet little place and there isn't too much happening. But anyway, this local family, who'd be tough nuts now, they had a family funeral in the town. It was a cousin I think and this little whippersnapper went in and started checking all the cars for tax, insurance and seat belts and illegal

parking and every whole bloody thing. We'd huge problems with them after that. He just didn't know when to hold back.

Gerry believed that, even though the young garda was sticking to the rules, he behaved badly because he should have drawn on his emotions to understand the distress of the bereaved family. His criticism suggests that there are situations when the demand to implement the rules should be over-ridden by sensitivity to the feelings of others, a perspective which highlights the importance he attaches to the world of relationships.

There are times when the delicate balancing act between the worlds of rules and relationships breaks down. In 2012, an Indian dentist, Savita Halappanavar, died as a result of a mistreated miscarriage. At Galway University Hospital, she asked for a termination to her pregnancy but was refused because of the Irish state's very restrictive rules on abortion. On an RTÉ radio programme after her death, five women who had been in the same situation told their stories. One woman, Jennifer, described the evident distress of doctors who were treating her. They knew her pregnancy was not viable and they also knew that the longer it progressed, the greater the chance that she herself would die. She describes how one consultant took her mother aside and said to her, 'I know what I would do if it was my daughter. You need to *read between the lines*. You need to do it urgently.'[2] Because Jennifer's mother was Irish, she knew that the rules of the state prohibited the consultant from openly telling her to take her daughter to the UK for a termination. However, because of the consultant's evident sympathy and her mother's capacity to read cultural nuance she knew that this is precisely what the doctor was telling her to do. The consultant's emotion and non-verbal signals were communicating something different from the rules, hence the advice to 'read between the lines'. Because immigrants come from another culture, they don't know enough about the world of relationships in their host society to be able to read the cultural nuances in these types of interaction. They can't 'read between the lines'. They take what service providers and supervisors tell them at face value and must, in some cases tragically, deal with the consequences.

As well as generating knowledge, the parallel worlds of rules and relationships also dictate different forms of trust. Trust is defined as the 'firm belief in the reliability, truth or ability of *someone or something*'.[3] The distinction between 'someone' and 'something' is critical to understanding these different forms of trust. A person who values relationships is inclined to put their trust in 'someone'; the person who values rules is more likely to trust 'something' – the principles or abstract regulations governing behaviour in a particular situation. Saoirse, who lives in Laois and is in a wheelchair, describes how these different forms of trust created a tension in her own family.

> My Mam and Dad are really very different people, and in some ways, my disability has made those differences more visible. When I finished the Leaving Cert, I badly wanted to do this PLC [Post-Leaving Certificate] course in the local college. So I had a chat with Mam and Dad about it. Dad knows everyone 'cause he runs a business in town and he was like, 'I'll go down to Paddy [the college principal] and I'll have a chat to him and we'll get you in, don't worry.' But my mother put her foot down and was like, 'No, she'll apply just like everyone else, she's just as entitled as anyone else!' Honest to God, they're like chalk and cheese. Anyway, I did apply as normal and I did get a place but I wouldn't be surprised if Dad had gone behind her back and had a quiet word with Paddy anyway!

Saoirse's mother put her trust in the fairness of a system based on rules; her father had little faith in the system, but he placed a lot of trust in his circle of relationships in the town, which he believed he could use to organise a place for her. Although Saoirse succeeded in getting a place through the world of rules, she suspected that her father's connections within the world of relationships might have played a significant part in her success, again highlighting the tension between these two worlds in Irish culture.

The tendency to place trust in relationships rather than rules creates particular challenges for immigrants who are located outside 'our own' in Ireland. Sharon moved from Birmingham to Dublin in 2007 to work in a software company. She says:

> I have to say that even though Irish people are friendly, I found it very hard to break in socially. Like, I've worked in lots of places and I would consider myself to be pretty competent socially and it just wasn't working. Then I happened to mention one day that both my parents were from Waterford. Well, it was like everything changed. It was like I was one of them immediately. I found it so much easier from there on in. *It's like people seemed to trust me more.*

When Sharon's colleagues discovered her family connections in Ireland, it gave her a link to their world of relationships. As a result, she feels more welcome and trusted within their circles of intimacy.

The forms of knowledge and trust generated by rules and relationships are also starting points for different methods of communication. In the world of rules, communication is generally written down and sent through traceable channels, for example letters or emails. When a summons is issued by the Irish courts, for instance, it is written down and recorded and the person who receives it must sign for the letter to prove that they have received it.[4] The contents of these communications are clear not only to the recipient but also to anyone else who can access them; in other words, they operate outside the realm of 'personal' relationships. Clodagh, a solicitor in Cork, comments:

> I find more and more that people are using email to communicate rather than picking up the phone or meeting them in person. It's like if they send you an email, then the problem is off their backs and on your lap because it's so visible and traceable. I much prefer a phone call. It's much more personal but it's getting harder and harder to operate that way.

Communication in the world of relationships is undoubtedly more informal; and because personal relationships build up over time, people who are in intimate relationships with each other can often even communicate through few or no words at all. Tony, a manager in an engineering plant in Limerick, describes his communication with his colleague, Frank.

> Frank and myself would be the longest here, we are the old stagers in this place. And often in meetings, if one of the young ones comes up with a suggestion that we just know won't work, we will catch each others' eye and then we both know that we will shoot it down in our individual ways. It's like an unspoken understanding. We wouldn't meet each other outside work or socialise together or anything, but in work, we can read other. We just know each other so well.

Staff meetings in Tony's firm are governed by rules. The CEO chairs each meeting, an agenda is set and the discussions are recorded in the minutes. But Tony and Frank use relationship-based communication to unite in objection to proposals through a method which subverts all these structures; a demonstration of the potency of relationship-based communication in the face of rules-based systems.

The closed nature of this type of communication can often leave immigrants to Ireland at a loss when they try to understand what is going on in particular situations. Ashley, an American student attending university in Dublin, describes her struggles with relationship-based communication in Ireland:

> When I started the course, I had two tutorials. One was great, a couple of other international students. We mixed really well but the second class was a nightmare. All the kids had gone to this private school in Dublin and they all knew each other, I felt like I stuck out. I just didn't understand the jokes. Sometimes, they would just start laughing for no reason. Well, no reason I could tell.

Because Ashley is located outside this tight social group, she is unable to read signals expressed through non-verbal communication between

Irish students in her tutorial group. Perhaps Ashley's presence also makes these students more aware of the intimacy they share with each other. Although there is no evidence that the other students are breaking any rules, Ashley feels uncomfortable and isolated in their presence. The exclusion of outsiders is the dark side of intimacy. More important, because communication within relationships can be conducted using few or no words, not even powerful outsiders, such as governments or auditing authorities, can supervise or monitor it. There are no checks or balances that can be applied to a hand gesture, a nod or eye contact between two people who have a relationship-based connection to each other.

BELONGING AND CONFLICT

Chapter 3 contrasted rule-based belonging (citizenship) with relationship-based belonging to family, community and nation, groups often described as 'our own'. The chapter also revealed that the term 'our own' was used to describe other groups and highlighted the strong emphasis in Irish culture on 'looking after our own'. Interviews for this research demonstrate that one of the reasons that 'looking after our own' is deemed so important in Irish culture is because membership of these groups tends to become part of the individual's identity. Kathy, who works in a multinational firm in County Limerick, provides a good example of this type of belonging in describing her participation in the Irish Girl Guide movement.

> I grew up going to Girl Guides and my mother was a Guide and now I'm involved with my own kids. I can honestly say that the Girl Guides in Ireland are a huge part of my identity. If somebody asked me what are the bits that make up Kathy I'd have to say that one bit of me will always be a Guide. If the Girl Guides came to an end tomorrow, I don't know how I'd cope. A bit of me would go with it.

The interweaving of group and individual identity may explain why the demand to 'look after our own' is so compelling for Irish people who belong to these circles of intimacy. Kathy continued:

One of the women I'm involved in Guides with, her daughter was very sick and had to go to Belgium for this operation. So we all got together to raise the money. We had cake sales, we did sponsored runs, we had coffee mornings, we did everything we could think of. In the end, the little one had the operation and now she's up, running around and in the Brownies herself. We had to make a big effort for 'one of our own'.

The world of rules also generates belonging to groups. In this case, however, belonging to these groups is often linked to the individual's commitment to some external set of principles or personal rules about a particular role or situation.[5] Commitment to the rules or principles tends to be a part of the individual's identity, but membership of the group itself isn't as important. Maeve, a bank clerk in north Cork, described this type of belonging when she talked about participating in the parents' council at her children's school:

After we moved here, I joined the parents' council up at the school. The membership changes every year and we do fundraising and bits and pieces. It's a nice way to meet all the parents of kids in the school and it's quite social, you know, but if the whole thing was abolished in the morning, it wouldn't bother me and I can't say that anyone I met through it has changed me as a person. I think I really just do it to help the school and the kids. I suppose it's really because I see myself as a good parent and that's what good parents do.

For Maeve, participation in the parents' council is based on her vision of being a 'good' parent, a principle which is much more important to her identity than her membership of the group itself – to which she doesn't seem particularly attached.

As well as influencing their participation in community and sporting organisations, Irish people also described how these different forms of belonging shaped their links with their occupational group. Fergal left a career in IT to retrain as a doctor. He describes the differences in his sense of belonging to the two professions:

I can't say that when I worked in IT, being in any one company changed me. I moved around a lot and I liked nearly all the companies I worked for, but I would never have said that working for company X or even being a micro-electronics engineer defined me as a person. With medicine it's totally different. Being a doctor is a big part of who I am, and even working in the clinic that I work in is a big part of who I am. If I left this job, I think I would be a different person. However, I sometimes miss IT. I think a lot of conflict happens in medicine because people's personalities, their egos, their identities are all tied up with their jobs. In IT, people were less involved so when things got rough, there was less personal bullshit to deal with.

Fergal has experienced two forms of belonging in the workplace and highlights the different forms of conflict each generates. In the world of relationships, the individual's identity overlaps with the group, so conflict can be emotional, personal and potentially damaging to the group. As a result, in groups where relationship-based belonging exists, there is less open confrontation, which is seen as risky. Instead, each individual gradually reveals their viewpoint in the hope that all members of the group will move towards a general consensus; a resolution which will not threaten their own identity or the survival of the group itself.

It became evident during this research that when members of a group based on rules disagreed, they tried to debate the source of the conflict by applying external evidence to support their position. If they still could not come to an agreement, they would try to find a compromise, and because the identity of each individual was separate from the group, they could do so without destroying the group or lessening the respect given to each person in the group. A number of the Eastern European immigrants interviewed came to Ireland with the expectation that this rules-based approach to conflict would operate in the workplace. For instance, Dorota comments, 'Where I grew up, you could have a meeting and people would say what's on their mind. The Irish psyche is not like that, you are not free to say what's on your mind. You are kind of reluctant to put your point forward, you know, when you say this is wrong or this is right'. Mikail says:

> Irish workplaces, by and large, are much better at using informal disciplinary methods than formal disciplinary methods. It's very unusual for a manager in my work to come and talk to you directly about a problem. More often they tend to find a roundabout way of communicating with the staff. I think it's because they all know each other. That's the way it works. It has advantages but they are outweighed by the disadvantages.

Ursula, who runs a pre-school in County Tipperary, even noticed these differences in approaches to conflict amongst Irish and Eastern European children in her care. She says.

> To be honest, you'd be aware of subtle difference all the time. The best example I can give is this Polish boy, Stefan, I had last year. He was so direct. If he wanted something he asked for it straight out and kind of stood up for himself and that. You'd often find that the Irish children would be pussy-footing around, you know. But this child was so focused. I want this now, when can I have it? … Even with that child's parents, they were lovely parents, lovely altogether, but if they wanted to ask you something, they just asked you straight out and they just wanted a quick answer and that was it. If they want to tell you something and you don't want to hear, well they'll just tell you and that's it. I felt you knew where you stood with them a lot of the time and the same with this little boy.

Interestingly, Alan, a manager in a biomedical firm in Limerick and a senior member of his local rugby club, describes how he applies a rule-based approach to conflict at work but uses a relationship-based approach at the rugby club.

> In work we have a lot of conflict but also a lot of time pressure so we really don't have the scope for lots of slow-moving debate

on stuff. Orders have to go out or we have head office in the States breathing down our necks. I just get everyone to set out their stall early on. If we can't get agreement someone has to back down. I prefer if it isn't the same person all the time. That creates bad feeling, particularly among the women! The rugby club is different. We've all known each other since Junior League stage and things can get very heated and emotional. Last year, we had to put together a rescue strategy or the club would have gone under. Things got cut that people feel very strongly about but I prepared the ground beforehand and nudged everyone along and we got it through in the end. We had to have support from everyone or else the whole thing would have fallen apart. I suppose because it's mostly voluntary and we all know each other so well, I felt that was essential.

Both the rugby club and the biomedical firm have rules which shape how conflict is managed, but it is Alan's understanding of the different worlds of rules and relationships that allows him to successfully manage conflicts in both contexts.

BEING FAIR AND BEING THERE

The model of belonging that lies at the heart of the world of rules recognises that while principles or ideas may become part of the individual's identity, relationships with other members of groups tend to exist outside their identity. Each individual is regarded as separate and unique; therefore, the most important quality of good behaviour is to respect the separateness of the individual. Separateness is respected by acknowledging their need for privacy. Sarah-Jane, who has worked in the software industry in the USA for ten years, describes how difficult she found her mother's funeral when she returned to Ireland – precisely because she wanted neighbours in the community to respect her privacy:

I suppose I left Ireland because I hated all that country thing of people being in your business, so I found it very hard when I came home for Mam's funeral. There were neighbours in the house all the time. I didn't ask them to be there, I didn't want them to be there, I just wanted some space to grieve and then the removal was a nightmare, oh God, every Tom, Dick and Harry, even the local politician. I thought I'd never survive it. I got on a plane back to San Francisco the next day and never looked back.

This respect for the separateness of the individual which is at the heart of the world of rules leads to a number of other related moral demands. First, if an act is to truly respect the separateness and wholeness of the other person, the individual who commits it should be happy if the act were reversed and applied to them. 'Do unto others as you would have others do unto you' reflects a golden rule found in many religious traditions.[6] Taking that respect for individual separateness further, the philosopher Immanuel Kant argued that the individual should be willing not only for the act to be reversed but for it to be applied to everyone.[7] Basically, 'Do unto others as you would have them do unto everybody.' An act that is applied to everyone in the same way is, of course, fair.[8] Therefore, this emphasis puts fairness right at the heart of visions of good behaviour in the world of rules.

In order to ensure fairness, abstract principles are often created to help the individual deal with specific situations. Once these rules have been created, anyone should be able to know what constitutes good and bad behaviour in that context. In the United States, for instance, 'good Samaritan' legislation provides a set of rules about how any individual should behave if they are confronted with another person who is in difficulty.[9] During this research, participants not only described situations in which they felt that formal rules supported fairness, they also outlined situations in which they had created their own informal rules to promote fairness. For instance, Turlough, a retired car dealer in the Mid-West, describes how rules shape his approach to buying Christmas presents for his grandchildren:

I had four children and now they're grown up so I've nine grandchildren who I love dearly. I really like to get them all something at Christmas but to be honest, I'd see some of them a lot more than others and then, some are quicker to ask for what they want. The squeaky wheel gets the most oil, isn't that what they say? Two years ago, my grandson Cian pointed out that some of the younger ones who are at home with us a lot were getting more than the others. So now, I set a thirty euro limit for each child and everyone gets the same. My own granny was a fierce woman for favourites and I remember resenting it intensely.

Following Cian's criticism of the personal approach to buying presents – typical of the world of relationships – Turlough has created a new rule for his Christmas shopping to make sure all his grandchildren are treated fairly.

In the world of relationships, definitions of good behaviour exist outside rules and are different for each relationship and situation. The individual's identity is not seen as discrete and separate from others'; instead, it overlaps with others', and this overlap becomes part of their sense of self. When someone you have an intimate relationship with is in trouble, their trouble affects you in a very personal way. The relationship demands that you respond to the other person's distress by 'being there' for them. Fionnuala, a nurse in Mallow, describes how she became aware of relationship-based good behaviour:

Nicola, my daughter, and her two best friends, Clodagh and Zoe, went to Sydney after graduation looking for work and one night Zoe got separated from the other two on the way home from a bar. She was sexually assaulted by a group of young guys. Afterwards, the two girls had to stay with her through the medical treatment and the police investigation. They've all come home since but to be honest, it's had a huge impact on Nicola and Clodagh. It's like each of them was attacked that night. They're still in contact with her all the time, trying to support her. They don't need to be asked to do it. They just know the right thing to do and to be honest, it's a lifeline for her at the moment.[10]

Because of the intimacy between Zoe and her two friends, they share her pain and respond to her distress at the point where their identities overlap. There is no need for her two friends to consult rules or abstract principles when deciding how to behave around Zoe. Their behaviour is dictated by their feelings, their love for Zoe.[11] It is their feelings that inform their good behaviour.

Given the identity overlap between individuals who are in intimate relationship with each other, when one person does something good for the other, they are also doing something good for themselves – their behaviour impacts positively on their own life. 'Love thy neighbour as thyself' is a relationship-based understanding of good behaviour which appears in the Christian and early Buddhist traditions.[12] In contexts that operate outside formal rules and regulations, the rewards for relationship-based good behaviour can be significant and the penalties for bad behaviour can be severe. Eimear, a Cork housewife in her mid-30s, describes how relationship-based bad behaviour can ultimately impact negatively on the wrongdoer:

> My father would be a difficult man. He wasn't physically abusive but he could be very nasty and mean. Growing up, myself and my brother, Shane, we really had to make our own way. Mammy would never stand up to him and we knew that anything we did, we would have to do under our own steam. Mammy died last year and now he's on his own. I live in Cork and Shane in Dublin and to be honest, neither of us would ever go back to our home town in Offaly. In fact, we go out of our way to avoid it. I suspect he's pretty lonely but he needn't bother looking to us for company, because quite frankly, he wasn't there when we needed him.

It would be difficult for a state agency to compel Eimear or Shane to care for their father, so he has to face the negative consequences of his own behaviour in the world of relationships. He was not 'there' for his children when they were young and now they are not 'there' for him. The material cost of this behaviour may be even greater if he becomes seriously ill or infirm. Conversely, a warm, loving and supportive parent may expect to have the same behaviour shown to them in their old age, behaviour which will have real material benefits for them.

The competing demands to 'be fair' and 'be there' created a lot of tension in the lives of interviewees. The experience of Carole, a secretary in a chemical firm in County Laois, provided one of the clearest examples of this tension.

> My son, Ben, needed speech therapy and the waiting list in our area is a mile long. Anyway, one day I rang up the secretary, Susie, in the clinic. Her mother was in school with my mother and I actually cried down the phone. I was at my wits' end, he [Ben] was just mute. So she bumped him up the list. I know there were probably other people waiting longer and maybe those kids needed it more but I just had to get him seen to. Any mother would have done it.

From a 'fairness' perspective, Susie did the wrong thing in changing Ben's position on the waiting list. There may have been other children who needed the treatment more or who had been waiting even longer. But from the perspective of relationships, of 'being there' for the other person, what Susie did could be viewed as 'good' because her actions alleviated Carole's worry about Ben.

Carole placed Susie in a complex situation by asking her to make this change. Whatever response Susie made to Carole exposed her to some risk. From a rule-based perspective, if the Health Information and Quality Authority (HIQA) had audited the clinic, Susie could have been disciplined for changing Ben's position on the list.[13] On the other hand, not conforming to a relationship-based vision of good behaviour would have exposed Susie to a different risk. If Susie ignored Carole's distress, she and her mother might see her as cold and unhelpful, a perception that could shape how they treat her in the future. If Susie or her mother needed a favour from Carole's family at a later date, they might not find that help forthcoming. Therefore, there could be a real material cost in ignoring Carole's distress in this situation.

An individual's ability to conform to relationship-based and rule-based models of good behaviour can have a significant impact on whether they see themselves as a 'good' or 'bad' person. Emily, a hairdresser in County Tipperary, describes how her response to the problems of her brother Kevin affected her self-image:

> All my family have had money troubles over the last few years. My father had a men's drapery shop which went under so that hit us all very hard. But my own business has ticked along and I've worked my socks off so I suppose I haven't felt it as much as my brothers and sisters. My sister Lorraine was made redundant and I lent her some cash to go to Australia. But my younger brother, Kevin, he wanted to go back to college to do a master's and he asked me for a loan and I said no. I suppose I was just sick of them all scrounging. And to be honest, I'm sorry now. He's drinking a lot and he has broken up with his girlfriend and his life has really gone downhill since that time. Even if he wanted to go back to college now, they'd hardly take him. I've always seen myself as someone that my family can turn to when they're in trouble. When I think about Kevin, I feel that I not only let him down but in some way I let myself down as well. I just feel bad about myself.

In refusing Kevin a loan, Emily broke no rules – indeed, she may have protected the credit status of her small business – but she does not feel 'good' about her decision. At some level, her own self-image and sense of being a good person is linked to her capacity to meet the demands of relationship-based models of good behaviour.

If a person repeatedly engages in good or bad acts, this behaviour can permanently shape their reputation: 'the belief or opinions that are generally held about someone'.[14] Rule-based reputation is enshrined in the legal concept of 'good name', and individuals can take legal action to defend their good name.[15] If an individual continuously breaks the law, the consequent damage to their good name will be reflected in their treatment by the criminal justice system. Even the Irish media use the term 'known to the Gardaí' to describe a person with an already damaged rule-based reputation.[16]

Relationship-based reputation is equally important, though its value is more difficult to measure. In their study of family obligations, Janet Finch and Jennifer Mason note that being considered 'good' by others in relationships is not a matter of simply saying that you are good. Instead, these claims are tested in everyday situations, for example when a sister asks to borrow money or a grandparent is asked to help with childcare.[17] Relationship-based reputation generated through these kinds of 'favours' matters because it can be used as a resource by the individual when they are faced with a crisis, particularly in situations where formal rules and regulations don't apply.[18] Siobhan, a single mum who lives in a big estate on the outskirts of Mallow, describes how relationship-based reputation has shaped her attitude to her two neighbours, Michelle and Clare-Ann:

> My daughter can't walk to school from here and I've no family living close by. So if I get sick or the car breaks down, I'm really dependent on the neighbours. Michelle beside me here is brilliant. She knows I'm on my own and if I'm out of action, she'll take her anywhere she needs to go. She couldn't do enough. She's great to all the neighbours. Clare-Ann across the road, however, seems to think I'm a bit of a loser. She never offers to help and I always feel she's looking down on me. Anyway, last March, she got sick and her husband was away and she'd nobody to take her kids to school. To be honest, I didn't even know. But if I had, I'm not sure I'd have offered, whereas I'd do anything for Michelle.

In adult life, an individual's inability to conform to either relationship- or rule-based models of good behaviour can have a profound impact on how they are perceived by others and how they feel about themselves. It can also have real material costs and benefits in terms of their capacity to manage the challenges of their daily lives.

Both Irish middle-class citizens and immigrants were aware of the tensions between 'being fair' and 'being there' in relation to models of good behaviour. A number of Irish interviewees acknowledged that 'being there' for 'one of our own' can impact on fairness to an individual located outside these networks. Eileen, an elderly lady with a chronic illness, says:

> My friend Noreen now, her son's a surgeon, a real big noise and when she got sick, she went to the consultant, a pal of his, and he sent her off to the Mater for this very new treatment. A few months later, I came down with the very same problem and went to the very same consultant and he was putting me on the waiting list for our local hospital and I said to him, 'Hang on a minute now, if I was your mother would you be recommending this treatment for me?' and he looked at me and said, 'Well, I suppose not.' That softened his cough for him, I'll tell you.

Shane, a young guard, also describes how relationship networks impacted on fairness in his workplace:

> Me and my friend, let's call him Tom, both got transferred to Dublin after Templemore. We are both involved in local GAA teams at home and we were both mad to get back down the country and out of Dodge. Anyway, his uncle is a guard in Waterford so he got on to him and he had a path beaten into the Chief Super. End of the day, he got his transfer back down the country to a town within an hour's drive of home. Just goes to show if you know the right people in any game, you're on to a winner. I'm still here and it's four years later.

Immigrants noted how the practice of 'being there' for those in circles of intimacy could impact on fairness. Tomaso from Uganda found that in the first week in his current job, his colleagues found it difficult to believe that he had got the job without 'knowing' someone: 'The first week I was working there, the people kept asking me how did you get here? Did you know anybody? And "Who is your uncle?" or "Who's your in-law?" They thought I was married to an Irish person and they were so surprised I never knew anybody.' After a while, he understood why he was being asked these questions. 'Where I work, you have a lot of what we call family dynasties. We have father, son, daughter-in-law all working at the same time and they try to keep the work for themselves. That's the way it works.' He also acknowledges that immigrants themselves are quick to develop their own networks of intimacy which involve 'being there' for members of their own national group. 'When I was there about four months, a Polish girl was taken on. Two years after, the husband of the Polish girl was taken on as well as the brother. So there you have the family thing again in a different group.'

Immigrants were not universally critical of 'being there' and highlighted examples of when the rules themselves were unfair or irrelevant and when the personal intervention of individuals had helped them solve problems. Agatha says:

> I had a problem with the Russian girl in our flat. She had stolen things where she worked and given my name and details instead of her own. So the Gardaí came looking for me and took me in for questioning. I was terrified. I felt that they didn't believe [me] and thought it was some kind of scam. I have never been in trouble with police in Poland. So I rang the lady I work for, her brother knows a garda and he spoke up for me. You need friends at those times.

Noelle, who works in a multinational company, described another incident where 'being there' delivered greater fairness:

> We have this woman working in payroll who, quite frankly, is a complete bitch. Anyway, this guy Luca gets hired. He's Eastern European, one of those crazy Balkan states, and she makes this huge deal about processing all his documents and takes forever about it. In the meantime, this guy is broke, has no cash and is starving. So in the end, we have this one manager, Tadhg, who is sound and he rings up your wan and basically tells her to fuckin' sort it now and of course, she does. If Tadhg hadn't done that, the poor fucker would be still waiting for his pay. And mind you, she wasn't breaking any rules by dragging her heels.

The recognition that personal interventions embedded within relationships can mitigate unfair or impotent rules was evident even among immigrants. Although 'being there' can promote favouritism and even facilitate corruption, there are still times when the rules do not deliver fairness and are not responsive to the challenges of particular situations. In these situations, interventions rooted in relationships can deliver greater justice.

CONCLUSION

As the Irish middle classes confront rules and negotiate relationships in their daily lives, it can be difficult to stand back and assess how these factors influence their deeper value system. Research presented in this chapter would appear to indicate that the world of rules is expanding, particularly in the Irish workplace. As the Irish middle classes become more educated, more integrated into global culture and further removed from circles of intimacy, their lives are becoming increasingly dominated by rules. Nevertheless, the research showed some evidence of a weak moral commitment to the implementation of rules in some contexts.

In contrast, relationships continue to be an important part of Irish culture, not only in the family but also in school, in the workplace and in the local community. A sense of belonging to groups often described as 'our own' helped many people locate themselves in Irish society, and belonging to these groups was an important part of their identity. However, this deep trust and binding sense of belonging to 'our own' did appear to exclude immigrants, who described situations where they felt less trusted and unable to understand relationship-based cultural nuances.

Most important, rules and relationships generate two distinct visions of 'being good'. In relationships, the importance of 'being there' for others in circles of intimacy was strongly associated with 'goodness'. Rules-based models of goodness placed greater emphasis on keeping rules because they promote a consistency which is fair. The tension between the demands to 'be there' and 'be fair' was evident in situations described by a number of Irish interview participants. It was clear that there were a number of situations where these two models of 'being good' could collide, with very negative consequences for all involved. There are also costs associated with not meeting either the moral demand to 'be there' or the moral demand to 'be fair'. Rules-based sanctions such as fines and the loss of legal good name are real risks. In the world of relationships, losing one's reputation in relation to 'looking after our own' can also have real material consequences. Both immigrants and Irish citizens described situations where 'being there' could impact negatively on fairness while at the same time citing examples where relationship-based personal interventions had delivered fairer outcomes. This delicate balance between the world of rules and the world of relationships was pivotal in shaping interactions in everyday life for the Irish middle class. It also plays a critical role in structuring how the Irish people engage with politicians at constituency level, a theme which is explored in the next chapter.

Chapter 5

EVERYDAY IRISH POLITICS

The Irish political system is broken and needs to be fixed. There is a crisis of competence in government, the Dáil fails to fulfil its most basic functions, the Seanad is irrelevant and the electoral system encourages TDs to behave like county councillors.

Dermot Desmond, February 2011

Two weeks before the general election of February 2011, businessman Dermot Desmond published *Ireland First: Political Reform – Effective and Efficient Government*, an online document accompanied by a major article in the *Irish Times*. For a close associate of former Taoiseach Charles Haughey and a key beneficiary of intimacy with political elites in the 1990s,[1] it was an odd intervention. However, the political reforms he advocated in his document suggested that Ireland's financial elite was placing the blame for the crisis firmly at the door of the politicians.[2]

On the left of the political spectrum, a slew of social movements were calling not only for political reform but also for a radically different approach to dealing with the rich elite itself. People Before Profit, the Socialist Party and the Workers and Unemployed Action Group indicated their opposition to 'solutions to the economic crisis based on slashing public expenditure, welfare payments and workers' pay'. The demands of their umbrella group, the United Left Alliance, included: 'end the bailout of the banks and developers'; 'scrap NAMA'; and 'tax the greedy not the needy'.[3] The centre-left Democracy Now stated that 'the bank bailout and its consequences in vicious austerity and the loss of sovereignty are immoral, unsustainable and both socially and economically disastrous'.[4] (Like the more right-wing National Forum, Democracy Now had difficulty fielding an array of candidates in time for the general election.) Nationalism was the final thread in this complex weave as Sinn Féin mounted a sustained and effective campaign stridently advocating anti-austerity policies.[5]

All this frenzied political activity created an expectation that the February 2011 general election, the first after the bailout, would be a watershed. In the German newspaper *Der Spiegel*, Carsten Volkery predicted that the election would bring 'a political revolution of historic proportions'.[6] The election did indeed turn out to be a watershed, but not in the way envisioned by the more idealistic political movements of 2011. Fianna Fáil suffered the worst defeat of a sitting government in the history of the Irish state and one of the worst defeats of any post-war Western European party.[7] Fine Gael became the largest party in Dáil Éireann (76 seats) and the Labour Party also made significant gains. Sinn Féin increased its proportion of the vote and its leader, Gerry Adams, was elected to the Dáil in the Louth constituency. Five candidates from the United Left Alliance were elected, along with a number of independent TDs from across the political spectrum.[8] All sitting TDs from the Green Party, which had been in coalition with Fianna Fáil, lost their seats. Summarising the outcome of the election, Sean Farrell *et al.* comment:

> Given the devastation of the Irish economy and the controversial bank bailout and subsequent intervention by the International Monetary Fund a few months before, it surprised no one that Fianna Fáil was swept from power. Even so, there was a consensus that the change in the Irish political landscape was one of historic dimensions. Commentators fumbled for comparisons ... Whatever the eventual ranking of history may be, the February results were unprecedented in Irish history.[9]

Despite the dramatic results, whether the election brought about a transformation of Irish political culture is debatable. The Fine Gael/

Labour coalition brought new personnel to key ministerial roles; but the terms of the bailout agreement allowed little scope for renegotiating the austerity programme, and none at all for structural default on the promissory notes agreed by the previous administration. Since 2011, by-elections, local elections and European elections have all given the impression of a political system still in massive flux and with no clear direction. Fianna Fáil has recovered to become the biggest party in local government, while the rise of Sinn Féin has continued. The most interesting question raised by this political turmoil is how it is affecting the long-term balance between rules and relationships in Irish political culture.

Studies of Irish politics in the second half of the twentieth century have consistently highlighted the dominance of clientelism in the Irish political system.[10] Voters use their relationships with politicians to deal with the rules-based systems of the state: in return, politicians are rewarded with votes. Using relationships to manipulate rules has historically been seen as key to electoral success in Ireland. This chapter begins by examining how the structure of the Irish political system has contributed to this rules–relationships balance. It explores the links between the everyday system of favours in Ireland (outlined in Chapter 4) and the understandings that inform interactions between politicians and ordinary voters. It also considers whether the bailout has brought about any shift in these assumptions. We shall see that while ordinary Irish citizens are deeply critical of the strong inter-elite relationships that contributed to the financial crash, they use many of the same behaviours and understandings of reality in their interactions with politicians at constituency level. In many cases, they do not recognise the links between their own relationship-based approach to political participation and the more destructive elite-level intimacy that contributed to the crash.

THE IMPORTANCE OF 'DOING TURNS'

The *Oireachtas Joint Committee on the Constitution (Third Interim Report)* found that Irish TDs spent 53 per cent of their time on constituency work and 38 per cent on legislative work. Fifty per cent of this constituency work involved making representations to rule-based systems on behalf of individual voters. The *2002 Irish National Election Survey* demonstrated the scale of public demand for this work: one in five people had made contact with their TD in the preceding five years. In the *2007 Irish National Election Survey*, 60 per cent of voters said that they expected their TD to provide a local service.

Even after the drama of the 2011 election, the newest generation of Irish politicians soon became aware of how important it was to attend to their relationships with voters through constituency work. Stephen Donnelly, a graduate of Harvard's Kennedy School of Government, successfully contested the 2011 election on the slogan, 'New Independent Expertise'. Here he describes a day during a week off:

> *Tuesday:* Spent the day in the constituency offices in Greystones. Started with clinics and moved on to working on individual constituent issues. These included children with special needs losing their teaching supports, people having their homes repossessed, schools changing patronage, domestic abuse, child custody, immigration, emergency accommodation for a mother and children, the household charge, development levies, rates, healthcare access for a toddler, withdrawal of community supports for the elderly, seed capital for start-up businesses, unsustainable debt, noise pollution and illegal dumping.[11]

Before the election, Donnelly clearly thought his primary contribution would be to national policy, but he quickly realised the importance of constituency work as part of everyday Irish politics.

The Irish electoral system, which is based on proportional representation – single transferable vote (PR-STV), has played a strong role in placing constituency work at the centre of Irish politics.[12] PR-STV essentially allows voters to subtly rank politicians from the same party who are running side by side at constituency level, creating an intense level of competition between politicians from the same party. A politician's performance in constituency work plays a big role in the voters' ranking process, and politicians themselves believe that it is the structure of the PR-STV system that requires them to be so responsive to the demands of voters. Bill, a Fianna Fáil politician, says:

> When the sitting TD is up in Dublin you have guys in the background who are doing work and if you look at the statistics you see in many counties and many constituencies where the sitting TD was defeated by a member of his own party who was a working councillor. It would be better if it was a single seat constituency.

Conall, a member of Fine Gael, agrees, arguing that the system creates huge mistrust within the party:

> The TD is supposed to be a legislator and a parliamentarian but the system has grown up here and underlying all this is a huge factor, which is the multi-seat constituency, because if I don't do all this, the fella will go down the road to the next man and he'll do it and he will get the vote. On my first day in the Dáil, I met one of the oldest and long-standing members of the party. He called me over and said, 'You're a nice young fella and I'd like to see you stay in politics. I tell you, never worry about the opposition but watch your own, boy.'

A 2010 Oireachtas survey bears out the truth of this advice. It found that for every extra candidate from their own party in their constituency, TDs engage in a higher proportion of constituency work. In 2007, TDs with no opposition from their own party colleagues spent 41 per cent of their time on constituency work; for TDs who faced two or more candidates from the same party this rose to 62 per cent. Most strikingly, TDs who had lost a seat to a fellow party member spent 66 per cent of time on constituency work, as opposed to 40 per cent among TDs who had lost a seat to a member of another party. As Fintan O'Toole succinctly writes, 'it is not war but friendly fire that Irish politicians fear most.'[13]

O'Toole also argues that many of the supposed benefits achieved by politicians are 'imaginary' because voters are entitled to these benefits anyway. Lee Komito appears to agree, writing in his study of brokerage in Dublin in the 1980s: 'The rhetoric of politics is clientelist, but the actual allocation of resource more closely follows the impersonal practices of the bureaucracy.'[14] However, interviews with ordinary Irish citizens and politicians conducted for this study suggest that clientelism does deliver positive outcomes for a considerable number of voters. There are some instances where politicians really can deliver, either because they understand the bureaucratic system better or because they have more information about the voter's circumstances, which they can use to make a more compelling case for their claim. Noeleen, a TD, comments:

> There were occasions and there are occasions where the intervention of a TD can help. I had this where people were shot down for various things like social welfare payments or pensions and you ring up to the Department and they produce the file for you. They would do that for the TD. And I'd state my case, and they'd say, 'But sure, Deputy, he or she didn't tell us this. If what you say is correct then they should have got the pension or payment or whatever.' And I said, 'Maybe they might be nervous of the official and they'd talk more freely to me', so they'd get the pension. So you can make a difference, because some of these systems are very cumbersome systems and not very responsive.

Alison works as a secretary for a TD in Laois. She points out, 'A lot of organisations in Ireland are not very efficient or fast-moving. What a politician can do is get in there and give everyone a kick up the backside in a polite way. Often, if that facility isn't there, people can suffer quite badly.' Alan, who manages a biomedical firm in Limerick, says, 'We would have a contact with the local TD off and on over the years. My wife applied for the carer's to look after her mother and then we had to adapt the house, so he helped us apply for a grant for that. He's a hard worker and it all comes back to him on election day.' The results politicians achieve by engaging with public services on behalf of constituents challenge the idea that the benefits of clientelism are imaginary, because rules-based systems in Ireland are often described as slow, unresponsive or, in some cases, unfair.

Given that strong relationships between politicians and business elites were highlighted as central to the banking crash, one would imagine that Irish voters would be more critical of these clientelist practices. However, over 80 per cent of the politicians interviewed for this study reported an increase in constituency work since the crash. Politicians are being asked to negotiate not only with state agencies but also with banks. Timmy, a politician in the Midlands, describes some of his dealings with the banks:

> I got a positive yesterday and I'm going to meet with someone in a bank next week about a constituent. It's a woman who's 80. She took out a life-time loan of €200,000 on a house that's now worth about €150,000. Her son lost his business and she doesn't want to involve other members of her family so, like, she's nobody; so, like, I wrote to the Central Bank for her and they kind of referred it back and said she should talk to the bank about it. So I offered to go in with her because I could see she was really nervous about it. I don't think the bank are going to do much for her. The Central Bank have already said that it wasn't illegal at the time the bank gave her the loan. I would have a lot more of that kind of thing, so that would be new.

Fiona, a young Dublin TD, describes another case:

> I think with the banks, people find them very complex to deal with. Like I had a successful outcome where a woman was going on maternity leave and the bank are supposed to work out some arrangement for you. And this woman had sent all the paperwork to the bank and had got no response. So I made representations and she got a response from them so, like, the main issue was that the bank was not replying to the person.

Despite the increasing volume of constituency work reported by politicians since the bailout, there is some evidence that voters are becoming more selective in the problems they bring to politicians. Fiona comments:

> Despite what people may think we don't get much local stuff like planning applications and that because the residents are actually distinguishing and going straight for who they know has a role in it.... The type of issues we tend to get are often to do with a national decision-making body but at the local level that could be the Guards. It could be the Department of Education, about the local school and an awful lot of individual cases – a lot of social welfare, a lot of health service.

Politicians do complain, however, that the reciprocal relationship – the 'turn for a vote' – is breaking down, particularly since 2010. According to Tony, who is based in County Cork:

> I find that there are people that you're after doing turns for and Jeez you nearly have to drag the vote out of them, that's been going on for ten or fifteen years now. I said to one woman one night and I was after doing her a good turn and she says, 'I won't be able to go to the voting booth.' 'What do you mean?' I says, 'Sure, Willie there will collect you any time that suits you.' And she was still humming and hawing and I said to her, 'By Jeez, you were able to walk up to the clinic the night you wanted me and you've a lift up now to the polling booth and you won't go to vote.' She'd no answer to that. I normally wouldn't say that but I was cold and we were about to finish and you will drop your guard on occasions.

Tony's comments highlight that there are lots of unspoken understandings that inform the interactions between politicians and voters. In the next section, the different forms of knowledge, trust, communication, belonging, conflict and 'being good' linked to rules and relationships (which were outlined in terms of Irish everyday life in Chapter 4) are used to illuminate some of these unspoken understandings. The research presented in this chapter draws on a series of interviews with politicians and Irish voters; all names have been changed to protect the identity of participants.

KNOWING, TRUSTING, COMMUNICATING

Chapter 4 described the open and transparent nature of rule-based knowledge and noted that individuals often need expertise and training to understand these rules. Basil Chubb argued that during the first forty years of the Irish state's existence, clientelist practices emerged because many citizens did not have sufficient knowledge to understand rules.[15] Desmond, who's retired from Fine Gael, shares this view.

> I think myself it was a lack of understanding of the system more than anything else. The TD or the local councillor was the one who was getting things done. Remember, they were an older generation with probably only primary school education and they hadn't much contact with the outside world and other than 'Up Dev' or 'Up Fine Gael', they didn't have much idea. They might have been a bit afraid, maybe suspicious, but I put it down myself to a lack of understanding of how the system works.

It would appear that not only a lack of understanding but a post-colonial expectation that rules were unfair informed this political culture. Xavier, a retired member of Fianna Fáil, says:

> I'd say to people, 'Sure there's no problem, I don't need to fill this in, you're entitled to it.' But they'd say, 'Unless you fill it in and send a letter with it, I won't get it.' Do you get my drift? They looked on the politician or the TD as being kind of a miracle worker. They just didn't see that they were entitled to it. They'd say, 'No, if you fill in the form I'll be certain I'll get it.'

Despite better education and a better general awareness of entitlements since the 1960s, politicians report that the level of constituency work has risen steadily. Xavier, from a rural political dynasty, argues that the younger generation of politicians are overwhelmed by constituency work.

> They can't keep up with it. There is an awful lot of problems now that we didn't have in my time. There is a lot of distress with banks which is taking up an awful lot of people's time, they are getting crucified, crucified.... Then you have the problem with the condition of the county roads, they are not built to take the heavy trucks that's using them.... Country people are more demanding and feel it's their right to go to their politician.

In engaging with voters about their problems with rules, politicians draw not only on reason but also on emotion and empathy, typical of the world of relationships. As Noeleen explains:

> I had cases where one person would come in a bad way with a problem and they're worried about it and you'd chat them out and tease them out and at the end of it, they'd say, 'You know, Noeleen, perhaps I'm worrying about nothing when you put it that way.' They'd come to you with the most intimate problems, family problems, personal problems, emotional problems, kind of like the work the Samaritans do. Now other TDs wouldn't do that. They'd say, 'What's the problem?', they'd write it out and they'd say, 'Okay, I'll see what I can do. Bye.' But that doesn't work that well, they expect sympathy, it's the human factor.

It is not only politicians who tend to draw on emotion in engaging with voters – the secretarial staff working in their constituency offices do too. Desmond says:

> I remember getting a thousand votes in certain areas in my latter elections. All because I had an office in town and I had a good woman in there and they'd say 'Aw, Mister O'Connor, we went down to his office, he wasn't there but his secretary was and we got

a nice letter from him. He wasn't able to do anything but he did his best and because of that, he gets Number One.' See the point? It all depends on how you handle it.

The importance of emotion as well as reason in these interactions suggests a leaning towards the world of relationships rather than rules in Irish political culture, a leaning reinforced by communication patterns between voters and politicians.

Research on twentieth-century Irish politics consistently stresses the importance of face-to-face communication. These face-to-face interactions took place at politicians' clinics, church gate collections, local branch meetings and on the doorstep during election campaigns. There is evidence that some elements of this face-to-face interaction are declining, due to urbanisation, modernisation and changes in Irish lifestyles. In the 1980s, Lee Komito commented, 'In a culture that emphasizes personal contacts as the basis for political support, clinics are good public relations.'[16] Senan, a long-standing Labour TD, notes, 'I often stood in clinics.... You might have a hundred people at a clinic, you'd be lucky now if you'd get five or six.' Church gate collections have also all but disappeared, particularly in urban areas. Tony comments, 'Cities are terrible, they don't support at all. Some places in cities, they don't even hold the collection.' The local cumann and branch structures have also declined considerably.[17] Retired TD Xavier comments:

> There isn't the same emphasis on those cumann meetings any more because Number One it's too time-consuming. Number Two, those cumann meetings weren't as well attended as they used to be, I'd remember cumann meetings where you'd have eighty and ninety people present in a small place. You'd be lucky if you'd get ten or twelve now.... After a cumann meeting, people would come to you and have a chat. There was a connection, whereas there isn't now.

Fiona says that the rise of social media has changed day-to-day constituency work:

Constituency work has definitely increased but it's less clinic. Now a lot of stuff comes in online through email or Facebook or Twitter. I've only recently gone on Twitter but you'd even get stuff on that ... I suppose that's one of the issues that we are much more accessible now than we were through technology and because of that you often get contact from people all around the country.... In order to have any kind of coping at all, I distinguish between my constituents and others who contact me or if I spot a hard case I might go back [to] them. But even if you just look at the constituency side, it's a huge amount. I'm literally deleting hundreds of emails a week. In order to have any kind of coping, I'm deleting stuff immediately that I know I'm not going to deal with. So yes, constituency work has definitely increased but it's less clinic.

However, she notes that once the initial contact has been made, face-to-face contact is still an important feature of the voter–politician relationship:

I get new people all the time but a lot of the same people would come back to us all the time. I meet them at the shops or at the school. They expect you to be responsive but I'm always surprised that people tend not to phone you at night. They tend to keep within normal hours.

Door-to-door canvassing is still a very important feature of Irish election campaigns. In his study of the 2002 general election, Michael Marsh found that 'there remains a clear association between the contact and vote.'[18] Fiona notes that the public not only expect personal canvassing but are also resistant to canvassing through phone and email:

As a politician you can't get round to everyone, but it's important that people perceive that they are being asked for their vote. If you are a candidate and you want to succeed, you have to create the perception that people are being asked for their vote. So like, you'd canvass as many people as you can. I canvass outside schools, supermarkets. I do the leaflets, I go to things … My party colleague did a bit of the texting but I resisted it because I was aware that it annoys people. I would have emailed people and I would have texted my own supporters…. There is a system where people use a much broader [way of] texting them but they got complaints and they don't like the thing of those automated calls, Mary Harney used those in the 2007 election and she got complaints about it.

This emphasis on face-to-face contact seems to clearly show not only the dominance of relationships in Irish politics but also the importance of *being asked for your vote*. By asking personally for a vote, politicians are acknowledging that the constituency relationship between politician and voter, while unequal, is still two-sided and one in which the voter still has some power. Irish voters seem to feel it important that this power is expressed personally, face to face, rather than simply at the ballot box. Face-to-face communication allows voters to assert their own power in the voter–politician relationship. The dominance of face-to-face communication and the amount of work that politicians do in managing rules for their constituents suggests that Irish politics at local level conforms to the weak rules/strong relationships model which caused the financial crash in 2010.

BELONGING AND CONFLICT

The vote is a core unit of the rules-based system of democratic participation. Democracy is based on the principle that if you are dissatisfied with a political party you can vote for someone else and help change the political system. However, some evidence suggests that before the general election of 2011, a considerable proportion of Irish voters did not use their vote in this way. Writing in the 1970s, Basil Chubb highlighted the strong emphasis on loyalty to relationship-based groups rather than ideas in shaping voter allegiances:

This loyalty was and is, to persons and institutions rather than to ideas. It reinforces powerfully the natural tendency of people generally in the past to adopt the political affiliation of their parents and to support their chosen parties consistently. Although it has often been suggested that the young today are politically more volatile than previously, parents' party preference is still by far the most reliable predictor of a young person's choice of party when he or she votes.[19]

Research by Michael Marsh on the results of the 2002 general election revealed how family allegiances impacted on voter behaviour in Ireland. He investigated the question of party identification – feelings of closeness to political parties. He found that participants who had two parents who supported Fianna Fáil or Fine Gael had a marked feeling of closeness to the same party. He concluded, 'for both of the main parties ... and spectacularly so for Fine Gael, feelings of closeness to the party show a strong tendency to be inherited from parents.'[20] Thus, 'the Irish political folklore that voting runs in families is indeed borne out in a very systematic way by the results of the 2002 election study.'[21]

Community relationships also played a significant role in establishing how people voted. In Dublin during the 1980s, Lee Komito found that:

Community contacts are used to create political bonds between politicians and voters. The personal loyalties created by politicians are useful in their attempts to maintain their standing in both the local party organization and the community at large. In the party arena, such supporters ensure re-nomination, help keep out rivals and help maintain a community presence. In the community arena, personal supporters also help the politician maintain his reputation for access and concern.[22]

One of the primary ways in which politicians demonstrated their loyalty to local family and community groups was by going to funerals. Abner Cohen highlights how in intimacy-based cultures, relationships between families are often underlined by the attendance of the 'big man' of the clan at the family events of other kinship groups.[23] Elements of these understandings are evident in the practice of funeral attendance in Irish politics, a practice which has declined in urban areas but remains important in rural areas. Irish politicians themselves have mixed feelings about the practice. Desmond, a retired Fine Gael politician, says:

> When I went into the Dáil, the first thing every TD would do every morning would be to get the morning paper and look at the deaths and I automatically sent a letter or a telegram of sympathy to every member of the constituency whose death was reported in the paper. I did it and so did everyone else. I wasn't long retired when I went to a funeral, of a family that was quite prominent in Fine Gael. I met a few people afterwards and they said 'Jesus, Desmond, we never thought you'd be here.' 'Why not?' I said, 'Sure they're very good friends of mine,' but they said, 'But sure why bother? You're no longer in politics now.'

Politicians complain that this practice is mocked in the national media; but if they do not attend funerals, particularly in rural areas, they experience strong disapproval. Kenneth, a former Fianna Fáil minister, explains:

> I remember when I was a minister being at a branch meeting one night and someone said to me, 'You'd want to be more alert and attending more funerals than you are,' and I said, 'Well, I'm a member of the government' and I said, 'But I do send anyone that you mentioned a personal letter and a mass card from me.'

The practice of attending funerals – deeply personal events for bereaved families – is near the apex of a system of face-to-face relationships which underpin Irish political culture and embeds it firmly within the world of relationships. In large urban constituencies, there doesn't appear to be the same pressure to attend funerals. Paula, a female TD, says, 'If someone from the community dies, there would be an expectation that you would be at certain funerals, and they're not family or anything like that. There is an onus to a certain extent but it's nothing like the pressure to go to funerals down the country.'

The depth of the connections established between political families and their constituents through attending funerals and so on may partly explain why political dynasties have historically been such an important feature of Irish politics. At the time of the Troika bailout in 2010, the three core cabinet members (Taoiseach, Tánaiste, Minister for Finance) were all members of political dynasties who had 'inherited' seats from their parents. In the subsequent general election, over forty politicians from Irish political dynasties contested seats. Seventy per cent of Fianna Fáil leaders and 71 per cent of Fine Gael leaders have come from political dynasties. The importance of family dynasties is striking even in the Irish Labour Party, where party identity is based more on ideology than on family: 40 per cent of Labour leaders had dynastic connections.[24] These connections extend beyond specific links between one politician and one family. Fiona notes that in Labour,

> It can relate to people who are absolute Labour stalwarts or it would be because you helped someone and they bring out their whole family to support you, they would be like your advocates almost. People don't necessarily vote in terms of family allegiances any more but there are definitely Labour families, who seem to influence fellow family members to vote for a particular candidate.

There is some evidence that the pattern of voter allegiances based on relationships has begun to change since the bailout and austerity process. Timmy comments:

> A party is a bit like a clan, though I think that's disappearing because you have a much more volatile electorate now. You still have the core supporters of the party, that would be a family thing, but the percentage of your vote, percentage of the electorate who are core party voters, is declining. I suppose it's because the younger generation are much better educated than their forebears.

So while voter allegiances in Ireland have historically been shaped by relationships, the trauma of the bailout seems to have substantially eroded this approach to voting.

Approaches to conflict between politicians and constituents are also changing. In the world of rules, conflict is openly named and compromises developed. In the world of relationships, however, differences of opinion are gradually revealed and eventually resolved through consensus. Politicians suggest that their approach to dealing with conflict with voters has historically been more typical of the world of relationships, with an emphasis on avoiding direct conflict. Conall says, 'The one golden rule on my canvass was under no circumstances start an argument at the door, or don't openly contradict someone; listen to them and use your own judgement. Not always easy to do, 'cause some people want a row.' This indirect approach to conflict can be underlaid with strong emotions. Xavier describes meeting an obviously upset supporter:

> This guy was a canvasser of mine. In the winter time, if you go abroad, it's difficult to get an Irish paper, you only really get it in the summer months. Anyway he said to me, 'I didn't see you at my mother's funeral.' In fact, I was very close to his mother. In fact the first Christmas card I'd get every Christmas was from her, I'd say I was closer to her than he was because he fell out with her. But I didn't say that to him because he was obviously upset.

At least six politicians described a marked increase in the level of anger they encountered on the doorsteps after the 2010 bailout. Paula says:

> Towards the end [of the 2007–2011 government] like, it would have been terrible for people in Fianna Fáil and I would have understood that and felt sympathetic ... It was even stressful for the opposition at that time. At the last election ... a lot of people [were] so disillusioned with politicians in general.

Sean comments, 'there is so much about a politician's role now that's quite stressful – an awful lot of work, people are quite aggressive to you … the internet is part of it. I think that we mightn't be the only ones experiencing it but there are particular things that are specific to politicians.'

Kenneth has also noticed this change in attitude towards politicians. 'People are more abusive on the one on one. You'd always get it, the thick-ended so and so who'd love to have a go at you in a bar or in front of people just to make himself feel good. You have to learn to leave it over your shoulder.' As a member of Fianna Fáil, he experienced particularly high levels of conflict on the doorstep during the canvass for the 2011 general election:

> The last election now where we got a lot of stick … Houses that we went into now, especially if they were working in the health services or the county councils, by Jesus they were very rude on the doorsteps, very rude on the doorsteps. Living in these big mansions of houses, by Jesus we didn't ask them to go into the bank and borrow all that money. When we got married, we had to start small and work our way up the line but they were talking about their pockets, you know. That's the way it's going now, the pocket is number one.

Kenneth's comments confirm that party loyalties which were embedded in the relationships-based groups of family and community were seriously eroded by the damage caused to the material circumstances of ordinary Irish citizens by the banking bailout and austerity process. This erosion appears to have created a larger space for rules-based loyalties and ideology in Irish politics in the future.

BEING THERE AND BEING FAIR

In the morality of Irish political culture, the entire system of clientelism prioritises 'being there' – the morality of relationships – over 'being fair' – the morality of rules. Voters who come to politicians looking for assistance do not really care whether the politician's intervention distorts the fairness of rules-based systems. Sheila describes applying for her medical card:

> I don't really care whether other people can get them or not. All I know is that I need one and in our health care, those who shout the loudest seem to get what they want and those who do nothing and say nothing get nothing. You have to get in there and fight. You can do that by having all your forms and documents in order but that's not enough, even if you can get it right. You need a bit of support on your side and that's where the politician comes in.

Bob explains why he rewards his local TD Timmy for 'being there' for him:

> Bottom line, if a guy is going to help one of my children get a job somewhere or help me get a grant to do something, people are going to support him and vote for him regardless of what's going on at national level. I think Irish people care about their own family first, then their community, other stuff comes far down the line after that. Maybe it's a bit different now with the recession but I'm not sure how it's changed really.

Politicians themselves are not only aware that engaging in constituency work is central to electoral success but also recognise that it is critical to being perceived as a 'good' politician. Conall says:

> If you weren't available [for constituency work], you'd be a one-term TD, been and gone. It doesn't leave a lot of time for parliamentary work, this is the whole problem. What one has to do is to try and balance the constituency work with the parliamentary work. It is difficult to balance the two. I've seen cases of brilliant parliamentarians, religiously tackling legislation, line by line and word by word, and they lost their seats because they didn't do the constituency work.

Even MEPs are expected to 'be there' to help constituents with their problems, as MEP Ger explains:

> One day a man called into my office and I was in Brussels at the time and he said 'Where's Ger?' and the secretary said, 'Ger's in Brussels in the European parliament,' and he said, 'Fuck Brussels, that's no good to me, I want my medical card.' That's what I've been trying to emphasise; to the person who comes in his medical card is hugely important, probably the most important thing to him and his family. Brussels is irrelevant in that context.

This constituent doesn't appear to care that his demand that his MEP be available to engage with the rules of the health care system for him personally may compromise his capacity to ensure Ireland's interests are fairly represented at European level.

By 'being there' for constituents over time, politicians build up a reputation for 'doing turns', which is central to being perceived as a 'good' politician. Senan says:

> You have to be seen to make the effort, if [you] don't, you'll get a bad name, you're not a good worker, you're careless, you know, your reputation would be affected … It's word of mouth … Eventually you'll lose your seat irrespective of what party you're in, that has been proved in all parties.

Enhancing relationship-based reputation seems critical for Irish politicians, and this reputation is largely based on the politician's constituency work rather than his or her contribution to rules-based national policy.

This leaning towards relationships rather than rules is so marked that a politician can in some cases ensure continued electoral success, even when his or her rules-based reputation is badly damaged. The tension is most evident in the continued success of Tipperary North TD Michael Lowry.

Case Study: Michael Lowry

Michael Lowry was first elected TD for Tipperary North in 1987 and retained his seat through a number of general elections, topping the poll in 2002, 2007 and 2011. In the early 1980s, he was a GAA administrator and became the youngest ever chairman of the GAA's Tipperary County Committee. During the 1980s, he established a refrigeration business, Streamline Enterprises, and in the early 1990s became Chairman of the Fine Gael Parliamentary Party and (in 1994) Minister for Transport, Energy and Communications. A succession of scandals linked to mobile phone licensing and his relationship with supermarket businessman Ben Dunne led to his resignation from cabinet in 1996 and he subsequently ran as an independent candidate. In November 2010, after a series of defections from the Fianna Fáil/ Green coalition government, he held the balance of power along with Kerry independent TD Jackie Healy-Rae.

Viewed from the perspective that those who break the rules are bad, Lowry's electoral success is inexplicable. He has been openly sanctioned by tribunals of inquiry for tax evasion, and his role in mobile phone licensing was highly dubious. Elaine Byrne summarises the report of the Moriarty Tribunal in relation to the latter:

> Lowry was the recipient of direct or facilitated financial contributions, as was his political party, by a businessman who benefited from a decision made by his department. Aside from the money-trail, a cocktail of irregularities within the evaluation process was complemented by the 'insidious and pervasive influence' of a minister.[25]

On any rules-based evaluation, this behaviour was 'bad'. However, constituents in North Tipperary who regularly vote for Michael Lowry have a different perspective, a perspective that views him as 'good'. Fionnuala, who lives near Thurles, comments:

Well, I come from a Fianna Fáil gene pool so I wouldn't have voted for Michael Lowry early on but to be honest, we have found him to be an outstanding constituency politician. He's the only one that you can go to who will get things done. I give him a vote in every election because he knows how to *look after his own.*

Attitudes to Michael Lowry in North Tipperary reveal directly the split morality of Irish political culture in which the relationship-based form of being good – 'being there' for others in the group – trumps obeying the rules. Towards the end of the research for this book, I put this question to Maurice, an older Lowry supporter in Tipperary North.

Niamh: Maurice, don't you think that by voting for Michael Lowry, an individual who has evaded tax and broken the rules, you are damaging the moral basis of the law in Ireland?

Maurice: Well, I don't know about that. I think we vote for Lowry because *he looks after his own.* He always put the voters of Tipperary North first. We can rely on him to do that and I suppose that's what we really reward him for. I suppose we feel that Dublin doesn't really give a shit about us but Lowry will always look after us.

So not only does Michael Lowry have a strong reputation for constituency work, but these 'turns' contribute to the sense that he belongs to the local community and he looks after his own. As we saw in Chapter 3, this has strong moral connotations of 'goodness'. It is also striking that in Ireland's highly centralised political system, Maurice does not appear to believe that fairer rules can be achieved anyway.

A DUAL MORALITY

It is significant that middle-class interviewees outside North Tipperary – who were, by and large, more critical of politicians such as Michael Lowry – still acknowledged that they often make contact with politicians about various issues. For instance, Feargal, a doctor in North Cork, says:

> I'm shocked at what austerity has done to our health care system. It was bad before, but now it's a complete disaster. I cannot believe that our political leaders put the interests of bankers and developers before everyone else. Our local A&E is like a North Korean field hospital and every time I send someone down there, it makes me angry.

Feargal is highly critical of the political elite's practice of 'being there' for bankers and developers, yet he expects his local politicians to 'be there' for him and his colleagues. He continues:

> The footpath outside our clinic was a disgrace and we are rate payers. I had brought it to the attention of the council and nothing happened. So I emailed our local TD and he came down and had a look at it. We have patients in wheelchairs and people with all kinds of mobility issues, so access to the clinic is really important. In fairness to him, he did get it sorted in the end and yes, I probably will vote for him next time because of it.

Rules-based systems are not perfect and interventions by politicians can sometimes make them more responsive. But these interventions can also undermine the fairness of the systems. While local interventions have nothing like the consequences of the rule changes that resulted from inter-elite intimacy, they are undoubtedly rooted in the same understanding of 'being good'. More important, there appears to be no clear sense of exactly when the 'good' practice of politicians 'being there' for their constituents changes into the 'bad' practice of politicians 'being there' for business elites.

CONCLUSION

Everyday politics in Ireland seems to lean more towards the world of relationships than the world of rules. However, rules are central to its operation. The key function of Irish politicians at constituency level is making representations to rule-based systems on behalf of voters, a practice which voters reward on election day. Despite criticism of politicians for 'being there' for bankers, businessmen and developers, few interviewees made a connection between these practices and their own interactions with politicians, which also centre on 'being there'.

There is some evidence that the benefits of 'being there' are not illusory and make a real difference when rules-based systems are over-stretched, unresponsive or simply unfair. Politicians themselves recognise this constituency work as central to political success and to building their reputation for 'being good', even if their representations distort 'fairness'. Most important, there appears to be huge ambiguity about the point at which the good practice of 'being there' for voters becomes the bad practice of 'being there' for business elites, a theme explored in the next chapter.

Chapter 6 ～

RULES, RELATIONSHIPS AND ELITES

Irish public life is fairly free of large-scale corruption. This is partly because of the intimacy of our society in which very little goes on that is not found out.[1]

Hibernia, 1974

In Chapter 2 we saw how the founding fathers of the state created a political culture that relied heavily on relationships. This tradition married a commitment to mass democratic participation, developed by O'Connell and Parnell, with the tight bonds of family and community which had emerged under colonialism. This political culture also emphasised frugality. Some strands of the nationalist movement, particularly those linked to Arthur Griffith's Sinn Féin, felt that an independent Irish state could generate economic prosperity, but as the structures of the new state stabilised in the 1920s and 1930s, the focus on economic growth took second place to nationalist goals and deference to Catholicism's ideological distaste for commerce. Tom Garvin writes:

> The Catholic Church's dislike of commerce and 'unbridled' capitalism echoed a general popular prejudice, encouraged in particular by people who pursued public-enterprise careers, against free trade and tacitly in favour of public enterprise. This in turn derived from an economic, or possibly anti-economic, political

culture that was fundamentally static and zero-sum in character, non-developmental and even anti-developmental in character.[2]

Historian J.J. Lee has argued that the net result of this ideological leaning was an acknowledgement that those living in independent Ireland would have to accept a frugal lifestyle as the price of political freedom.

> De Valera had compared Ireland before independence to 'a servant in a big mansion'. If the servant wanted his freedom he must give up the luxuries of a certain kind which were available to him by being in that mansion … If he goes into the cottage he has to make up his mind to put up with the frugal fare of the cottage.[3]

By the 1950s, this indifference to economic prosperity had led to a level of emigration that threatened the survival of families, communities and ultimately the nation itself. Desmond, a retired Fine Gael politician who remembers this period, said:

> Well, you see, you had World War II and after the war, things were in a bad shape, there was fifty thousand a year emigrating. I remember the railway station and it was packed with people leaving … Dr Whitaker then came along and Seán Lemass and it was a question of having to face up to the situation that if this level of emigration was going to continue we'd be in queer street. There'd be nobody left. The survival of the nation was threatened … survival, that's the word.

That threat to survival led to a sharp change in economic policy. Now the focus was on integrating Ireland into global capitalism. Fianna Fáil Taoiseach Seán Lemass, who led the process, commented:

> We are not prepared to watch calmly the de-population and impoverishment of our country. We desire political and economic freedom so that we can take action to protect our vital nationality

interests. Unless we are prepared to see the scattering of our people over the face of the world and the destruction of our nation, we must take steps to preserve and develop here the industries which mean employment for our people in their own country.[4]

An important component of that change was a shift in attitudes to money, profit and material goods. The distaste for commerce that had been a theme of early Irish nationalism was replaced by a sense that the entrepreneurs, those who created jobs and those whose activities led to economic development, were the new heroes, the people who were really 'good' in modern Ireland.

Analysts of Ireland's poor economic performance criticised the conservatism of Irish culture and the distaste for commerce in Catholic social teaching.[5] Failing to understand and prioritise commerce and entrepreneurship was also repeatedly highlighted as a reason for Ireland's early economic failure. These explanations were strongly resonant of the work of modernisation theorists such as David McClelland, who pointed out that many relationship-oriented societies do not value achievement and entrepreneurship.[6] The individual's position in these societies is often determined on the day they are born and bears little relation to their own capacity for hard work or innovation. In contrast, in a society that values achievement, the individual's position depends on how they use their talents and resources to achieve status and wealth, rather than on their position in relationship-based groups such as the family and community. In this type of society, individuals will be more likely to strive in ways that generate economic growth. This analysis was affirmed by academic experts on the Irish context, such as historian J.J. Lee, who highlighted the absence of a 'performer' ethic in Irish economic activity.[7]

Alongside these academic debates came a new popular celebration of the 'entrepreneur' which became increasingly prevalent in Irish society during the 1960s, 1970s and 1980s. The most important vehicle for this 'celebration of the entrepreneur' was *The Late Late Show*, a weekly talk show hosted by one of Ireland's most influential broadcasters, Gay Byrne. Byrne's programme impacted on a range of modernisation processes in Ireland and, among other things, was a platform for celebrating entrepreneurship. For instance, John Concannon, Managing Director of JFC Manufacturing, attributed the success of his company to a slot he got on Byrne's programme in the 1980s:

> I invented a product for feeding calves, called the Triple Bucket. I needed publicity. At the time, they reckoned if you got on the *Late Late Show* you were set.... The segment was supposed to be two minutes long, but in the end it went on for 12 minutes. That was the starting point. Everything that followed came from that one appearance.[8]

Michael Burke, who founded Stira, a folding attic stairs company, in 1982, also credits his eventual success to Byrne's support. He says, 'we were invited on Ireland's most popular current events programme, *The Late Late Show* hosted by Gay Byrne. The show was dedicated to showcasing new, up and coming Irish businesses. The response from that show was incredible and catapulted us on to the national stage very quickly.'[9]

A significant part of Byrne's cultural influence in this context was not just publicity for the products but a celebration of the entrepreneurs themselves. He frequently stressed that these individuals were the kind of risk-takers and innovators Ireland needed. Unlike the priests and politicians whom he alternately mocked and fawned over, the entrepreneur was a figure to be admired and valued in Irish society. Yeats's caricature of the businessman as the 'fumbler in the greasy till',[10] a model that neatly matched Catholic distaste for commerce, gave way to an ideology identifying the entrepreneur as the central driving figure of the Irish economy. At the same time, there were strong links between this celebration of Irish entrepreneurship and earlier Irish models of 'being good' that centred on family and community. After they had introduced their product, Byrne would invariably ask the entrepreneur, 'How many jobs have you created?' The key dividend from entrepreneurship in Irish culture was job creation, which enabled families and communities to stay in Ireland while building long-lasting economic prosperity. Thus, the entrepreneur – not the priest or small farmer – was now the key figure in maintaining relationship-based groups in Ireland. The idea that the entrepreneur is 'good' because his or her activities support job creation continues to be powerfully evident in Irish culture, a feature evident in the public response to the troubles of Cavan businessman Sean Quinn.

Case Study: Sean Quinn

In 2008, the *Sunday Times Rich List* identified Sean Quinn, with an estimated wealth of €4.7 billion, as Ireland's richest man. Quinn attributed his initial success to contacts made through the GAA, an organisation of which his brother Peter ultimately became president.[11] Starting with a quarry business in the 1970s, his interests expanded over the next thirty years to hotels, glass, plastics, insurance and banking.

By 2008, Quinn had a 15 per cent stake in Anglo-Irish Bank, the most troubled and corrupt of Ireland's toxic banks. When the bank was wound up, Quinn and his family lost €2.8 billion of their fortune. It emerged that Quinn had obtained loans to support the bank's share price, and Quinn Insurance was fined by the Financial Regulator. In 2011, although he was permanently resident in the Irish Republic, Quinn filed for bankruptcy in Belfast. In 2012, following applications from the Irish Banking Resolution Corporation (IBRC), Quinn and his sons were served with thirty court orders to reverse asset-stripping measures. IBRC argued that Quinn and his family were attempting to put their wealth and assets beyond its reach. In November 2012, he was jailed for nine weeks for continued asset-stripping.

For those who believe that the rules governing financial exchanges should be obeyed, Sean Quinn is clearly an example of a 'bad' man. Fintan O'Toole, writing in the *Irish Times* in July 2012, criticised 'Quinn's outright defiance of the courts and determination to hang on to public money'.[12] He noted the damage done to the Irish economy by Quinn's reckless trading:

> Take all the money raised this year by cuts in child benefit. And from cutting the school clothing and footwear allowance. And all the cuts to jobseekers' benefit, rent supplement and fuel allowance for the elderly. Throw in the restrictions of one-parent family allowances to children under seven. Pile on all the cuts in back-to-education allowances and community employment schemes. Take all of that money from the pockets of the poorest people in Ireland this year and you still haven't reached the amount that Sean Quinn agrees he owes the Irish tax-payer.[13]

Noting Quinn's apparent lack of shame at breaking the rules, O'Toole concludes:

> Quinn is openly, flagrantly and quite proudly trying to hang on to this money that belongs to us. As he said on Sunday, he took a 'very conscious decision' to do 'everything in our power to take as many assets as we could'. The basic intention is very simple – to transfer assets from the Irish people to the Quinn family.[14]

But many people did not share O'Toole's view of Sean Quinn. On Sunday 29 July 2012, four thousand supporters of the bankrupt businessman, including key figures from the Catholic Church, the GAA and Irish politics, attended a rally supporting the Quinns in their home community in Ballyconnell, County Cavan. Amid a forest of GAA banners from local clubs, speaker after speaker highlighted Quinn's role as a family man, a prominent employer in the local community whose businesses in the Cavan and border region had helped families and communities remain intact. Speakers also highlighted his contributions to the GAA. Tyrone GAA manager Mickey Harte described Quinn as 'the most humble man who did as much as he could for people and caused little harm'.[15] Fr Brian D'Arcy said, 'The main reason I'm here tonight is because as Christians and good neighbours we have a right, a duty to stand by one of our families and neighbours when they are in trouble. And nobody will take that away from us.'[16]

Quinn was portrayed as a victim, as a good man, 'one of our own', in contrast to the immoral rule-based activities of the state. Placards at the rally claimed 'Cowardly Kenny[17] supports Illegality' and 'Let the Quinn case go to Brussels, there is no justice here'. In the *Irish Times*, former GAA president and Fine Gael MEP Sean Kelly was quoted as saying that it was 'part of the ethos' of the GAA to get behind 'a decent family' who were living in the community and going through a difficult patch. He concluded that one of the great strengths of the GAA is that 'we stand by our own.'[18]

So for Quinn supporters, the morality of relationships trumped the morality of rules. They were, in effect, demonstrating that the 'good' person stands by their 'own' and that this moral imperative takes precedence over conforming to rules – which are fundamentally less important and less moral. It is worth noting that a number of the prominent GAA speakers at this rally, such as Mickey Harte and Jarlath Burns, were not actually citizens of the Republic of Ireland, so they, as individuals, did not have to pay for the consequences of Sean Quinn's activities. Yet they evidently felt that being members of the 32-county relationship-based group of the nation qualified them to speak publicly on the matter.

Emphasising the goodness of the entrepreneur who contributes to job creation fails to acknowledge the sometimes exploitative relationships that can lie at the heart of entrepreneurial capitalism. Examining the links between economic activity and intimacy in families and communities in west Clare in the 1930s, Arensberg and Kimball found that many of the commercial transactions between farmers and local tradespeople were reciprocal. For instance, the farmer usually had an account at the local shop, where he would buy dry goods, cloth, etc. He might have been able to buy goods more cheaply elsewhere, but having an account at the shop allowed him to build a reciprocal relationship with the shop owner which could be useful – financially, politically and socially. Likewise, the shopkeeper providing credit to the farmer gained a whole range of benefits for his family in terms of the broader network of social relations within the community.[19]

The commercial transactions of Gay Byrne's entrepreneurs were much more typically capitalist and, therefore, potentially more exploitative. One of the most striking examples was Geoff Read, a young businessman who set up his own bottled water company and who was praised by Byrne on the *Late Late Show* in 1984. His company, Ballygowan Bottled Water, was selling a commodity – water! – previously freely available to the residents of Newcastle West, County Limerick. His daring in selling something that had been free was initially mocked and then quickly celebrated as his company began to turn significant profits.[20] The principle of exchange that had governed earlier commercial transactions, and which had blocked economic growth, had been replaced by the principle of extracting money from the consumer for various commodities, whether they needed them or not. This shift from exchange to extraction, which facilitated economic growth, went hand in hand with a shift in the perception of how a 'good' person should behave in Ireland. Worryingly, this value shift happened at a time when increasing wealth was opening a gap between ordinary people and business elites in Irish society, a gap which had already begun to reshape Irish political culture.

ELITES AND ECONOMIC CHANGE

All political systems have elites. From the earliest days of the state, Irish society had a pattern of both public and private inter-elite relationships. These connections were particularly evident in the Church–State relationship, exemplified by the link between de Valera and Archbishop John Charles McQuaid.[21] Catholic social thought actively promoted corporatist political structures in which inter-elite relationships were seen as 'good', a model evident in the structure of the Irish parliament's second house, the Seanad. However, very few of these inter-elite structures delivered the type of personal financial gain that became a feature of inter-elite relationships in Ireland from the 1960s onwards.

The introduction of foreign direct investment, increased industrialisation and accompanying economic growth led to the emergence of a new stratum of financial, business and corporate elites in Irish society. Because the recording of wealth in Ireland has historically been so vague, it is difficult to map the links between this new wealthy group and older Irish commercial and agriculture elites. However, there are some sources of data which provide concrete evidence of the economic profile of this elite stratum of 'our own'. In his 1966 study of the *Distribution of Personal Wealth by County*, Patrick Lyons found that in Ireland 'just over 70 per cent of the adult population own no net wealth', and that slightly more than two-thirds of personal wealth in Ireland was 'possessed by those who own more than £5000 of net wealth, but they account for only 5.1 per cent of the total adult population'. This wealthy group lived mainly in Dublin, particularly Dun Laoghaire, and Counties Meath, Wicklow and Kildare. Data from the Revenue Commissioners from the 1970s indicates that in 1978, 2189 individuals owned gross wealth over £600 million. These individuals controlled gross wealth equal to approximately 9 per cent of GNP. By 1988, *Magill* magazine was able to list the fifty richest people in Ireland. The vast majority of this group made their money from manufacturing, property dealing, construction and land ownership. The concentration of wealth at the highest strata of Irish society became much more marked during the Celtic Tiger period: Denis O'Hearn writes, 'in terms of ratio of the income share of the richest ten per cent to the poorest ten per cent, Ireland was, in the mid 1990s, the most unequal country in Europe and second only to the United States in the OECD.'[22]

Alongside the emergence of a new business elite, there was a significant generational shift in Irish politics as the Civil War generation in the main political parties retired. De Valera, who had dominated politics after independence, was very open to arbitration with powerful interest groups; thus his brand of politics resulted in the privileging of the agenda of those who were already materially wealthy. However, power rather than direct financial gain was the driving force behind his elite connections. De Valera himself had an ambiguous relationship with money: he was strongly influenced by Catholic social teaching, which prioritised frugal family life over material gain, and when he was elected president at the end of his political career, he refused to draw his salary.[23]

With the changing of the guard in Fianna Fáil during the 1960s, the Civil War generation was gradually replaced by the notorious 'men in mohair suits', whose flaunting of their material wealth set them apart from the relationship-based groups of family and community. No politician better exemplifies this value change and new elitism than Charles J. Haughey. From his earliest appearances in the Dáil, he impressed older colleagues with his clear commitment to modernisation; but the core aim of this modernisation was to gain material wealth – for the nation as well as for him personally. T. Ryle Dwyer writes:

> Haughey stood out amidst the ageing members of the Fianna Fáil hierarchy. Young, highly educated and enthusiastic, he attracted attention as a man of the future. By repeatedly calling for more research and development, he was basically advocating change and modernization, and this set him apart from the conservative orthodoxy of his party elders. Yet profit was still the basic motivation behind the policies he advocated. 'Once and for all, let us get rid of this cant that there is something illegal, immoral or wrong in profits' he declared.[24]

During his tenure as Minister for Justice, for Agriculture and for Health, there were undoubtedly benefits to his modernising zeal, even if it was driven by a firmly materialistic vision. However, in his personal life he exhibited a desire to distinguish himself, to stand apart from his peers and constituents that was symptomatic of the new, wider elitism that was already beginning to erode the relationship-based moral structure of Irish political culture. Elaine Byrne writes, 'The puritan revolutionary ethic of the first generation of political leaders in independent Ireland was evident in the austerity which characterized their private lives.'[25] Part of the purpose of leading an austere private life was to link political leaders with members of the relationship-based national group, with 'our own'. Although in real terms they were elites, their frugality appeared to make them one with the rest of the Irish population. In contrast, at the time Haughey entered politics, the younger generation of politicians wanted to separate themselves from the group in ways that often, paradoxically, mirrored the lifestyle of the old Anglo-Irish class. Ryle Dwyer writes:

> Haughey was inevitably seen as a friend of the rich, and his ostentatious lifestyle exacerbated the impression. Fianna Fáil had once been proud that it consisted of the men with the cloth caps, but the Minister for Justice was representative of a new breed in the party. A wealthy businessman who owned racehorses and rode with the hunt, he came to be classified as one of the men in the mohair suits. He enjoyed his prosperity and flaunted it.[26]

This new elitism was strongly reflected in the style of fundraising that emerged in Irish politics during the 1960s and was closely associated with Haughey's growing dominance in the party.

The fundraising committee Taca, established in 1966, was designed to be, in Fianna Fáil politician Kevin Boland's words, a 'top hat' organisation that held dinners which facilitated close relationships between business, construction, financial elites and politicians. Significantly, ordinary Fianna Fáil cumann members were excluded from these occasions – they were clearly not ranked in the 'top hat' category. Elaine Byrne notes that while Taca was wound up in the late 1960s, the goal of political fundraising through inter-elite relationships remained firmly in place; it just took less visible forms. Kevin Boland writes pointedly about the moral implications of connections between politicians and financial elites: 'These people were making an investment on which they expected a return and they intended to call the tune.'[27]

The heady pace of urbanisation in Ireland during this period created a raft of opportunities for planning and development-based 'favours' between business and political elites, particularly in the greater Dublin area. The subsidisation of sectors of the Irish economy that resulted from EU membership also created plenty of opportunities for back-handers, false payments and the distribution of licences and contracts associated within this new capitalist circle of intimacy. Some of the money went directly to fund political parties during the 1960s and 1970s, but, more important, this activity created new circles of influence at the top of Irish society.

The ties binding politicians to local families and communities were loosening during this period and face-to-face contacts had to be supplemented with roadside posters and television advertising. These features of modern political campaigns appealed to an increasingly educated and mobile electorate – and they cost money. When Jack Lynch became leader of Fianna Fáil, a helicopter was used to canvass the country during the campaign. 'Our own' were changing rapidly and Irish politicians were positioning themselves physically and metaphorically above them, not among them.

The contrast with de Valera's positioning of himself within the relationship-based groups is striking. Xavier, a retired Fianna Fáil politician, describes de Valera calling to his mother's house:

> He was a man who would call into a TD's house when he was passing in the summer months. I remember him speaking Irish to my mother. My father hadn't much Irish, very basic, and there was another politician, who shall remain nameless, who said, 'Níl aon Ghaeilge ag Sean' and my father said, 'Níl, I had a gun on my shoulder when you were learning Irish.'

This exchange is very revealing about the boundaries of intimacy within Fianna Fáil. For de Valera, being able to speak Irish signified belonging to 'our own' in Fianna Fáil; for Xavier's father, it was demonstrated by having taken up arms in the war of independence and the Civil War. Neither of these politicians had achieved their position on the basis of money.

More important, the process of calling to the house itself represented a gesture towards the wider circle of intimacy within the Fianna Fáil party.

The contempt for the ordinary voter and the ordinary Fianna Fáil supporter that was implied by this new 'top hat' helicopter culture was only fleetingly visible. An incident at one major Fianna Fáil rally at the Northside Shopping Centre in Dublin, which was attended by Jack Lynch and Charles Haughey, is very revealing. One shop owner complained to P.J. Mara, Haughey's associate, that the rally was obstructing business. Ryle Dwyer writes:

> P.J. Mara suggested that he get lost, but the man persisted in complaining. 'Would you ever go and fuck yourself,' Mara snapped. Indignant, the man went to Haughey. 'I want to complain about the way I was treated by your Director of Elections, Mr Mara.... He told me to "fuck off".' 'And I'm now making it official,' Haughey replied.[28]

This type of response was clearly not meted out to Taca supporters as Haughey climbed his way towards the top of Irish politics in the early 1980s.

ELITES AND IRISH POLITICS

Much of what we know about the impact of the new wealthy elite on Ireland's political culture comes from the evidence gathered by tribunals of inquiry, particularly during the 1990–2010 period. The Beef, McCracken, Moriarty and Flood/Mahon Tribunals uncovered a dense web of intimate relationships between politicians, property developers and Irish business elites which led to significant levels of corruption in planning, licence regulation and the agri-food industry. Along with this intimacy, the tribunals revealed the extraordinarily weak response of rules-based institutions to corruption and the willingness of politicians and financial elites to bend or break the rules to accommodate individuals within their circles of intimacy.

The 1963 Planning Act had left numerous loopholes in planning law which were ripe for exploitation. During the early 1970s, commentators in the media were already raising questions about land transactions and the granting of planning permission for construction and development. A key factor in these developments was the weakness of the rules on conflict of interest. The Local Government Act 1946 had rescinded Section 36 of the Application of Enactments Order 1898, which directed that local authority members could not take part in discussions on any matter in which they had a personal interest. Therefore, the rules introduced by the independent Irish state governing planning were actually weaker and provided greater opportunities for relationship-based corruption than was the case under colonial rule. Elaine Byrne comments:

> Conflict of interest legislation was far more robust when Ireland was under British rule. Thus, councillors who pushed through rezoning were not legally obliged to decline their occupation as auctioneers. They were not required to disclose their close relationship with those developers who sought to have land rezoned. Ultimately, this absence of statutory disclosure requirements allowed a carte blanche approach by elected representatives.[29]

Neither local nor national politicians were keen to strengthen the rules. When Fianna Fáil councillor Niall Andrews proposed a motion in Dublin City Council in 1974 which would oblige councillors to declare their interests, no one seconded the motion. The establishment of An Bord Pleanála should have provided an opportunity to strengthen the rules and limit political discretion in planning matters, but as the system of appointments to the board relied heavily on political patronage, this opportunity to boost the rules-based dimension of planning was largely lost.

Elaine Byrne argues that the 1980s and 1990s marked one of the most intense periods of political corruption in the Irish state's history and asserts that this period can be viewed as an example of 'state capture'. State capture is defined by the World Bank as a 'type of political corruption in which private interests significantly influence a state's decision-making processes to their own advantage through illicit and unobvious means'.[30] The series of scandals which emerged during this period contribute to this impression of state capture. Decisions which were subsequently scrutinised for evidence of state capture include the allocation of a commercial licence to Century Radio, the privatisation of Irish Sugar, the sale of land involving Telecom Éireann and the Beef Tribunal. Surprisingly, there was a good deal of public awareness about this corruption. An MRBI poll in 1991 found:

> A total of 89 per cent agreed that 'there is a Golden Circle of people in Ireland who are using power to make money for themselves'. Some 81 per cent agreed that the people in this Golden Circle were made up in equal measure of business people and politicians. Some 76 per cent thought the scandals were part and parcel of the Irish economic system rather than one-off events. A total of 83 per cent thought that the Greencore, Telecom and Goodman scandals were merely 'the tip of the iceberg' while 84 per cent said business people involved in corrupt dealings and fraud get off more lightly than other criminals.[31]

The late 1990s and early 2000s saw the establishment of more tribunals. The McCracken Tribunal investigated donations to Charles Haughey and the relationship between businessman Ben Dunne and former Fine Gael minister Michael Lowry. The Moriarty Tribunal focused on the links between Lowry, Dunne and businessman Denis O'Brien.[32] The Flood/Mahon Tribunal, which became the longest-running tribunal in the history of the state, returned to the thorny question of planning and issued a number of interim reports, including one which contributed to the resignation of Taoiseach Bertie Ahern in April 2008, before issuing its final report in March 2012.

Before the decision to provide the Irish banks with a guarantee in September 2008, there was widespread public awareness of problems relating to inter-elite relationships in Ireland. Yet there is little evidence of public demand during the 1990s and early 2000s for reform of Irish politics – despite the revelations of the tribunals. It would appear that the similarities between this elite intimacy and the relationship-based intimacy which underpins everyday political culture in Ireland were so great that they created an ambiguity in public attitudes towards corruption. As a result of this ambiguity, political parties and individuals involved in corrupt activities were continually re-elected during the Celtic Tiger period. Indirectly, voters sent a message to corrupt political elites that their behaviour was 'not that bad' because it reflected their own prioritising of relationships over rules. This indulgent attitude towards rule-breakers was to cost Irish citizens dear when the Celtic Tiger boom finally imploded.

VOTERS, ELITES AND POLITICAL INTIMACY

Knowing, Trusting, Communicating

Chapter 4 highlighted the distinction between rule-based knowledge (written down in an open and transparent form) and relationship-based knowledge (communicated face to face). In Chapter 5 we looked at the tendency of voters to use relationships with politicians to manage rules. In the elite political context, relationships are used by elites not simply to bend or break the rules, but often to rewrite the rules. This practice generates a much deeper form of corruption than everyday local political intimacy, although it is embedded in the balance between weak rules and strong relationships which operates across Irish culture.

Case Study: Export Credit Insurance

A typical example of this deeper corruption emerged from the findings of the Beef Tribunal. In 1986, the Department of Industry and Commerce decided to withdraw all state-granted export credit insurance to Irish companies exporting to Iraq because of concerns about the imminent outbreak of war. The decision was paralleled around Europe. In March 1987, after a general election, the new Minister for Commerce and Industry, Albert Reynolds, decided to revoke this decision. On 9 April 1987, Larry Goodman, chairman of the Goodman Group and a close 'friend' of Reynolds, met him to discuss 'the desirability or necessity for the provision of export credit insurance'. Within a week of this meeting, Reynolds had reinstated export credit insurance for companies exporting to Iraq. Of these companies, Goodman's was by far the largest. By changing the rules, Reynolds went against the explicit advice of officials from the Departments of Agriculture, Finance, and Industry and Commerce and of the Insurance Corporation of Ireland (ICI), which administered the scheme. In September 1987, Reynolds doubled the export credit ceiling to £150 million. It was clear that Reynolds made these decisions following representations from Goodman. He subsequently admitted to the Beef Tribunal, 'You can take it from me that … Mr Goodman or Mr Britton [Goodman executive] or both, took every opportunity to look for the maximum export credit.' In October 1988, as Elaine Byrne notes:

> Reynolds informed his department that the cabinet had decided the previous June that under the provision of the Insurance (Export Guarantee) Act 1988, the Iraqi export credit ceiling was to be increased to £270 million. More ominously further increases *'should be at the discretion of the Minister for Industry and Commerce'.*

In total, the state paid out £67 million under the scheme, £27 million of which was never recovered. In addition, following a meeting with Taoiseach Charles Haughey, it was announced that the Goodman Group would receive cheap subsidised loans, of which £81 million was drawn down, in exchange for providing employment which never materialised. At the time when these decisions were being made, Charles Haughey had appeared publicly on Irish television to launch an austerity programme involving massive cuts in the public health system and the education system. He opened his speech, 'As a community, we are living way beyond our means.' By invoking the relationship-based unit of community to describe Irish society he was suggesting that everyone had a common interest in restoring the national finances – but this was not actually the case. At the top of Irish society was a small business elite who were actively exploiting the limited national resource base for personal gain and who were supported by the same politicians who located themselves within 'our own' and dressed up their decisions in the language and morality of intimacy.

In describing the relationship between Goodman and Reynolds, Elaine Byrne comments:

> Reynolds swore four times to the Tribunal on oath that Goodman was 'never ever a guest of mine at a Cáirde Fáil dinner' (the annual Fianna Fáil President's dinner). However, an *Irish Independent* article on 12 December 1987 reported that 'Albert and Kathleen cut quite a dash on the dance floor. And they had Ireland's most important "Baron" as their guest. Larry Goodman, beef baron extraordinaire, even ventured onto the floor for a couple of twirls.'[33]

Members of the golden circle felt that this intimacy would provide them with protection against the rules. Former Goodman executive Patrick McGuinness told journalist Susan O'Keeffe, 'There was also a feeling that we were invincible, that we had the right connections at the right places, that could basically control any investigation that would be put in place.'[34] In this assessment, Goodman executives were proved largely correct.

REWRITING RULES

The export credit insurance scheme tells us a lot about the balance between rules and relationships at the elite level in Irish culture. Goodman and his executives knew the rule-based systems of the state very well, but they trusted their relationships with senior politicians more. Because Goodman knew Reynolds and Haughey personally, he trusted that they would change the rules in his favour. Describing lobbying Haughey about one particular rule change,[35] he told the tribunal that he was not 'going along asking Mr Haughey to remove it', but 'if Mr Haughey chose to do something about it, that was great.' It seems that Mr Haughey did do something about it: at a later cabinet meeting, his proposal to change the rule was accepted. Byrne notes, 'This cabinet decision was not recorded on the usual pink slip used for cabinet decisions.' The absence of the pink slip highlights how relationships had undermined even rule-based recording at the top of Irish politics.

We saw in Chapter 5 the importance placed on face-to-face communication in everyday political culture. Despite the increasing use of social media and technology, Irish voters still like to be asked for their vote. They also like to feel that a politician will engage with them face to face in constituency work if they need their help. When we communicate face to face, each person can read the other's non-verbal signals, enabling us to develop greater knowledge of each other. This knowledge draws on reason and emotion and, critically, it can be used to build long-lasting relationships of reciprocal obligation. Charles Haughey's Taca was the first political entity to recognise the commercial saleability of this face-to-face intimacy. Unlike ordinary voters, who had to attend the local clinic, he offered people with money a chance to engage with politicians in a closed, intimate, 'top hat' environment. The success of Taca led to a range of other ventures – including exclusive dinners and golf classics – by Irish political parties, all aimed at facilitating face-to-face communication between politicians and business elites.

The most controversial example of elite political face-to-face communication came during the late Celtic Tiger period. George Taylor describes political fundraising at the Galway races:

The Galway horse races were the social event of the Irish calendar: a heady mixture of gambling and politics, where travelling by helicopter confirmed you had finally arrived. While it often felt like a re-run of the fall of Saigon, the 'real action' was to be found on the ground, or rather the tent, where Fianna Fáil politicians rubbed shoulders with the elite of Ireland's property developers and bankers.[36]

A table for ten in the Galway tent could cost up to €4,000. This sum, according to journalist Matt Cooper, 'provided access to the elite, and even a sense of being part of their set. Government ministers would always be present.'[37] Access to the tent was tightly controlled. Not only was the ordinary race-goer excluded, so was the ordinary member of Fianna Fáil – despite Taoiseach Bertie Ahern's claim that it was 'for ordinary Joe Soaps' from 'all walks of life'.[38] Even after he closed the tent, Ahern's successor, Brian Cowen, denied that it provided anyone with the 'inside curve'. However, the opportunity to engage in face-to-face communication with politicians was precisely what was being offered in Galway. Senan, a Labour politician, concludes:

> It created an elitist core with the tent at the Galway races. It became a bad word and became associated with things that did damage to Fianna Fáil for the very reason that Mickey So and So who was out in Carraroe or in Spiddal and who was breaking his backside putting up posters and everything else, he wasn't in there.

Relationships had always been at the core of Irish politics. In earlier times, these relationships were between a politician and a family or community, and the core transaction was intimacy with the politician in exchange for a vote. In contrast, elite intimacy traded face-to-face communication with politicians for money and access to elite spheres of influence. The moral basis of intimacy in Irish political culture had become profoundly distorted and the scale of changes to rules emerging at this elite level was completely different from the requests made at local clinics.

Case Study: Golf

In early 2008, it started to become clear that there was a potential crisis in Irish banking, and specifically in Anglo Irish Bank. Businessman Sean Quinn had engaged in an enormous gamble involving contracts for difference (CFDs) in relation to the bank's shares. Tom Lyons writes, 'In May 2008, [Brian] Lenihan was appointed Minister for Finance when Cowen finally became Taoiseach. Lenihan was briefed by his civil servants in his first month in office that Quinn was a large gambler in Anglo CFDs and this had stability implications for the State.'[39] By September 2008, the Irish state had decided to offer a blanket state guarantee to the Irish banks, a decision that contributed to the collapse of the Irish economy in late 2010. But very little is known about the circumstances in which this decision was taken. There is a surprising absence of documentation on the decision. Both former Information Commissioner Emily O'Reilly and Rob Wright, author of the official report on the Department of Finance's response to the crisis, have complained about the absence of a rules-based paper trail. However, in January 2011, details began to emerge of face-to-face communication that may have had an effect on the decision.

Two months before the guarantee, Taoiseach Brian Cowen had played a game of golf with Seán FitzPatrick and three other former directors of Anglo Irish Bank. (Cowen also later took a mobile phone call, when he was in Malaysia, from FitzPatrick.) Cowen subsequently denied that the bank had been discussed during the golf game. However, as Leo Varadkar of Fine Gael commented, 'This game of golf with Fintan Drury and Brian Cowen and Seán FitzPatrick must have gone on for three or four hours … it would seem strange to me that they did not discuss the condition of the bank at the time.'[40] In September 2008, Cowen's government offered a blanket guarantee to all the Irish banks, a guarantee which benefited Anglo Irish Bank more than any other institution.

Seán FitzPatrick publicly admitted that he believed that face-to-face communication is the most effective means of sourcing 'advice to support financial decision-making. Although he consulted the websites of the *Financial Times* and the *Economist*, he acknowledged that "for the real McCoy you can't beat the 19th hole on the golf course."[41]

It is impossible to know what was said on the golf course, but the lack of documentation explaining the context and rationale for the bank guarantee led many to suspect that face-to-face communication played a significant role in choosing the guarantee to resolve the banking crisis. The Irish bank guarantee placed the bulk of responsibility for the consequences of banking mismanagement on the Irish taxpayer – there were none of the structural reforms of banking systems that had accompanied other bank guarantees in countries such as Sweden.[42] In the *Irish Independent*, Ailish O'Hora highlighted public disquiet about the lack of documentation on the guarantee: 'We're blue in the face from hearing there's no paper trail in relation to what happened in the run-up to the night of the bank guarantee. That's simply not good enough. Either the civil servants took notes or they didn't. And if not, why not?'[43]

The Galway tent and the Anglo golf game have become part of the popular lore of the Irish economy's implosion between 2007 and 2010. However, these iconic incidents are part of the wider balance between weak rules and strong relationships in Ireland. Like everyday political culture, elite political culture seems to lean more strongly towards relationships than rules. Unlike everyday politics, however, access to elite circles of intimacy is tightly controlled and, in most cases, must be bought through money or influence. These closed circles exclude not only ordinary citizens but also ordinary political party members. Finally, the scale of rule changes being demanded at this level is far greater than the rule changes requested at constituency level and often involves rewriting the rules to make them instruments of exploitation rather than fairness.

BELONGING AND CONFLICT

Chapter 5 looked at the role of family relationships in shaping a sense of belonging to Irish political parties. We saw how family allegiances and the attendance of politicians at key family events, particularly family funerals, influences voter behaviour. Basil Chubb notes that Irish politics was strongly shaped by loyalty to relationships rather than to ideas.[44] At elite level, relationships are also hugely important; however, the role of loyalty appears to be quite different. An analysis of political donations since the 1960s highlights quite strikingly the extent to which business elites contributed to all political parties, not just Fianna Fáil. In the beef industry, for example, Elaine Byrne notes that while Fianna Fáil received nearly £300,000 from beef barons between 1987 and 1991, Fine Gael received almost £140,000 during the same period.[45] Larry Goodman also donated £20,000 to the Progressive Democrats (PDs) before the 1987 election. More recently, in 2001, controversy arose when businessman Denis O'Brien donated £50,000 to all four major political parties, Fianna Fáil, Fine Gael, Labour and the PDs (although Labour returned the donation).[46] This pattern of multiple donations is not only an effective way of hedging your bets; it also reaffirms the importance of money as the key factor in belonging to Ireland's golden circles.

Putting direct political connections aside, some Irish business elites are also shrewd enough to publicly stress that they belong to local intimacy-based groups in order to tap into relationship-based models of 'being good'. In *The FitzPatrick Tapes*, banker Seán FitzPatrick recognised how cleverly the businessman Sean Quinn built this image of relationships-based goodness linked to family and community. Describing his first impression of Quinn, he says:

> He was one of those hail-fellow-well-met, 'ah sure I will go down there and play the old cards, five and six lads for ten bob or whatever it was' ... He was always producing that and would nearly be blessing himself ... He was very human, but ... I didn't easily like him.[47]

It was perhaps FitzPatrick's long experience of 'relationship banking' with the Irish construction industry which made him recognise how manipulative this approach could be in terms of the Irish value system.

In Chapter 5, a number of politicians explained how they tried not to engage in arguments with voters or say no to them in the course of constituency work, even when they knew they could do nothing for them. This unwillingness to say no is also evident at the elite level. During the 1970s, industrialist D.S.A. Carroll argued that the tendency of Irish politicians to avoid saying no had led to a political culture in which there was a serious gap between words and actions. His comments about the disastrous consequences of this approach in the 1970s could easily have been written about later periods in Irish politics. He says:

> Successive governments have proposed policies which they then have failed to pursue, have made offers to the electorate which they could not afford, and have responded to factionalist demands of narrow and immediate interest, to the detriment of the broader and long-term interests of the factions themselves, apart altogether from the nation as a whole.[48]

Carroll notes that in this political culture, the powerful voices had the most influence on policy:

> Businessmen and business organizations have contributed much to this deterioration in our affairs, because they have demanded from government measures, aid and support which further distort the economic system and which involve still further intervention by the public sector in our economy. In doing so, of course, they have been behaving no differently from all the other interests in society. Trade unions, farmers' organizations, political parties have all become more strident in their clamour for the immediate advancement of their own narrow interest.[49]

He predicted that an approach to economic management that was driven by the constant desire to achieve consensus would end in disaster, concluding:

> With attempts at consensus, as opposed to leadership in national affairs, the result is inevitable. The only consensus possible is one which postpones to a later date fundamental matters of a painful kind. Any consensus reached between factional interests must, in the nature of factions, relate to short-term means rather than long-term ends. Inevitably, expediency dictates that the most powerful faction secures those things which will pacify it now, regardless of the subsequent cost.[50]

Before the banking collapse, some politicians tried to pacify rather than confront a banking and construction sector which was heading for disaster. Kathleen Barrington describes the onslaught of communications from leaders in the banking sector to Minister for Finance Brian Cowen and Taoiseach Bertie Ahern during 2006 seeking changes to the Asset Covered Securities Act that would make it easier for them to raise money for lending.[51] Cowen received communications from Pat Farrell of the Irish Banking Federation (and a former general secretary of Fianna Fáil). He also received letters requesting the changes from David Kelly of AIB Mortgage Bank, Michael Doherty of WestLB and Austin Jennings of Bank of Ireland Global Markets. Officials in the Financial Regulator's office had deep reservations about these changes, which they communicated to the senior politicians. However, the pressure from the banking sector intensified: Brian Goggin of Bank of Ireland, David Drumm of Anglo Irish and representatives from DEPFA, a German bank based in the International Financial Services Centre (IFSC), all added their voices to the lobby.

As the Regulator continued to question the changes, the tone of these communications switched from easy charm to aggressive impatience. What is striking from the documentation obtained by the *Sunday Business Post* under Freedom of Information legislation is the politicians' unwillingness to say 'no' outright to the bankers – even though they clearly had reservations about the change. Barrington comments, 'The documents which we have obtained under [the] Freedom of Information Act suggest that [the] Financial Regulator was voicing concerns about the new legislation but that Cowen and his department were bowing to the bankers.'[52] The consequences of this decision for the Irish economy in 2007 were significant. Barrington concludes:

> It paved the way for banks to lend even more into an already overheated property market, effectively putting more air in to an enormous property bubble just before it burst – leaving first the banks and then the country teetering on the brink of insolvency. Ironically, the explanatory memorandum issued by the Department of Finance to accompany the bill seemed very reassuring: 'The bill will not give rise to any additional cost to the exchequer.'[53]

By trying to shore up a consensus rather than provide leadership based on a rational assessment of the overall needs of the group, political elites were the handmaidens of economic collapse. They abandoned their role as the protectors of the interests of the entire group in their anxiety to cater for the needs of those in their elite circles of intimacy. Therefore, 'being there' not only trumped 'being fair' but completely undermined their capacity to provide credible leadership.

BEING THERE AND BEING FAIR

In everyday Irish political culture, politicians and voters highlight the importance of politicians 'being there' for their constituents. A politician's capacity to 'be there' to negotiate with rules-based systems is central to their electoral success locally and their reputation as a 'good' politician. At the level of inter-elite relationships, it is also clear (as shown, for example, in the books of Simon Carswell, Shane Ross, Matt Cooper and Fintan O'Toole) that elites expect politicians to 'be there' for them. As with ordinary voters, the demand to 'be there' appears to take precedence over being fair to the group. At the elite level, politicians who built a reputation for 'being there' for business elites – Charles Haughey and Michael Lowry, for example – were rewarded. However, there are a number of stark differences between the relationship-based model of 'being there' at the everyday level and the model of 'being there' at the elite level.

In everyday political culture, voter–politician intimacy is based in the local constituency. Any voter can ask a politician in their constituency to make representations on their behalf. In inter-elite intimacy, the context is not the local constituency but informal circles of intimacy, which usually revolve around social meetings. Access to these circles is heavily controlled by power and money. So the politician offers a different quality of intimacy to the elite individual than he or she does to the ordinary voter.

Ordinary voters tend to ask politicians to negotiate for them with rules-based systems. These negotiations sometimes involve requests to bend or break rules in ways that make these systems less fair. However, as the tribunals show, while some politicians bent or broke the rules for their elite friends, the most profound damage was caused by politicians who rewrote the rules for those in their elite circles of intimacy. If we accept that the purpose of rules is to create a consistency that supports fairness, the process of state capture utterly distorts and inverts the purpose of rules, making them instruments of oppression and exploitation rather than fairness.

The politician who does a 'turn' for a voter in everyday Irish political culture will be rewarded with a vote, and their actions will contribute to their reputation as a 'good' politician from a relationship-based perspective. Politicians who do 'turns' for elites also gain considerable rewards, accruing financial contributions for their party and boosting their personal status within elite spheres of influence. Unfortunately, as their relationships with business elites become stronger, the connection between the politician and the local voter weakens. In describing this two-tier political system in other post-colonial countries, Beekers and van Gool comment:

[P]olitics tends to become a kind of business with two modes of exchange: connections and money. The state is a pie that everyone greedily wants to eat … With the stark centralization of power and wealth at the level of the state, ordinary people … may find themselves far removed from the centres of resource allocation and therefore easily miss out on getting their share. Once in office … rulers face little constraints to care for ordinary citizens. In fact, from the ruler's perspective, denying ordinary citizens unregulated access to markets and public goods and services is a perfectly rational strategy, since it encourages individuals to seek the ruler's personal favour to secure access to these.[54]

Xavier, a retired Fianna Fáil politician, noticed this weakened relationship between politicians and ordinary voters, particularly during the period 2003–2007. 'Some of them [politicians] got cocky, they got too big for their boots. A number of them had been around for a long time but there was a number of younger people as well, male and female … I didn't like the way they got so hoity toity.'

Irish party politics is highly centralised and most power lies with the cabinet. Bill, a Fianna Fáil TD at the time, argues that an increasing elitism could even be seen in the relationship between cabinet ministers and ordinary Fianna Fáil politicians:

We had a weekly parliamentary party meeting and the point was raised that we hadn't access to the ministers. Bertie was after already pretending to lay down the law that on a Wednesday morning … when leader's questions was over, which is about quarter past eleven, we'd normally go in for a cup of coffee in the bar and the ministers were to make themselves available. He had to reprimand them after a number of months again because they weren't coming for the coffee. They were shying off!

Given the two tiers that emerged in Fianna Fáil during his tenure as leader, it is striking that Bertie Ahern was himself so adept at locating himself within intimacy-based groups, particularly his local community. In his autobiography, he says:

One of the strengths of Ireland through the ages has been that communities have been strong and people look out for each other. That is something I have always valued in my own life. Since childhood, I have been part of a community in Drumcondra where people are embraced, where they are not unknown to each other or living in a vacuum ... For me, a good community makes a good society and a good society makes a good country.[55]

Despite his attachment to his local community, Ahern presided over a political culture which used the 'goodness' associated with family and community to dress up political activities that primarily served business elites who were not only increasingly removed from 'our own' but also actively exploiting 'our own'.

CONCLUSION

Chapter 1 argued that the trauma of colonialism created a split in the Irish psyche. This split divided the worlds of rules and relationships and generated two distinct modes of understandings of reality, one linked to rules, the other to relationships. Meeting obligations within relationships was regarded as more moral than simply conforming to rules, which under colonial rule were not viewed as moral anyway. Civil servants in late nineteenth-century Ireland had to balance their obligations under rule-based systems with their more important moral obligations to family and community. After independence, relationships continued to be a dominant feature of Irish politics, economic activity and public administration. However, the potential for corruption in these systems was mitigated by the cohesiveness of Irish society, with intense loyalty to groups described as 'our own'. This cohesive society was dominated by the rules of the Catholic Church as well as the state. Although this structure had many oppressive elements, the Church's emphasis on frugality and distaste for commerce did help to keep corruption in check.

During the 1960s, this delicate balance between rules and relationships unravelled. The lack of prosperity generated by the frugal vision of economic development led to a crisis in Irish society which in turn led to a shift in attitudes to money, consumption and profit. With policy changes came new opportunities for making money in a society that was also experiencing secularisation and a shift away from the values of the Church. Ireland's new business elites needed favours from the state to further their business interests, favours that were nested in the long tradition of intimacy that had been central to Ireland's political culture since the foundation of the state. However, the moral basis of this intimacy was different: it was based on exchanging money – not votes – for intimacy. Intimate connections were lifted out of the context of families and communities and taken to elite social occasions where access was tightly controlled and had to be bought. While traditional political intimacy in Ireland had sometimes involved bending and breaking the rules, this burgeoning inter-elite intimacy produced state capture, where political elites rewrote the rules to benefit business elites. Because these relationships were shrouded in the intimacy-based behaviours associated with 'being good' at everyday level, they have been tolerated by an Irish population who employ similar behaviours themselves in their interactions with politicians and have little faith in the capacity of rules-based systems to deliver fairness.

Chapter 7

RULES AND TWO-TIER AUSTERITY

Every austerity measure is in fact a covert bailout.[1]

The trauma of the banking crash and the loss of economic sovereignty in 2010 pushed the delicate balance between rules and relationships in Irish society into a state of flux. In late 2010 and early 2011, people questioned as never before Irish attitudes to wealth and property and the relationship between politicians and business elites. The ground-breaking results of the 2011 general election and the 2014 local and European elections revealed the continuing turmoil the economic crisis had created. The 'necessary pain' inflicted by rules-based systems under the austerity programme led to a renewed concern about the fairness of rules.

Chapter 1 examined the role of colonialism in generating a sense in Irish culture that rules are inherently unfair. The top-down nature of the Troika bailout and the different rules for elites and for ordinary citizens which emerged as part of the austerity process reawakened these memories. Having been told during the boom years that the rules governing markets were effective, Irish citizens found themselves having to pay for the reckless behaviour of those who managed markets. The cost of the bank bailout was funded by a programme of severe cuts to services and welfare under which, as Martin Power notes, every austerity measure was, in fact, part of the bailout.

This chapter explores how the attitudes of ordinary Irish citizens to rules evolved during the bailout and austerity period in Ireland.

AUSTERITY AND FAIRNESS

Critics of IMF structural adjustment policies in Africa, Asia and South America have for many years pointed out that the rules of austerity programmes can create a two-tier society. Economist William Easterly quotes one critical review:

> When the International Monetary Fund (IMF) and World Bank arrive in southern countries, corporate profits go up, but so do poverty and suffering. Decades of promises that just a little more 'short-term' pain will bring long-term gain have exposed the IMF and World Bank as false prophets whose mission is to protect those who already control too much wealth and power.... In country after country, structural adjustment programs (SAPs) have reversed the development successes of the 1960s and 1970s, with millions sliding into poverty every year. Even the World Bank has had to accept that SAPs have failed the poor, with a special burden falling on women and children. Yet together with the IMF it still demands that developing countries persist with SAPs.[2]

After the banking crash of 2008, some European nations began to experience the 'necessary pain' of austerity rules for themselves. There is a good deal of evidence to suggest that these programmes have contributed to greater inequality. In its comparative study of austerity across Europe, Oxfam found that:

> Austerity programmes implemented across Europe – based on short sighted, regressive taxes and deep spending cuts, particularly to public services such as education, health and social security – have dismantled the mechanisms that reduce inequality and enable equitable growth. The poorest have been hit hardest, as the burden

of responsibility for the excesses of the past decades is passed to those most vulnerable and least to blame.... Almost one in 10 working households in Europe now lives in poverty.[3]

Economic analysis of austerity in Ireland also showed that the process was uneven, but there was much debate about which groups had been hit hardest. Discussing its impact on Irish incomes, Callan *et al.* comment:

> The overall fall in income was just under 8 per cent between 2008 and 2011 but the greatest losses were strongly concentrated on the bottom and top deciles. On average, the real income of the lowest decile in 2011 was 18 per cent lower than in 2008, while the average income of the top decile was 11 per cent lower.[4]

Oxfam's own case study of austerity in Ireland suggested that the rich fared slightly better:

> In 2010, those in the lowest income band saw their disposable income fall by more than 26 per cent while those in the highest income band saw their disposable income rise by more than eight per cent. The 2013 budget led to a 1.3 per cent increase in taxes for a worker on an annual salary of €20,000. Meanwhile a worker on €100,000 experienced a 0.2 per cent increase in taxes. Those on €200,000 or more paid 0.1 per cent more. As a result, even when tax increases are chosen over cuts to social support as a means to reduce the budget deficit, those on lower incomes are the ones hit the hardest.[5]

The Economic and Social Research Institute (ESRI) published a series of reports exploring the uneven impact of austerity on different social classes and age groups. In her analysis of the Central Statistics Office's (CSO) 2013 Household Budget Survey, Petra Gerlach-Kristen found that the financial crisis 'had affected younger households much more than older ones';[6] younger workers were significantly more likely to become unemployed and had higher levels of debt. These findings mirrored research by Alan Barrett and Vincent O'Sullivan, who also found that the elderly had fared better during the early years of the austerity process.[7] More worryingly, as the austerity process deepened, budgetary policies became more regressive and had a sharper impact on the poor. In reviewing the ESRI commentary on the 2012 budget, Fiona Reddan of the *Irish Times* noted:

> When the most recent budget, in December 2012 is looked at in isolation, it demonstrates that taxes have become more regressive. It introduced a number of indirect tax measures and as a result, the research shows that those on the lowest incomes took the greatest hit. Indeed for the poorest 40 per cent of households, incomes fell by about 2–2.5 per cent as a result of the measures.[8]

Analyses of the impact of austerity on Irish society suggested that not all groups had felt the same level of 'necessary pain', and there is evidence that the most vulnerable felt the pain most. If the objective of rules-based systems is to achieve fairness, that objective was not achieved under the austerity programme.

Popular responses to austerity in Ireland between 2010 and 2014 suggest that many ordinary Irish citizens and their representative groups felt that the rules of austerity were unfair. For example, the National Youth Council of Ireland described the 2012 budget as 'unfair and austere'.

> Budget 2012 was always going to inflict pain but for some there was more pain than for others.... Although we expected this budget to be a difficult one given the economic context, the impact of the budgetary cuts announced over the last two days will have devastating consequences for many children and young people especially those living in low income families.[9]

Writing in the *Irish Times*, pensioner W.J. Murphy revealed that some elderly people also viewed austerity as unfair: 'surely the problem is how austerity is unfairly implemented hitting as it does the easy targets ... let us campaign, not so much for "taking less in taxation" but for a fairer system in which those that can afford it pay their fair share.'[10] In the UK newspaper for Irish emigrants, the *Irish Post*, Joe Hogan noted:

> For all those who have gone through austerity relatively unscathed, there are those who have lost jobs and houses and those facing a life of debt in a property worth a fraction of what they paid for it.... It's down to the lottery of an insanely unfair economic system and Ireland is by any measure, a more unfair society than most.[11]

Sean Healy of Social Justice Ireland said, 'austerity, however, has been exposed ... because poor and middle-income people have borne an unfair share of its consequences.'[12] The Society of St Vincent de Paul concurred:

> The Society of St Vincent de Paul sees at first hand the impact that the economic crisis has had on struggling households.... Those who have already borne the brunt of cut backs and are unable to take any more, must be protected. To this end, Government must tackle the burden of reducing bank debt, reduce the non-core costs of providing public services and ensure that those who can afford it take more of the burden of the crisis on their shoulders.... SVP is challenging the unfair burden which has been placed upon those least able to afford it.[13]

At least 64 per cent of the middle-class citizens who were interviewed for the final segment of this research in 2012–2013 saw austerity as unfair. Laura from Tipperary, a secretary and mother of two, comments:

> It just feels like there's one rule for some and one rule for others. When you hear about some banker getting a big bonus or some civil servant getting a massive pension and the government say they can do nothing about it. There doesn't seem to be the will there

but there's plenty of will when it comes to property tax and cuts to welfare. It's just not fair.

Colm, an unemployed architect, agrees:

> There's a whole generation who got away scot free. They had the jobs and the pensions when times were good. Most of them owned their homes before the boom really hit. It's a completely different story for us. Most of my college friends are gone and the ones that are still here are up to their oxters in debt or doing half-baked jobs for fuck all. There doesn't seem to be any attempt to be even-handed about the whole thing. You're either screwed or in easy street.

In that final interview series from 2012 and 2013, two particular issues, debt and justice, cropped up repeatedly when participants discussed the unfairness of austerity and its rules-based systems.

AUSTERITY AND DEBT

In 2008, it was clear that the state faced a looming debt crisis that threatened the viability of the banking system at two levels. The six major Irish banks had given large loans to developers in the construction industry. As the property bubble burst in 2007–2008, it was obvious that the value of these loans would never be realised. The bankrupt developers could not repay the loans and the scale of these losses threatened the viability of the entire Irish banking system. The state moved quickly to shore up the banks by giving a blanket guarantee of bank debt. In 2009, it established NAMA (the National Asset Management Agency), essentially a 'bad bank' which would take responsibility for these loans. Although immense secrecy surrounds the activities of NAMA, it became clear early on that the agency's strategy was to engage with bankrupt developers and write off large amounts of their debt in exchange for deals on property, assets, etc. These debt write-offs were paid for by the Irish taxpayer, so through NAMA, the debt of bankrupt developers essentially became Irish sovereign debt serviced by the ordinary people of Ireland. At the outset, economists nationally and internationally criticised the NAMA approach to debt management and questioned the justice of transferring private debt to the public purse.[14]

At the same time, a second debt crisis was looming. As the Irish economy went into recession and unemployment began to rise in 2008 and 2009, it became clear that many ordinary mortgage holders would not be able to service the debt they had incurred when buying massively over-priced properties during the Celtic Tiger years. From 2003 to 2007, Irish banks had used an extremely light-touch lending system, offering 100 per cent mortgages in some cases to customers who could not hope to service this debt in the long term. Siobhan, who works for the Money Advice and Budgeting Service (MABS), says:

> A lot of younger people had no real experience of recession and they thought the boom would go on for ever. Builders and labourers in particular were making ridiculous money, €1200 a week in some cases. They were given loans on this basis even though their income levels were completely unsustainable.... The banks lent ridiculous amounts of money but people spent this money. Very few of the people we see just have problems with mortgage arrears, it's credit card bills, personal loans, the whole nine yards.

The mania for buying property highlighted by experts such as Peter Nyberg was a particularly important factor in this boom. Siobhan says:

> There was this mad pressure to buy a house, to get on the property ladder, to be an owner. There was this notion of ownership as a bulwark against God knows what, maybe it was just a form of security. The length of time these loans were being given over was crazy.... There was no culture of saving at all amongst those earning the high wages. Somehow they believed that it was going to go on for ever and once you had bought one property, the best thing to do was to buy another one and another one.

The lack of realism about the individual borrower's capacity to repay these loans was also clear to Fiona, a TD, who now deals with lots of individuals with mortgage arrears in her constituency work:

> I think there was a collective delusion. This thing about a credit-fuelled construction boom, people did buy into that. The whole property thing … I remember calling to one woman who was 24 (and I was in my thirties when I bought my first house). I remember this 24-year-old saying to me how she really wanted to get on the property ladder and how she was the only one without a house and, like, her job wouldn't have been that good, she was working in a retail outlet. I sent her advice about affordable housing but I know someone who bought a one-bed apartment for €300,000 through affordable housing, like what would that be worth now?

The property mania of ordinary mortgage-holders – like that of developers – did play a role in their own financial downfall. However, the state was much slower to react to their plight. By June 2012, 144,000 mortgages were in arrears. Central Bank figures revealed that almost 95,000 residential mortgages were in arrears of three months or more, and a further 49,000 home mortgages were in arrears of less than 90 days.[15] Despite being bailed out by the Irish taxpayer, the banks themselves were extremely slow to engage in debt resolution processes with individuals in mortgage arrears. Having resisted calls by the IMF to confront the mortgage arrears issue, the government finally passed the Personal Insolvency Act in 2012, although it didn't become fully operational until 2014.[16] The Act introduced three approaches to debt resolution: debt relief notices; debt settlements; and personal insolvency arrangements. People who engaged with these processes would be able to write off part of their debt.

The most striking distinction between NAMA and the new personal insolvency schemes is the different approaches taken to the personal circumstances of bankrupt individuals. Officials at NAMA appeared to believe that it was not their job to regulate the personal spending of bankrupt developers. In an interview in 2012, Frank Daly, the chairman of NAMA, commented:

> We go through people on the basis of their business plans, their level of co-operation, not what clothes they wear, not what clubs they go to, and not where they dine or anything like that. It's a purely business relationship. It's never personal. NAMA has made it very clear – there are views on lifestyles all right, but we're not policemen in the sense of checking up on what they're at. There are people who would say, why should so and so's children be going to private school, why should so and so be driving this car rather than a Mondeo or a Cortina or whatever.... You know if we go down into that sort of policing in detail, then it becomes personal.[17]

Despite this hands-off attitude to the personal circumstances of their clients, it became clear in 2013 that not everyone who engaged with NAMA was happy to co-operate with their light-touch approach. Christine Connolly and her husband, developer Larry O'Mahony, took a case to the High Court over agreements they had reached with NAMA regarding outstanding loans. Under the agreement, Ms Connolly had been allocated €6500 per month in expenses for herself and her three children. In the High Court, Ms Connolly claimed that she needed a further €3750 to cover the costs of renting a four-bedroom home in Dublin 4 (€3000–3500), school fees and extracurricular activities for her three children (€1644), monthly car expenses (€820) and golf club subscription (€165). Her action against NAMA was successful and she was awarded €9000 expenses per month.[18]

The contrast with the approach taken to the personal circumstances of indebted individuals under the state's personal insolvency regime is striking. All three models of debt resolution are based on intense scrutiny of the personal lives of individuals, with specific guidelines on how much people in each category can spend per month. In its *Guidelines on a Reasonable Standard of Living and Reasonable Living Expenses*, the Insolvency Service of Ireland (ISI) states that a single adult of working age should have a monthly food allowance of €250.98 with the proviso that 'the expenditure on food is based on a balanced, nutritious diet'.[19] The monthly allowance for social participation, which includes all social and sporting activities, is €126.10. There is some flexibility in the scheme, but the onus is on indebted individuals to negotiate any specific changes. For instance, ISI comments:

> As a general principle, the ISI wishes to see debtors retaining the autonomy to make their own choices as to what is best for them, though necessarily within the constraints of reasonableness and the overall expenditure limits. Thus, while the focus groups have decided that cable or satellite television subscription are not necessary and that allowance for a SAORVIEW approved set-top box or television is sufficient, a debtor may choose to retain such a subscription by prioritising it within his or her budget.[20]

Both NAMA and the personal insolvency regime are based on rules-based systems that aim to resolve debt, yet they seem to have markedly different approaches to the personal circumstances of indebted individuals. The two-tier nature of this approach has been highlighted both by public commentators and by participants in this study. Commenting on the rent allowance given to Christine Connolly, journalist Michael Clifford says:

> The judge obviously agreed that these folks shouldn't be expected to slum it beyond the boundaries of desirable Dublin 4. A few months back, a row broke out over guidelines in the new Personal Insolvency Act, about whether or not people availing of it should be permitted allowance for cable TV. The act is designed mainly for the 'little people' who can't pay mortgages taken out on family homes. While the little people are expected to lower their basic standard of living, those who bestrode the property bubble are allowed to carry on as if the illusory wealth had never vanished into thin air.[21]

A commentator on the NAMA Winelake blog agreed.

It's very clear that the ruling classes in this country consider themselves and their friends to be above the laws which apply to everyone else. This applies to bankruptcy and insolvency as well as everything else. Nowhere is this made clearer than in the Personal Insolvency Act itself. The act is divided along classical class lines. Working class debtors are subjected to harsh Debt Relief Notices. Middle class debtors are subjected to stringent Personal Insolvency Arrangements. And Upper class debtors with potentially unlimited amounts of unsecured debt … their lifestyle, cost of living and even cost of sending their dependent children to university must all be protected first before their creditors can get a slice.[22]

In his blog, economist Brian Lucey highlighted the distinct approach of the two regimes in the following table:

You are a NAMA Family	*You are a regular Family*
Bad luck, bankrupt, eh?	Bad luck, bankrupt, eh?
Phew, you're in luck …	You're sh!t out of luck …
Your reasonable standard of living is defined by the High Court by expensive barristers	Your standard is set down in a leaflet by the Insolvency Service
You can claim (2 adults, a car, three second level school kids) €9k per month as reasonable	You can claim (2 adults, a car, three second level school kids) €2461 per month as reasonable (per Table 6)[23]

The view that there is a two-tier approach to the rules of austerity in Ireland was also shared by interviewees for this study. Timmy, a local councillor in Co. Laois, who was interviewed in 2011 describes the impact of this two-tier approach on beliefs about rules.

In some ways, I think NAMA are doing a good job, in other ways though, it's very damaging to morale. I'll give you an example. I'd a couple come to me the other day who were about to lose their house. Usual story, his business gone bust, mortgage arrears, two teenage kids. The wife just basically cried through the whole conversation. I really don't think there is anything I can do for them. The bank wants the house and I don't think they'll budge. But these people live in the same ward as my neighbour Felim[24] who was part of a development consortium which now owes over €20 million to the banks. Well, this guy's been NAMAed so he's still living in his nice house and his kids are still going to college and everything's ticketyboo for him as far as I can see. Why should he get off scot free when those poor bastards who only owe about €200,000 will lose the little bit they've left? NAMA might be delivering for the Irish taxpayer but you can't say it's fair.

Michael-Joe is a farmer who is struggling with his own repayments to the bank. He says:

I'm very suspicious of NAMA. You can't help feeling that if it was all fair, we'd know all about it. It's seems like those bastards are very good at tying things up in the courts with legalese for ever and this thing of transferring houses to the wives quite frankly gives me the sick. Do you think if I transferred this farm to my wan the bank would stop writing me letters? Jesus one of them's worse than the next and the phone calls, when they start ringing you, that's fifty times worse. I'm telling you, it's one rule for some!

The contrasting approaches to the personal circumstances of indebted people under the rules of NAMA and the personal insolvency scheme have reinforced rather than challenged a deeply held suspicion that the rules are unfair and that they privilege elites. This suspicion makes it more likely that ordinary Irish citizens will continue to favour the weak rules/strong relationships balance that was causal to the economic crash.

AUSTERITY AND JUSTICE

Interviewees also highlighted the unfairness of rules in relation to justice and white-collar crime. In the immediate post-bailout period, there was intense criticism of the slow pace of the state's investigation of bankers, particularly those involved in the collapse of Anglo Irish Bank. Bernie Madoff, an investment broker in the United States, whose activities had played a significant role in the US banking crash, was sentenced to 150 years in prison in June 2009, less than seven months after his arrest on 11 December 2008. In contrast, the pace of investigation into the activities of Irish bankers and investors was frustratingly slow. In July 2010, the Office of the Director of Corporate Enforcement (ODCE) in Ireland admitted that in the ten years the office had been in existence, no one prosecuted for a white-collar crime had ever been jailed. Kevin Prendergast, corporate compliance manager for the ODCE, warned that it would be at least two years before any prosecution in relation to Anglo Irish Bank took place because of the 'incredibly high' proof thresholds for white-collar crime in Ireland.[25]

By May 2011, High Court Judge Peter Kelly was beginning to lose patience with the investigation when he refused an application from the Gardaí and the ODCE for a further six-month extension to their joint enquiry into the management of Anglo Irish Bank. In the flurry of recrimination that followed the judge's cry of 'When will it ever end?', corporate enforcer Paul Appleby admitted that he had no power to compel ten key witnesses to co-operate with his enquiries.[26] The government introduced the Criminal Justice Act 2011 with the aim of tackling some of these obstacles to white-collar investigations. The Act created new categories of offences in relation to banking, finance and company law, and gave the Gardaí greater investigative powers. However, by 2013, the outgoing Financial Regulator, Matthew Elderfield, was calling on the government to further tighten the laws relating to white-collar crime. Asked if he believed that the current laws dealing with individuals suspected of white-collar crime were up to scratch, he replied 'no'. He also commented:

I think in due course we'll be able to take some actions against individuals – and we are pursuing a couple of cases – but I wish it had happened faster.... The white collar set-up in and around capabilities, resources, powers, constitutional interaction – I don't think in the round that it's working sufficiently well.[27]

Elaine Byrne has noted, 'although the Criminal Justice Act 2011 identifies new categories of white-collar crimes, and enhances powers to gather evidence, it did not appear to quicken the painfully slow pace of criminal investigations arising from the 2008 banking crisis.'[28]

In 2014, three key individuals involved in the collapse of Anglo Irish Bank finally came to trial. The trial focused on specific issues relating to trade in contracts for difference (CFDs) with which businessman Sean Quinn had gambled on the bank's share price. After fourteen hours of deliberation, the jury found that Sean FitzPatrick was not guilty of breaching Section 60 of the Companies Act 1963.[29] Two other Anglo executives, Willie McAteer and Patrick Whelan, were found guilty but did not receive custodial sentences. The fact that none of the bankers involved in the Anglo crash went to prison was the subject of some debate after the trials. Pearse Doherty of Sinn Féin appeared to tap into the public mood when he said:

I can't help but think tonight of the many good people I have met over the years who said to me that they know no banker will ever serve a day in prison for what they did to this State ... two bankers were found guilty of a corporate crime, the only bankers to date to have been convicted. Their sentence – community service. We have seen in the past that if someone cannot pay their TV licence, they've faced jail sentences and often served those sentences. People have been sent to prison for unpaid fines. If they simply couldn't afford those fines, or chose to feed and clothe their children over paying them, that was seen as their problem.[30]

Doherty's comments highlight the willingness of the criminal justice system in Ireland to impose custodial sentences on those breaking the law even for non-violent crimes. In March 2012, Paul Begley of Begley Bros, Blanchardstown, Dublin was sentenced to six years in prison for labelling imported garlic as apples to avoid paying a higher rate of customs duty.[31] While his sentence was commuted to two years in 2013, in the same year the annual report of the prison service showed a 10 per cent increase in the number of ordinary citizens being sent to prison for not paying fines. In 2012, 8,300 people were jailed for non-payment of fines, an increase of almost 800 on 2011.[32] By 2014, six out of every ten people sent to Cork prison were being jailed for non-payment of court fines: the prison, designed for 143 inmates, was actually holding 230. The governor of Cork prison, Jim Collins, acknowledged the unfairness of custodial sentences in this context:

> People given short terms for fines don't need to be in prison: take 50c off their dole instead.... Sending them to jail does not do anything. Prison should be for those who are dangerous and a risk to society.[33]

Like the two-tier treatment of debt, comparing the Irish state's response to non-violent crimes committed by the rich and the poor reinforces the impression of a two-tier system of rules. In 2011, legal expert Shane Kilcommins noted the potential damage to the public's confidence in the law, the rules of the state, generated by these disparities. He said, 'The biggest risk we face by failing to hold people to account, if the evidence supports it, is that the public will see a two-tier system of justice that allows the rich and powerful to be immunised from the full reach of criminal law.'[34] His fear that this two-tier approach to justice was weakening confidence in the rules was confirmed in 2013 by a poll of Irish farmers carried out by the *Irish Examiner*.

> [M]ore than nine out of ten farmers believe that not a single banker will see the inside of a jail cell after the banking crisis. A staggering 93% of farmers said they had no faith in the justice system's ability to jail anyone over the crisis. The view was more or less equally

shared by men and women, with older farmers more pessimistic than their younger counterparts.[35]

This scepticism about justice and the belief that a two-tier system exists was also evident in the comments of individuals interviewed during the final stage of this research in 2012–2013. Alan, who works for a multinational firm in Limerick, commented:

> If I behaved in work every day, the way those Anglo bankers behaved, I'd be out on my ear. And if I behaved at home with our household budget, the way that those bankers behaved, the wife would have me out on my ear. If I don't pay my parking fine or my TV licence I could go to jail. I'm caught every way I look and these guys seem to get away with everything.

Clodagh, a solicitor in Cork, says, 'To be honest, I think it's really bad for the law. People don't see it as fair. They think that rich people will get some fat-cat solicitor to get them off the hook for everything while everyone else has to take their chances. People have said that to me when I told them I was training to be a solicitor.' Clearly, the state's approach to debt and non-violent crime has created a strong feeling that a two-tier system of rules is operating as a part of austerity. Despite this cynicism about rules, however, Irish citizens continue to recognise that rules are important. Indeed, in the post-bailout era, there has been some evidence that attitudes towards rule-breaking and bending, the famous 'nod and wink' culture that underpinned Irish attitudes to rules, is changing significantly.

WELFARE, TAX AND PENALTY POINTS

In December 2013, according to informal briefing papers from the Department of Social Protection, reports of social welfare fraud were up 2500 per cent since 2008. These reports related to people claiming welfare while working, lone parents cohabiting and welfare payments being claimed by those living outside the state.[36] The *Irish Examiner* had earlier noted, 'gone are the days when this crime – and that's the correct term – was greeted with knowing nods, winks and grudging admiration for certain people who knew the system inside out and could "get away with it".[37] Most of these reports of social welfare fraud came from anonymous tip-offs to the Department of Social Protection from ordinary Irish citizens. Perhaps a greater public intolerance for rule-breaking indicated a shift in attitudes to rules. But the state's response continued to imply a two-tier approach. In 2012, Sinn Féin called for a social welfare amnesty similar to the tax amnesties for the wealthy of the late 1980s and early 1990s, but this call was rejected. Sinn Féin's spokesman concluded that there was 'one yardstick for the poor and another for the rich' and noted that when social welfare recipients were overpaid small sums, the state insisted on getting the money back. In contrast, 'no attempt had been made to recover the €160,000 that was overpaid in error to the director designate of the HSE, Tony O'Brien.'[38] Journalist Colette Browne noted that the government's robust application of the rules to those involved in social welfare fraud differed sharply from government attitudes towards the wealthy.

> While the Tax Justice Network was able to compile data for 145 countries, our own Government has persistently said it is unable to estimate the amount of money that is lost via tax evasion and avoidance each year. Strangely they have no such qualms about guesstimating, in the most creative ways, notional levels of welfare fraud each year and using the resultant pie-in-the-sky figures to stoke up prejudice and justify arbitrary cutbacks.[39]

Some have argued that this soft approach to tax evasion and avoidance reflects popular attitudes,[40] but there was some evidence that popular attitudes to tax avoidance by some wealthy individuals were changing. In his book *The Frontman*, Harry Browne chronicled some of the negative public attitudes towards U2 lead singer Bono after the band moved part of their tax affairs to the Netherlands in 2006, a move that became increasingly controversial in the post-bailout period. He comments:

The tax issue clearly did him 'reputational damage' but for many people it did no more than provide a hard factual reason for the soft, emotional dislike he aroused. Some anti-Bono graffiti sprang up around Dublin, mostly referring to the tax issue, like the doggerel in Clanbrassil Street that mocked both his financial status and physical stature: 'Bono is a jerk/He never had to work/He doesn't pay his tax/He always wears stacks'.[41]

This type of commentary suggests that tax avoidance by some wealthy individuals was being viewed less positively by the Irish public and that the 'nod and wink' attitude to rule-breaking and rule-bending was unravelling.

The delicate balance between rules and relationships was thrown into even more turmoil by a huge controversy over the allocation of penalty points under the Irish state's traffic management system during the late austerity period. In September 2012, two Garda whistleblowers, John Wilson and Maurice McCabe, alleged that the penalty points system wasn't working because both ordinary members of the public and elites from various sectors were using their relationships with gardaí to get penalty points cancelled. In December of that year, four independent TDs highlighted the matter in the Dáil. It subsequently emerged that one of these TDs, Deputy Luke 'Ming' Flanagan, had also had points cancelled.

The controversy resulted in internal and external investigations of the Gardaí, which ultimately led to a review of the entire penalty points system. A Garda Inspectorate report found that there were 'consistent and widespread breaches of policy by those charged with administering the penalty points system'.[42] And it was not just elites but ordinary members of the public who were bending and breaking these rules.[43] Gerry, a garda in Cork, argues that this controversy demonstrates shifting attitudes to the rules.

There are guards in this country who have been absolutely pestered by family, friends, politicians, and neighbours to have their points cancelled. Even the report shows there are so many points cancelled, everyone was doing it. Don't get me wrong, I think we have to have a system, particularly for speeding. But I'd like to ask that fella Ming, 'At what point did the wind change? When, between the time he had his points cancelled and the time he stood in the Dáil calling us all corrupt, when did this become wrong?'

Gerry's question is a good one. Clearly the wind was changing and the delicate balance between rules, relationships and 'being good' was shifting in the post-bailout period. The 'penalty points' controversy, as well as changes in attitudes to social welfare fraud and tax avoidance, suggests that the strong association between looking after 'our own' and 'being good' was weakening. At the same time, breaking and bending rules was increasingly being characterised as wrong.

CONCLUSION

During the colonial era in Ireland, a belief developed that rules were inherently unfair, favoured the interests of elites and helped them to extract resources from everyone else. As a consequence, there has historically been a stronger link in the Irish value system between 'being there' for those in circles of intimacy and 'being good' than between conforming to rules and 'goodness'. This value system contributed to the creation of two parallel worlds in Irish society: the weak rules which governed public and economic life operated side by side with strong relationships. While these two parallel worlds have co-existed harmoniously during periods of Irish history (largely by absorbing the stronger rules of the Catholic Church into state-based systems), in 2008 they collided spectacularly.

In the aftermath of the financial crisis, official reports were deeply critical of the weak rules-based systems governing the Irish economy. At the same time, journalists uncovered the dense network of strong relationships which had allowed politicians, developers and banks to manipulate and, in some cases, rewrite the rules to promote their own interests rather than the interests of ordinary citizens. One would imagine that the austerity which was inflicted as a result of this weak rules/strong relationships balance would have led to a sustained public demand for stronger rules and greater restraints on intimacy. However, these changes have been slow to emerge, and an analysis of the operation of rules-based systems under austerity reveals why.[44]

Instead of re-configuring rules to promote fairness, a move which might have increased popular confidence in rules, the austerity programme and post-bailout recovery has been managed using a two-tier approach which closely mirrors the unfairness of rules in the earlier colonial era. The two-tier approach to dealing with debt and non-violent crime in particular has reinforced rather than challenged popular cynicism about rules. Yet despite this cynicism, there appears to be an increasing public recognition that rule-breaking and bending is not 'good'. This is evident in changing attitudes to tax avoidance, social welfare fraud and the penalty points controversy. While the austerity programme has resulted in the development of a new, stronger set of rules to deal with debt and white-collar crime, the two-tier nature of the system has reinforced rather than challenged popular belief that rules are unfair. Under colonial rule, people believed that rules favour elites and that only relationships can mitigate unfair rules. The rules-based systems which have become stronger under austerity have not dismantled this belief and Irish citizens are once again turning to relationships to mitigate the harshness of rules. The two-tier nature of austerity in Ireland, a feature of austerity programmes across the globe, has therefore nullified the chance that lessons can be learned from the crisis and popular confidence in the fairness of robust rules established. However, attitudes to rule-bending and rule-breaking have changed in Ireland – despite the unfairness of the rules of austerity – suggesting that Irish citizens recognise that rules are important and can potentially be a way of creating greater fairness in society.

Conclusion ∾

| PAST AND PRESENT

In a dark time, the eye begins to see.

Theodore Roethke

The imposition of the austerity programme in Ireland during 2010 was initially met with muted protest. In the same year, a similar bailout was imposed on Greece and there was widespread social unrest, even riots.[1] In reviewing this initial response, political scientist Eoin O'Malley says, 'If we reacted it was with surprising acceptance of our lot. We became model *Austerians*.'[2] This absence of protest in response to the initial imposition of austerity measures puzzled some commentators. In 2013, economists Donal Donovan and Antoin Murphy speculated that 'the Irish are realists at heart'.[3] Others were not so sure that this early muted response was due to realism. Writing in the same year, French media analyst Julien Mercille commented, 'Sometimes we get the impression that the Irish have lost any hope of getting out of economic crisis and life under austerity.'[4] As Mercille subsequently noted, there had, in fact, been a succession of protests in response to austerity, including campaigns against the removal of medical cards from pensioners,[5] student protests against increases in tuition fees,[6] protests against the introduction of the Household Charge in 2012.[7] The level of protest actually increased after Ireland had exited the bailout programme, with a confrontational campaign against the introduction of water charges achieving international prominence in 2014.[8] These protests all focused on specific new charges and cuts, but there were also a smaller number of protests against the entire programme of austerity. These protests included Occupy camps in Dublin, Cork, Limerick, Galway and Waterford, the long-running 'Ballyhea Says No' campaign in Cork, and left-wing protests under the umbrella of the United Left Alliance and the Anti-Austerity Alliance. However, these broader protests against the programme of austerity as a whole received less mass public support. Why?

Both Mercille and sociologist Gavan Titley have criticised the Irish media for promoting the idea that 'there is no alternative' to austerity. In examining media coverage of one of the most hard-hitting austerity budgets in December 2010, Gavan Titley listed the five key mantras – 'incontrovertible facts and truths' – which dominated mainstream media discussion of the budget:

- The country is broke (bankrupt)
- We're all in this together
- We have to move on, going forward
- The tough love of the IMF/EU is actually good after a period of 'mismanagement'
- … There is no alternative.[9]

Another reason why protest during the early austerity period was so muted may have been that many Irish citizens expressed their dissatisfaction through the ballot box, the ultimate rules-based expression of discontent. The defeat of the Fianna Fáil–Green Party coalition in the 2011 general election was one of the worst of any post-war European government.[10] The local, European and by-elections of 2014 provided little further comfort for Fianna Fáil: they did badly in the European and by-elections, but recovered significantly at local level. There was a big rise in support for Sinn Féin in both the European and local elections. The Anti-Austerity Alliance increased their presence in local government significantly, while the government parties of Fine Gael and Labour experienced a marked decline in support, with Labour experiencing a particularly sharp public backlash. After the election, Labour minister Pat Rabbitte said, 'In Ireland, people don't march down Grafton Street and break windows, but by God, they vent their vengeance in the ballot box.'[11] Labour's Minister for Education, Ruairi Quinn, said, 'Unlike Greece, Spain and Portugal where there were riots in the streets and all sorts of disruptions, the people held their breaths and waited for the ballot box and dropped the grenade into the ballot box.'[12]

In their study of austerity in Ireland, Kieran Allen and Brian O'Boyle suggest that another factor may have contributed to anti-austerity protests being initially so muted. Much of the economic growth of the Celtic Tiger era had been built around a close alliance between politicians and trade union leaders through the model of social partnership. Once the banking crisis emerged, they argue, these union leaders were too close to political elites to express dissent – they had been co-opted 'into serving the needs of capitalism'.[13] Emigration, particularly youth emigration, was also a factor. Young people played an important role in anti-austerity protests throughout Europe,[14] but it is estimated that over 41 per cent of the 308,000 people who emigrated from Ireland between 2009 and 2013 were aged between 15 and 24. This level of emigration not only diffused the anger created by austerity but made the process itself easier to manage. The emigrant newspaper the *Irish Voice* notes that in 2012, the unemployment rate of 14.6 per cent would have been significantly higher without emigration.[15] A selection of letters from Irish emigrants published in the *Irish Times* during the austerity period reveals no shortage of the kind of anger that would fuel further serious social protests. Sarah Moore, a nursing graduate who emigrated to England in 2010, wrote:

I moved because my native country has nothing to offer me because of the self-interest, the naked greed, the cronyism of those in positions of power in Government and in financial institutions. These are the people who robbed a whole generation of a future in

Ireland and they are still making decisions about our country. Are we the most compliant nation on Earth?[16]

This anger among the Irish emigrant population was not new. The following week, in the same paper, Tom Healy, who left Ireland for England in 1962, revealed:

> For a few years, I entertained the hope that I might be able to return and tried to do so, only to run up against the barriers which made people like me in the Ireland of the time unable to find work. I refer to cronyism and insider relationships which plagued Ireland of the time and appear never to have gone away.... Those of us who leave provide a safety valve that allows the rotten shower in power to avoid having to create a more just and fair society. It might well be better to stay at home and raise hell to change the odiously corrupt system which existed when I was young and which seems to have changed but little in the almost fifty years since I left.[17]

Perhaps it would have been better for Irish society if Tom had stayed, but both he and Sarah Moore left, taking their potentially transformative anger with them.

A less developed theme which runs through the commentary is the idea that the initial lack of protest was linked to Ireland's colonial history. Though this analysis has not been developed in detail, a link has been suggested repeatedly by historian Tim Pat Coogan, who wrote in 2013:

> Over the New Year I've been pondering the implications of a discovery I made while researching my book on the Famine namely that one of the principal legacies to Ireland was what the psychiatrists called 'learned helplessness'. The belief that no matter how one tried there was nothing to do in the face of catastrophe save succumb to it or emigrate. There was no possibility of getting back at those who brought about the disaster. In the case of the Famine and in today's Ireland, people are either accepting whatever

burdens have been placed upon them with varying degrees of despair or they are getting out.[18]

This idea was also highlighted by geographer Rory Hearne on the forum Ireland After Nama. He commented, 'perhaps it is our … post-colonial inferiority and tendency to "tip our cap to the landlord", that we believe the crisis is our fault.'[19] His comments were echoed by the youngest member of the Irish Council of State, Ruairí McKiernan: 'it may be that our inheritance of colonialism and repression has given us a fear of rocking the boat – something that is convenient for those with power.'[20]

Although this muted response had, by late 2014, given way to much more confrontational protests, it was not the first time this theory had been mooted. Considering the response of the Irish public to cutbacks by Irish governments in the 1980s, psychologist Vincent Kenny argued that the memory of the high cost of protest under colonialism may have made Irish citizens more compliant. He commented that colonialism creates a tendency to 'appear to be at least superficially compliant' because 'open rebelliousness tends to meet with immediately harsh measures.'[21] The role of memory in inhibiting social protest has also been noted by Fredrick C. Harris, who has argued that the memory of violent suppression of black protests militated against civil rights protest emerging in some parts of the American South during the 1960s. 'Depending on what is remembered the collective memories of marginal groups may either facilitate group action or discourage it. Past events symbolizing the cost of challenging structures of oppression may weaken the possibility of collective action.'[22]

It's easy to see how the bailout might have reawakened memories of the cost of protest during the colonial era. The bailout involved ceding a substantial portion of Irish sovereignty, the freedom that had been painfully won less than a hundred years before, to an external power. This external power then imposed a series of harsh fiscal measures, creating immediate pain for the local population. With their periodic appearances in Ireland to monitor the progress of austerity, the Troika team made no effort to conceal their superior position in relation to the Irish public. This neo-colonial approach to bailout was noted by Belgian MEP Derk Jan Eppink, who complained, 'The Troika acts like a governor and visits its colonies in the South of Europe and tells them what to do.'[23] The Troika's rhetoric around imposing austerity on Ireland and other states mirrored very closely the colonial idea that a country that submits will meet with approval. In 2010, Jean-Claude Trichet, President of the ECB, told Greece that it should follow the example of the more acquiescent Irish: 'Greece has a role model and that role model is Ireland,'[24] while German Chancellor Angela Merkel told Taoiseach Enda Kenny that Ireland had set an 'outstanding example' of how to implement austerity.[25]

Despite the lack of initial protests during the early austerity period, there was, early on, a deep fundamental anger about the injustice of the bailout which harks back to debates about the fairness of rules-based systems under colonialism. While it was clear in 2008 that some form of bank guarantee was needed in Ireland, the lavish scale of the Irish bank guarantee has been extremely controversial.[26] The subsequent refusal of the Troika to countenance any write-down of the debt incurred to service the bank guarantee is widely viewed as unjust when compared to the experience of countries outside the eurozone, such as Iceland and Denmark, where banks were allowed to fail. The injustice of the bank guarantee and promissory notes scheme has been acknowledged not only by prominent financial commentators but also by A.J. Chopra, who led the Troika delegation to Ireland in 2010. In an interview in late 2013, he said, 'It is unfair to impose the burden of supporting banks primarily on domestic taxpayers while senior unguaranteed bank holders get paid out. This not only adds to sovereign debt but it also creates political problems, making it harder to sustain fiscal adjustment.'[27]

Because the bailout programme involved a transnational power effectively taking control of Irish sovereignty, the parallels with colonialism were obvious; but the research for this book has demonstrated that the roots of the crisis lie to a much deeper extent in colonialism. The trauma of colonialism created a split between rules and relationships within which two distinct understandings of reality developed. These parallel worlds co-existed side by side and were dominated by different attitudes to knowledge, trust, communication, belonging and conflict. Most important, each of these parallel worlds had its own morality. Following the rules has historically been a strong feature of the Irish value system, particularly when those rules were reinforced by the authority of the Catholic Church. However, 'being there' for those circles of intimacy described as 'our own' has an even stronger link to 'being good' in that value system.

The strength of intimacy in Irish public life was evident from the earliest years of the state's existence. However, any tendency for intimacy to lead to corruption was muted by the emphasis on frugality in both Catholic ideology and the nationalism of the Civil War generation of politicians. From the 1960s onwards, this bulwark against corruption eroded significantly. Attitudes towards profit, consumption and material wealth changed with modernisation and integration into the global economy. At the same time, the ties that bound political elites to local communities and families were weakening under the pressures of urbanisation and modernisation. With this transformation, dramatic new scope was created for relationship-based corruption among business and political elites, who became more removed from the rest of the population. The exploitation of the resources of the Irish state that resulted from these relationships has been well catalogued by the tribunals of inquiry of the 1990s and 2000s. Yet, despite all the widespread evidence of corruption available before 2008, this information did not yield a significant popular demand for the rules to be strengthened or formal restraints on intimacy to be created prior to the bailout. I suggest that we must dig deeper into the legacy of the Irish colonial experience to explain the absence of a sustained public demand for reform in response to these behaviours.

RE-ENACTMENT

Chapter 1 looked at the parallels between the individual experiences of trauma and the cultural trauma generated by wars, colonialism and other disasters. Research on cultural trauma places a strong emphasis on remembering events that took place as a way of healing and making sense of these experiences afterwards. However, the understanding of trauma at the individual level has moved far beyond this model. Remembering is simply a first step for survivors of trauma. Victims – in particular victims of childhood abuse – must come to terms with all the distortions in their understandings of reality that have come about as a result of the trauma.

One of the most common distortions in the behaviour of abuse survivors occurs because of disassociation, which is a way of coping with abuse. During the abusive experience, the victim may outwardly appear to acquiesce, negotiating with their abuser in order to lessen the abuse experience. Their real feelings about their abuse become split off and they develop another interior world where they experience their real feelings about the abuse. But sometimes even these tactics do not succeed and victims retreat into a passive helplessness in which their capacity to perceive danger and wrong-doing, their 'fight or flight' mechanisms, become disabled. Even after the trauma is over and the abuse is over, this split reality and passive helplessness may shape how they behave and how they perceive reality. As a consequence, the survivor may find themselves repeatedly in situations which mirror the circumstances of the original trauma or abuse experience.

Research on individual trauma provides deep insights into why some Irish people tolerate corruption and why other Irish people engage in corrupt activities. In his research on the experiences of adult survivors of trauma, Bessel A. van der Kolk notes the tendency of abuse survivors to find themselves in situations which repeat many of the aspects of the original abuse. The influence of early trauma experiences on the adult lives of victims has been noted since the earliest years of psychology in the work of Freud, Charcot, Janet and others. In reviewing this research, van der Kolk notes:

> Some traumatized people remain preoccupied with the trauma at the expense of other life experiences and continue to re-create it in some form for themselves and for others. War veterans may enlist as mercenaries, victims of incest may become prostitutes and victims of childhood abuse seemingly provoke subsequent abuse in

foster families or become self-mutilators. Still others identify with the aggressor and do to others what was done to them.[28]

Not only are survivors of childhood abuse more likely to become victims of abuse in adult life, but some survivors are also more likely to become abusers themselves. In describing the adult relationships of abuse survivors, van der Kolk cites research by Carmen *et al.*, who suggest that some childhood abuse victims, particularly boys, tend to 'identify with the aggressor and later victimize others', whereas other victims, often girls, 'are prone to become attached to abusive men who allow themselves and their offspring to be victimized further'.[29] Strikingly, these findings have been mirrored in studies of monkeys and mice which have also had early 'abuse' experiences.[30] Van der Kolk notes that 'nonhuman primates subjected to early abuse and deprivation also are more likely to engage in violent relationships with their peers as adults, as in humans, males tend to be hyper-aggressive and females fail to protect themselves and their offspring against danger.'[31]

Both these re-enactment behaviours provide some insight into Irish attitudes to corruption. When the process of disassociation fails to avert disaster, some victims of abuse may succumb to learned helplessness, which disables the mind's capacity to perceive danger and wrongdoing. This is why monkeys and mice who have had early abuse experiences may allow an aggressor to attack them or their young without responding appropriately. Elizabeth G. Vermilyea writes that as a result of trauma:

> [victims] may unconsciously disconnect the internal mechanisms that facilitate awareness of danger. When these fight or flight mechanisms are constantly activated to no avail, they may be ignored over time. Most survivors learn to shut down awareness of emotions to protect themselves from overwhelming emotional pain and betrayal.... When a survivor has to constrict awareness of danger and access to emotions in order to survive, s/he essentially disables self-protective mechanisms.[32]

She notes that childhood victims of abuse often tend to be re-victimised in relationships in adult life because their danger systems are disabled. She concludes, 'With emotions and awareness of danger disabled in the service of survival, the now-grown survivor is lacking crucial tools that are necessary in adult relationships. S/he cannot access feelings that tell how s/he is doing in relation to someone else, therefore, s/he may become involved with dangerous people without realizing it.'[33] The trauma creates a blind spot in the individual's capacity to perceive danger and wrongdoing in later life.

A blind spot can be defined as 'an area in which a person lacks understanding or impartiality'[34] or 'a tendency to ignore something especially because it is difficult or unpleasant'.[35] One of the chief legacies of childhood abuse is blind spots in the individual's judgement. If someone hasn't dealt with their childhood abuse experience, they may struggle to evaluate and respond to the dangerous or inappropriate behaviour of others. If the behaviour of another adult in their environment mimics the behaviour of their original abuser, they may find it even more difficult to respond appropriately. They may in adult life remain in abusive situations for long periods because the abusive behaviours re-awaken their feelings of helplessness and they cannot respond appropriately.

Is it possible that the memory of colonialism has created a blind spot about corruption in Irish culture? Despite the harsh austerity that has resulted from 'insider intimacy', do Irish citizens struggle to respond with appropriate anger because they have difficulty perceiving the 'wrongness' or the potential dangers of these activities? The process of colonialism was abusive at several levels. It generated a traumatic degree of violence and a profound threat to the survival of the group in the form of mass starvation. The associated denigration of Irish culture was rooted in an ideology that suggested that these processes were somehow justified because of weaknesses in the culture of the colonised. The result of this abusive system was the positioning of the Anglo-Irish colonising elite at the top of Irish society, a group whose wealth was generated largely by extracting resources from Irish tenant farmers and workers.

Even after political independence in 1922, the legacy of this cultural trauma remained at many levels of Irish society. The uneasy tension between the parallel worlds of rules and relationships in the new Irish state was resolved by combining the rules of the state with those of the Catholic Church, one of the few rules-based systems in which the majority Catholic Irish population believed. While this approach to rules meant repression for minorities and incarceration for those who did not conform to the Church–State standards of sexual behaviour, it did create a stable nation state with a functioning civil service and criminal justice system. However, the rhetoric of the revolutionary generation, particularly Éamon de Valera, made it clear that the relationship-based units of family and community – not the individual citizen – were the bedrock of the new state. The patronage politics generated by this intimacy was muted somewhat by the state's lack of wealth, the distaste for commerce and the emphasis on frugality in Church–State ideology.

By the late 1950s, however, Ireland's lack of prosperity had generated such large-scale emigration that the survival of the group was threatened. This threat led to a sharp shift in attitudes towards money and wealth which recalibrated the balance between rules and relationships at the highest level of Irish society. The grip of the Church began to loosen as families and communities were transformed by modernisation. In the midst of all this change, the Civil War generation of politicians retired and were replaced by a younger group who recognised that elite intimacy at the political level was a valuable commodity that could be sold to those who could pay. By engaging in corrupt activities which resulted in the extraction of resources from the larger group, were these individuals identifying with the aggressor? A tendency to mimic the behaviour of the original abuser is another response to abuse trauma identified by Bessel van der Kolk. Like those who re-enact the abuse victim role, they are engaged in recreating the original abuse experience; but because they re-enact the role of the aggressor rather than the victim in this process, their experience is one of triumph rather than repeated failure to prevent abuse. They are rewriting the abuse experience with a different ending, one where they emerge the winners.

Despite the success of this elite in embedding their activities within the morality of intimacy which highlights 'being there' for others in circles of intimacy, these individuals actually came to occupy a position which closely mimics the earlier aggressor, the Anglo-Irish colonial class. However, rather than using the rules of colonialism, they used relationships to extract resources from everyone else. The individual whose lifestyle provides the clearest example of this identification with the aggressor response was Charles J. Haughey. Haughey's career is exceptional not only because of the scale of his corrupt activities but because of his open desire to reproduce the lifestyle of the Anglo-Irish. He spent most of his career living in a Gandon mansion typical of an Irish country aristocrat. He liked gourmet food, bespoke clothing and regular breaks in Europe's elite watering holes. Patrick Gallagher, whose father, Matt Gallagher, was deeply enmeshed in Haughey's affairs, said, 'Haughey was financed in order to create the environment which the Anglo-Irish had enjoyed and that we as a people could never aspire to.'[36] Unlike de Valera, who went out of his way to distance himself from the oppressor and align his party with the 'men in the cloth caps', Haughey wanted to be the oppressor. This tendency was noted by Thomas Kinsella in his poem 'Nightwalker'. It is believed that he was describing Haughey in the lines, 'It is himself! In his silk hat, accoutred in stern jodhpurs … climbing the dark, to his mansion in the sky.'[37] Describing the sale of Haughey's mansion after he died, Liam Collins commented, 'some say he bought the house because he wanted to model himself on a fun-loving Munster earl with his mansion, his love of horse-riding and hunting with hounds.'[38]

Most of the political leaders who followed Haughey embedded themselves more subtly within the Irish cultural blind spot relating to rules and relationships, successfully screening their position as extracting elites. Many of the individuals involved in these activities were clever enough to recognise that they were successful because their activities were nested within an everyday morality that had a strong association between 'being there' for those in circles of intimacy and 'being good'. In a number of prominent cases, including those of Sean Quinn and Michael Lowry, which we discussed in Chapters

5 and 6, these individuals would repeatedly and publicly stress their commitment to their families and communities and their ties to organisations rooted in the community, such as the GAA. One of the best examples of this 'intimacy' rhetoric is a speech given by former Taoiseach Bertie Ahern to the Fianna Fáil parliamentary party in Sean Quinn's Slieve Russell Hotel in Cavan in September 2005, three years before the bank guarantee. He said:

> We are in power not for its own sake but to bring this island together and make it an even better place to live, to work, to raise a family – to be young in hope and grow old with dignity – an Ireland of unity, prosperity and community. ... We will be poorer as a country if we ever lose the vibrant sense of community that is the force of everyday Irish life. Our policies in government should and will be directed to encouraging an Ireland where communities come together, *where people are there for one another* and where technology never replaces the warmth of human contact.... We must also strengthen the essential character of Ireland as a country with a unique gift for warmth, for fun and always *being there* when our neighbour needs us.[39]

Ahern was quick to nest his government's approach to managing the economy within this vision of intimacy where people *are there* for one another. He continued:

> The Government will never put at risk the prosperity that the Irish people are building. Our strong economy is the beginning not the end of our ambitions. It is the base from which we can build the brave society we aspire to create. At the heart of that brave society is an ideal central to the country we live in and the culture we come from. For Ireland, community is the thread that holds together the fabric of our society and our future.[40]

It could be argued that in formulating his vision for Ireland, Bertie Ahern was telling his parliamentary party and the wider Irish public what they wanted to hear. But the reason they wanted to hear it was because it appealed strongly to their relationship-based vision of good behaviour, which prioritises 'being there' for others in the family and community. The triumph of this moral vision over a model of good citizenship which stresses conformity to rules is one of the most profound elements of the Irish post-colonial legacy. The impact of 'being there' on fairness to everyone else was not something which Ahern discussed. Neither did he outline the considerable differences between how politicians had, since the 1960s, 'been there' for business elites and their approach to 'being there' for ordinary voters.

STRENGTHENING THE RULES?

Since Ahern's speech in 2005, the Irish public has been forced to radically question the practice of 'being there'. As the American poet Theodore Roethke observes, 'In a dark time, the eye begins to see.'[41] Some post-bailout debates about corruption show an increasing awareness of Irish culture's blind spot about rule-breakers. One influential commentator, Fintan O'Toole, has suggested that the solution to endemic corruption is to dramatically increase the scope of rules in Irish public life. In his book *Enough is Enough: How to Build a New Republic*, O'Toole outlines fifty key actions that could change Irish society; almost all these actions involve changing rules. He acknowledges that:

> Large-scale constitutional change is certainly necessary to enable many of the key transformations I suggest here: to establish powerful local government; to change the voting system for national elections; to establish real accountability of government to parliament; to renovate or abolish the Seanad, to clarify the right to freedom of conscience and to make clear once and for all that the rights of private property do not outweigh the common good.[42]

Central to O'Toole's vision of rules is the idea of transcendence – the idea that administering rules-based systems is based on reason alone; there is no influence from local cultures and therefore the rules are difficult to bend around relationships.[43] The model of a transcendent rational bureaucracy operating above the flawed intimacy culture of Irish society is appealing, but in practice, it would be almost impossible to achieve. Guy Peters notes, 'public bureaucracies are sometimes portrayed as running roughshod over their societies, but they are bound by many thin but strong bonds to their societies and their values.'[44] O'Toole's faith in rules appears to be based on a belief that those who would create and administer the new rule-based systems would be operating from outside Irish culture, the culture that produced the distortion between rules and relationships in the first place. But bureaucrats do not exist outside the culture of their own country. They are socialised in the same way as all other citizens and respond to the same cultural values as their fellow citizens. In describing his research on bureaucracy, Michael Herzfeld writes:

> During fieldwork, I came to know and like a host of officials (including police officers), bureaucrats, academic and artistic celebrities and politicians and I came to realise that they usually worked with the same assumptions and experienced the same constraints as other citizens.[45]

Indeed, the model of transcendent rational bureaucracy has already been implemented in Ireland through the austerity programme itself and is widely felt not to have delivered the 'fairness' that is supposed to be central to rules-based systems.[46] Those who aspire to increase the volume and scope of rules do so in the hope of eliminating intimacy entirely from public institutions in Irish society. However, one important public institution in Ireland, the healthcare system, has already been reformed to remove intimacy from its structures, and the outcome of this reform does not necessarily reinforce the case that rules alone can deliver the required transformation of Irish society.

In 1970, eight regional health boards were established in Ireland to manage the healthcare service. Each health board was headed by a chief executive and typically about half the members of the health boards were appointees from city and county councils. By the late 1990s, there were concerns about the role of political intimacy in the management of the health system. Following the publication of two expert reports in 2005, the health boards were abolished and replaced with one large bureaucratic organisation, the Health Services Executive (HSE), which reported directly to the Minister for Health. The reform was supposed to remove intimacy from Irish healthcare and make the system fairer and more efficient. By the end of the austerity period, there was evidence that this reform has not been successful. In 2014, a damning report on the HSE's financial management found that no manager was actually responsible for its considerable financial over-runs. The PA Consulting analysis found that the HSE's financial systems were 'overly resource intensive and inflexible' and that 'budget holders are rarely accountable for success or failure in achieving budgets.'[47] The reformed HSE does not appear to have had any notable success in delivering a fairer healthcare system. Striking inequities in healthcare have not been addressed. For instance, a comparative report by the Organisation for Economic Co-operation and Development (OECD) found that while Ireland spent less (as a proportion of GDP) on health than any other country in Western Europe, Irish hospital consultants were the third highest paid in the OECD (after New Zealand and Luxembourg).[48]

The inflexibility and inefficiency of the HSE's rule-based systems was highlighted by a number of participants in the final phase of interviews for this book in 2012–2013. Caroline, whose daughter is seriously ill, says:

> Jodie has this very rare brain condition and she has to go to Scotland for treatment. I've tried explaining all about this to the HSE and I've shown them all the medical reports and so far, we've got nothing, no help, no support, nothing. It's like because her condition is so rare, they have no box to tick. I'm been sent from pillar to post and no one seems to give a rat's ass. They only care about their bloody forms.

Caroline's description of her fight to get care for Jodie contained many of the 'heartless, interest-directed, buck-passing bureaucrats' identified by Michael Herzfeld in his studies of bureaucracy.[49] Because of this lack of responsiveness, ordinary citizens are still appealing to politicians for help in negotiating with the HSE. Alison works as a secretary for a TD in Laois:

> Take that girl in Sligo who missed out on a liver transplant because they couldn't get a bloody helicopter going. If she'd been in our constituency and got on to us, we'd have raised the roof to get her going. Her situation seemed to get lost in the maze. It's a heartless maze. They don't really give a shit about people.

Tony, a former member of the Southern Health Board, also believes that the change to the HSE has not delivered fairness or efficiency:[50]

> Now I know I've a vested interest 'cause I was on the old health board but to be honest, it was a better structure than what we have now. At least on the health board, the relationships between health officials and councillors could be seen, the press attended board meetings and councillors could talk about the complaints of the people they represented. Now we are still beating a track to them day in and day out but nobody knows who's connected to who and the top brass are untouchable in a way that they weren't before and just as capable of pulling strokes for each other as any other group.

Essentially, Tony is suggesting that the health board model of administration created a visible space for both rules and relationships. Its replacement with an opaque, bureaucratic organisation has pushed intimacy underground without delivering any greater fairness in the administration of rules-based systems.

The perception that rule-based reform made the HSE less fair has been further reinforced by evidence of patronage among HSE officials themselves. In 2010, the *Irish Examiner* reported that in Cork, four children of senior managers were appointed as clerical officers in HSE South. In Limerick, 'the spouses and children of five senior staff at HSE Mid-West were interviewed last week for positions as temporary community welfare officers.' In Cork, none of the positions was advertised internally or externally, while in Limerick:

> The vacancies were only advertised internally on May 28 and were confined to suitably qualified existing HSE staff. However, the *Irish Examiner* is aware that children and husbands of existing HSE community welfare officers actually secured some of the positions. It has also established that one applicant, with no family connections to the HSE, whose CV had been kept on file, was not called for an interview.[51]

These incidents do not bode well for those who suggest that rule-based changes alone will recalibrate the balance between weak rules and strong relationships in Irish society.

Aside from increasing the scope and the volume of rules, a number of commentators have suggested that politicians should no longer get involved in making representations for their constituents. After losing his seat in the 2011 general election, former minister Conor Lenihan commented:

> It is wrong that TDs are spending so much of their time on individual queries in relation to individual citizen issues. One of the best ways we could reform the Dáil and reform the way it works for the country is to actually ban TDs from taking individual representations. We should give very strong powers to the Ombudsman to correct that on behalf of the citizens … I would assess at a very conservative estimate that 40 per cent of a TD's work is devoted to individual representation and that's not even good for the communities they serve. It's the community that needs to be represented not the individual.[52]

Lenihan's acknowledgement that making representations for individuals can impact on fairness is welcome. However, there is a significant danger that eliminating constituency work at local level will widen the already large gap between politicians' practices of 'being there' for big businesses that operate as 'groups' and their approach to 'being there' for ordinary citizens who operate as individuals.

While the proposal to strengthen the Ombudsman's power is welcome, the resources of the Office of the Ombudsman are very modest in comparison with the vast number of elected representatives at local, European and national level in Ireland. Second, the Office of the Ombudsman tends to intervene after a rule-based system has made a mistake, while politicians can intervene while a decision is in progress and respond with the kind of immediacy not possible for an ombudsman. Finally, making a complaint through Ombudsman structures requires a range of technical skills and a high degree of literacy. The face-to-face contact provided by politicians is easier to access for groups such as the elderly, many of whom are not IT literate, members of marginalised communities and ethnic minorities, who may have issues with literacy and numeracy. So while referring problems to the Office of the Ombudsman can help some individuals, it is unlikely that these structures could provide a genuine alternative to the relationship-based constituency work currently offered by politicians to ordinary voters.

If simply increasing the volume and scope of the rules will not solve Ireland's problems with endemic corruption and if Irish society is unwilling to dispense with responsive intimacy-based constituency work, what can be done to reconfigure the Irish value system? If the distortion of attitudes to rules and relationships is rooted in Ireland's past, should the past be the starting point for changing attitudes to corruption? In an article on the Irish Famine, historian David Lloyd argues that one of the dangers of applying the trauma model to history is that it leads to an unhealthy or melancholic preoccupation with the past in which citizens of the post-colonial country lose sight of the fact that colonialism was actually survived. He notes that neither individuals nor cultures actually recover from trauma, rather they are transformed, changed forever by these experiences; and he concludes, 'the changed live on in strange ways.'[53]

Rather than focusing on the past, the focus, he argues, should be on the present and on understanding both the positive and negative elements of the transformation brought about by colonial trauma. Throughout this study, returned migrants, recent immigrants and members of the Irish middle classes made many positive comments about the 'warmth' of Irish culture, which they described as one of the most attractive and engaging aspects of Irish society. This warmth is undoubtedly linked to the value placed on intimacy, relationships and the 'personal', which is a positive part of the post-colonial legacy in Ireland.

In dealing with the more negative elements of this legacy, and specifically the tendency for intimacy to generate corruption, it is worth returning to lessons learned by individual trauma survivors in learning to cope with the legacy of their abuse experiences. There is a growing therapeutic emphasis on 'noticing' for trauma survivors. Abuse survivors, it is argued, simply need to be more aware of their blind spots and of how the abuse has created distortions in their behaviour and their understandings of reality.[54] It is possible to argue that even without mapping the links between intimacy, morality and corruption – conducted as part of this study – this 'noticing' is already beginning to take place in Irish culture. In the dark time of austerity, the problems with the balance between weak rules and strong relationships in Irish culture have been perceived.

This noticing was evident in the penalty points controversy of 2014: people questioned not only the quashing of points for celebrities but also the quashing of points for ordinary citizens. Noticing was also apparent in the critical commentary of tax avoidance and increased reporting of social welfare fraud during the 2010–2014 period. A more formal recognition of the distortion in the balance between rules and relationships could be put in place by a popular and political commitment to *making the intimacy visible*. Mechanisms that facilitate transparency, such as conflict of interest registers, etc., could be more widely introduced. Intimacy-based constituency work at a local level could also become more transparent. Intense efforts also need to be made to reach out to immigrant communities so that they too feel that they can avail of intimacy-based support in Irish public life.

In relation to rules, greater popular demand for fairness in rule-based systems will only emerge if it is demanded through the ballot box and in all available public forums. The importance of demanding fairness from rules-based systems, particularly those which dominate the economy, has become even more critical as Ireland has become more tightly locked into monetary union through the European Stability Mechanism (ESM). There is evidence that macro-economic policy at European level is not being managed to promote fairness or redistribution of wealth but rather to shore up existing hierarchies and inequalities. Even Colm McCarthy, who played a prominent role in implementing cuts in the early austerity period, acknowledged in 2014 that 'Germany has by common agreement had a rather good eurozone crisis.'[55] He comments, 'If the worldwide financial crisis had been resolved through the distribution of losses to savers and investors, as in textbook capitalism, rather than to taxpayers in debtor countries, Germany would have taken a substantial hit.' Instead, the flawed rules which govern the eurozone have allowed Germany to shield itself from the worst consequences of the crisis. He continues:

> The design flaws in EMU Mark 1 are largely Germany's fault: the European Central Bank in particular operates to a rule book based on the Bundesbank model, and it is no accident that its headquarters are in Frankfurt…. The flaws have been recognised by some German politicians but there has been no admission of authorship.[56]

He concludes that these flaws have contributed to a deepening sense of injustice relating to the rules which govern monetary and economic policy, not only in Ireland but across the eurozone:

> This makes it hard for people to endure lectures from German economists and politicians about fiscal rectitude, market discipline and 'reform' in peripheral countries. Germany wrote the rule book, has benefited therefrom and has resisted reform where it matters – that is reform of the flawed eurozone structures. Any meaningful reform would include market discipline for unsecured creditors.[57]

During the Celtic Tiger period, Irish cynicism about the rules of capitalism reached its zenith with the success of Ireland's International Financial Services Centre (IFSC). Ireland's corporate tax law structures continue to facilitate tax avoidance by multinational corporations, but international tolerance of these local 'rules' is waning. Despite accommodating big business through its 'rules', Ireland increasingly finds itself on the 'raw' end of global capitalism. It has been forced into structural adjustment policies which openly place the needs of markets before people. *Making the intimacy visible* in Irish society itself may turn out to be the easy part of recalibrating the balance between weak rules and strong relationships in the Irish value system. Ensuring that rules-based systems become fairer in an international context where rules are profoundly distorted – and are becoming more so – will prove to be much more difficult. Nevertheless, surely the most critical lesson of the bailout is that while 'being there' is valuable, 'being fair' is an even more important part of 'being good'.

REFERENCES

Introduction

1. R. Ingle (2011), 'Will everything be okay?', *Irish Times*, 19 February.
2. D. Donovan and A. Murphy (2013) *The Fall of the Celtic Tiger: Ireland and the Euro-Debt Crisis.* Oxford: Oxford University Press.
3. D. McDonald, *Irish Independent*, 8 February 2011.
4. J. Reilly, *Sunday Independent*, 6 February 2011.
5. E. MacConnell, G. Deegan and E. O'Regan, *Irish Independent*, 25 January 2011.
6. In January 2007, it was reported that the ratings agency Standard and Poor's had placed Ireland sixth in the global wealth league, beating the USA (11th) and the UK (18th). *Irish Independent*, 'Ireland rated sixth richest country in global wealth league', 21 January 2007.
7. J. Authers (2012) *Europe's Financial Crisis.* London: FT Press.
8. S. Ross (2010) *The Bankers: How the Banks Brought Ireland to its Knees.* Penguin; M. Cooper (2011) *How Ireland Really Went Bust.* Dublin: Penguin Ireland.
9. F. O'Toole (2010) *Ship of Fools: How Stupidity and Corruption Sank the Celtic Tiger.* Faber & Faber, p. 3.
10. G. Taylor (2011) 'Risk and financial Armageddon in Ireland: the politics of the Galway tent', *Political Quarterly* 8(4): 596–608.
11. K. Regling and M. Watson (2010) *A Preliminary Report on the Sources of Ireland's Banking Crisis.* Dublin: Government Publications (Prn A10/07000); P. Honohan (2010) *The Irish Banking Crisis: Regulatory and Financial Stability Policy 2003–2008: A Report to the Minister for Finance by the Governor of the Central Bank*, available at www.socialjustice.ie; P. Nyberg (2011) *Commission of Investigation into the Banking Sector in Ireland*, www.bankinginquiry.gov.ie. Another important report that highlighted the weakness of rules-based systems is R. Wright (2010) *Strengthening the Capacity of the Department of Finance: Report of the Independent Review Panel.* Dublin: Department of Finance, http://oldwww.finance.gov.ie.

12.   P. Nyberg, *op. cit.*, pp. 96–7.

13.   Quoted in B. Clarke and N. Hardiman (2012) *Crisis in the Irish Banking System.* Dublin: UCD Geary Institute Discussion Paper Series, Geary WP 2012/03, p. 19.

14.   N. Murray (2010) 'No Minister, we didn't all party', *Irish Examiner*, 6 December.

15.   N. O'Connor (2012) 'Enda makes U-turn on mad remarks as ministers back him', *The Herald*, 28 January.

16.   M. Kelly (2009) *The Irish Credit Bubble.* Dublin: UCD Centre for Economic Research Working Paper Series, WP09/32.

17.   K. Whelan (2010) 'Policy lessons from Ireland's latest depression', *Economic and Social Review* 41(2): 225–54.

18.   G. Crow (2002) *Social Solidarities: Theories, Identities and Social Change.* Milton Keynes: Open University Press.

19.   J. Macionis and K. Plummer (1997) *Sociology: A Global Introduction.* London: Prentice Hall, pp. 67–74.

20.   B. Misztal (1996) *Trust in Modern Societies: The Search for the Bases of Social Order.* Oxford: Polity Press; I. Honohan (2005) 'Metaphors of Solidarity', European Consortium for Political Research (ECPR) Workshop, Metaphors in Political Science, Granada, April 2005.

21.   D. Ó Cronín (2008) *New History of Ireland, Vol. 1: Pre-historic and Early Medieval Ireland.* Oxford: Oxford University Press.

22.   P. Bickle (ed.) (1997) *Resistance, Representation and Community: The Origins of the Modern State in Europe 13th–18th Centuries.* Oxford: Oxford University Press.

23.   M. Weber (1921, 1978) *Economy and Society*, ed. G. Roth and C. Witich. Berkeley: University of California Press; É. Durkheim (1893, 1964) *The Division of Labour in Sociology.* New York: Free Press.

24.   H.P. Muller (1994) 'Social differentiation and organic solidarity: the division of labour revisited', *Sociological Forum* 9(1): 73–86.

25.   T. Kasulis (2002) *Intimacy and Integrity: Philosophy and Cultural Difference.* Honolulu: University of Hawaii Press, pp. 118–25.

26.   For instance, if an individual skips the queue in a doctor's surgery where the rule is that everyone is seen in order of arrival, the rule-breaking impacts negatively on everyone else in the queue, who have to wait longer.

27.   The names of all three individuals and the location have been changed in this narrative.

28.   Elaine Byrne notes, 'Early Dáil debates denoted corruption as an evil depravity which undermined democracy and called for those who violated their citizenship duties to be deprived of citizenship.' E. Byrne (2012)

Political Corruption in Ireland 1922–2010: A Crooked Harp? Manchester: Manchester University Press, p. 25.

29. J.P. O'Carroll (1987) 'Strokes, cute hoors and sneaking regarders', *Irish Political Studies* 2(1): 77–92.

30. E. Byrne, *op. cit.*

31. These studies include, for example, C. Arensberg and S. Kimball (1940) *Family and Community in Ireland.* Cambridge, MA: Harvard University Press; A. Humphreys (1966) *New Dubliners.* London: Routledge and Kegan Paul; D. Hannan (1972) 'Kinship, neighbourhood and social change in Irish rural communities', *Economic and Social Review*, 3(1): 163–88; C. Whelan and T. Fahey (1995) 'Marriage and the Family' in C. Whelan (ed.) *Values and Social Change in Ireland.* Dublin: Gill & Macmillan; F. Kennedy (2001) *From Cottage to Crèche: Family Change in Ireland.* Dublin: Institute of Public Administration (IPA); R.R. Seward, R. Stivers, D. Igoe, I. Amin and D. Cosimo (2005) 'Irish families in the twentieth century: exceptional or converging?', *Journal of Family History* 30: 410–30; M. Corcoran, J. Gray and M. Peillon (2010) *Suburban Affiliations: Social Relations in the Greater Dublin Area.* New York: Syracuse University Press; M. Fine-Davis (2011) *Attitudes to Family Formation in Ireland: Findings from the Nationwide Study.* Dublin: Family Support Agency and Trinity College Dublin.

32. Broader studies of values in Ireland have, however, noted the importance of family in the Irish value system. See C. Whelan (ed.) (1995) *Values and Social Change in Ireland.* Dublin: Gill & Macmillan.

33. The category of 'middle class' is notoriously difficult to define in social research. This study takes as its starting point definitions of middle-class occupations used for the 2006 Irish Census which were developed by the Central Statistics Office (CSO) in Ireland (see Appendices 7 and 8, Broad Level of Occupational Groups used in Census 2006 Classification, www.cso.ie). However, this approach was broadened in light of the findings of Savage *et al.* in their analysis of the middle class in the UK, which used data gathered from the BBC's *Great British Class Survey.* This analysis highlights the distinction between the middle class and the elite in British society, a distinction absent from British class analysis conducted during the 1980s and 1990s based on John Goldthorpe's seven-class model developed at Nuffield College, Oxford University. Savage *et al.*'s framework not only takes account of the distinction between the elite and the middle class (using the salary scale of £89,000 as a starting point) but also uses a range of other criteria for identifying an individual as middle class. These factors include cultural capital and social capital. These concepts, which were developed by Pierre Bourdieu to understand class distinctions, have been employed

by Bennett *et al.* in class analysis in Australia and the UK, and Lamont in a comparative study of the USA and France. Using Savage *et al.*'s scale, the middle class are distinguished from the elite (who were also interviewed for Chapter 7 of this study). The process of defining a research participant as middle class began with questions about occupation and continued with questions about cultural and social interests. According to the Savage *et al.* criteria, middle-class participants in this study could be described as members of the (2) Established middle class, (3) Technical middle class or (4) New affluent workers. Participants were asked about their occupation in 2007 as a starting point in allocating their class position. Workers in the construction sector who were earning high wages during the 2003–2007 period were included in the middle-class cohort, although many of these workers experienced rapid downward mobility between 2008 and 2013. Despite the popularity of terms such as the 'squeezed middle' and the 'coping classes', the main cohort for this study could actually be described as the socially included: Irish citizens who in normal economic circumstances would have an expectation of being in work and fully participating in Irish society. Residents of socially excluded and marginalised communities were not included in the study. These communities were identified using Haase's Deprivation Indices and micro-analysis of the various regions available. Members of elites were ruled out of the middle-class cohort using the following method. Standards in Public Office define the salary point of €87,258 as the point where public disclosure regulations for public servants become mandatory. This salary point was using as a benchmark for elite entry. Participants were simply informed of this salary point as an elite entry point and asked if they fell into this category. If they did, the interview did not proceed. (This only happened in two cases.) See Standards in Public Office (2013) *Guidelines on Compliance with the Provisions of the Ethics in Public Office Acts 1995 and 2001* (10th edn), www.sipo.gov.ie. For further discussion see T. Bennett, M. Savage, E.B. Silva, A. Warde, M. Cal-Gayo and D. Wright (2008) *Culture, Class and Distinction*. London: Routledge; T. Haase, J. Pratschke and J. Gleeson (2012) *All-Island Deprivation Index*, available to download at http://trutzhaase.eu/deprivation-index/all-island-deprivation-index; M. Lamont (1992) *Money, Morals and Manners*. Chicago: University of Chicago Press; M. Savage, F. Devine, N. Cunningham, M. Taylor, Y. Li, J. Hjellbreke, B. La Roux, S. Friedman and A. Milnes (2013) 'A new model of social class: findings from the BBC's *Great British Class Survey* experiment', *Sociology* 47(2) 219–50. It should be noted that apart from expert participants, every attempt was made to secure middle-class interviewees who were either practising or non-practising Catholics. Given the emphasis on religion in Weber's work on rules and relationships, it was felt that members of religious minority groups might have a different understanding of the tension between rules and relationships in Irish culture.

34. I wish to thank Deirdre O'Riordan for her assistance with this stage of the research project. Of the migrant interview cohort, 15 were women and 10 were men. Interviewees were from a range of countries including Poland, Hungary, Czech Republic, Romania, Russia, Italy, Iraq, Singapore, Nigeria, Ghana, Brazil, Pakistan, Malaysia and Hong Kong. Of the Irish interview cohort 17 were women and 19 were men. All were adults in employment.

35. The *Irish Times* was particularly prominent in popularising the term 'squeezed middle' and ran a series of articles on 'Ireland's Squeezed Middle' in February 2012, for example C. Kenny (2012) 'We were a typical middle-class Irish family but fell victim to the recession', *Irish Times*, 11 February. The *Sunday Independent* has used the term 'the coping class' to describe broadly the same group.

36. This second stage of the research began with four mixed-gender focus groups, each including four newly unemployed individuals. It continued with 35 interviews with Irish people at various levels in the Irish workforce (16 women, 19 men). The series concluded with 11 re-interviews with migrants from the first stage of the study.

37. Michael Lowry is an independent TD for Tipperary North who has been re-elected despite being publicly criticised in the report of the Moriarty Tribunal.

38. In 2012, it was estimated that there were 18 unfinished 'ghost estates' in County Laois, of which three were in Portlaoise, the main town in the county. 'Ghost estate bill hits €4m', *Leinster Express*, 30 May 2012.

39. P. Gerlach-Kirsten (2013) *Younger and Older Households in the Crisis*. Quarterly Economic Commentary, Economic and Social Research Institute Research Note 2013/1/4, www.esri.ie.

40. R. Lydon and Y. McCarthy (2011) *What Lies Beneath? Understanding Recent Trends in Irish Mortgage Arrears*. Central Bank of Ireland Research Technical Paper 14/RT/11; L. Delaney, M.Egan and N. O'Connell (2011) *The Experience of Unemployment in Ireland: A Thematic Analysis*. UCD Geary Institute Discussion Paper Series WP 2011/16.

41. The meetings I went to were held in Cork and Limerick between November 2010 and March 2011. A fieldwork diary of observations was assembled after attendance at each meeting.

42. The final stage of the research began with five mixed-gender focus groups with Irish citizens on the theme of 'Rules and Austerity'. This was followed

by 13 interviews with politicians at local, national and MEP level. This interview cohort included retired politicians from Fianna Fáil, Fine Gael and Labour. Five experts in debt management were interviewed, including people working for the Money Advice and Budgeting Service (MABS), Citizens' Information officials, bank managers and accountants. This stage concluded with 41 interviews with middle-class Irish citizens, including ten revisit interviews with unemployed Irish people from the Stage Two research cohort.

43. Excerpts from interviews conducted during all three stages of the research are quoted throughout this book: all names and identifying information have been changed. Interview schedules and confidentiality agreements used in research conducted for this project were approved by the University Ethics Committee of University College Cork and grounded in guidelines developed by the International Sociological Association and the Sociological Association of Ireland. All interviews and focus groups were recorded, apart from the 18 interviews with politicians and debt experts. Due to the sensitivity of the material, interviewees in this cohort were given the option of note-taking by interviewer during the interview process rather than recording, an option which was taken up by five research participants.

44. For a detailed analysis of the timeframe of the publication of reports of tribunals see E. Byrne, *op. cit.*

45. There is considerable debate about the origins of this phrase. Recently, it's been associated with US motivational speaker Tony Robbins. However, the quote seems to have much earlier origins and has been attributed at different times to Henry Ford, Albert Einstein and Mark Twain.

Chapter 1

1. L.B. Smedes (1984) *Forgive and Forget: Healing the Hurts We Don't Deserve.* New York: Harper.

2. C. O'Callaghan (2011) 'The Queen in the PostColony', www. IrelandafterNAMA.ie, 18 May 2011.

3. M. Brennan (2010), 'Mansergh defends Cowen and Ahern in Cromwell row', *Irish Independent*, 26 November.

4. A full transcript of this debate was published on the website www. broadsheet.ie: see 'The funniest radio ding dung you'll read this week', www. broadsheet.ie/2011/12/02/matties-dirty-protest/, accessed 20 November 2013.

5. C. Daly (2012) 'Resistance to the Household Charge', www.journal.ie, 16 January.

6. Minihan refers here to the ratification of the European Stability Mechanism (ESM) treaty in Ireland in 2012. G. Reilly (2012) 'Ireland to formally ratify ESM treaty after Supreme Court clearance', www.thejournal.ie, 31 July 2012.

7. Quoted in 'The Irish Revolution', http://theirishrevolution.wordpress.com/2012/01/29/campaign-against-austerity-treaty/.

8. T.P. Coogan (2013), www.timpatcoogan.com/blog/, 3 February.

9. P. Leahy (2013), 'Exiting the bailout', *Sunday Business Post*, 19 February.

10. L. MacNally (2013), 'Banking on austerity', *Mayo News*, 16 April.

11. J. Reilly (2013) 'Jimmy McEntee fronting new "Land League"', *Sunday Independent*, 29 September 2013.

12. E. Brown (2013) 'The bank guarantee that bankrupted Ireland', *Huffington Post*, www.huffingtonpost.com/ellen-brown, accessed 20 November 2013.

13. N. Hussain (2003) *The Jurisprudence of Emergency: Colonialism and the Rule of Law*. University of Michigan Press, p. 10.

14. Ibid., p. 11.

15. R. English (2006) *Irish Freedom: The History of Nationalism in Ireland*. London: Macmillan, pp. 127–40.

16. Hill and Lynch write that in Ireland, police 'acted as the "eyes and ears" of the Dublin government in every town and rural area. Policemen in other parts of the United Kingdom were under county or borough control and they were much more limited in function than their Irish equivalents.' UCC MultiText Project in Irish History: *Society and Economy 1870–1914*, http://multitext.ucc.ie.

17. UCC MultiText Project in Irish History: *Emancipation, Famine and Religion: Ireland under the Union 1815–1870*, http://multitext.ucc.ie/d/The_Union.

18. E. Byrne (2012) *Political Corruption in Ireland 1922–2010: A Crooked Harp?* Manchester: Manchester University Press, pp. 19–25.

19. D. Lloyd (2000), 'Colonial trauma/post-colonial recovery', *Interventions* 2(2): 212–28, p. 214.

20. Quoted in F. O'Toole (2013) *A History of Ireland in 100 Objects*. Dublin: Royal Irish Academy.

21. R. English, *op. cit.*, p. 62.

22. M. Levene (2005) *Genocide in the Age of the Nation State* Vol. 2. London: I.B. Tauris, pp. 55–7.

23. B. Behan (2008) *Confessions of an Irish Rebel*. London: Random House.

24. http://politics.ie/forum/history/12820-oliver-cromwell-pimp-child-sex-trafficer.html, 30 March 2007.

25. J. Crowley, W. Smyth and M. Murphy (2012) *Atlas of the Great Irish Famine*. Cork: Cork University Press.

26. C. Ó Murchadha (2011) *The Great Famine: Ireland's Agony*. London: Hambledon Continuum; T.P. Coogan (2013) *The Famine Plot: England's Role in Ireland's Great Tragedy*. London: Palgrave; J. Kelly (2013) *The Graves are Walking: The History of the Great Irish Famine*. London: Faber & Faber; www.rte.ie/radio1/blighted-nation/.

27. www.timpatcoogan.com/blog/, 3 February 2013.

28. R. Haslam (1999) 'A race bashed in the face: imagining Ireland as a damaged child', *Jouvert: Journal of Post-Colonial Studies* 4(1): 1–26; S. O'Connor (1994) 'Famine', *Universal Mother*. Chrysalis/EMI Records.

29. J. Herman (1992) *Trauma and Recovery*. New York: Basic Books, p. 8.

30. J. Walsh (2011) *Contests and Contexts: The Irish Language and Ireland's Socio-Economic Development*. Bern: Peter Lang.

31. W.S. Trench (1868) *Realities of Irish Life*. London: Longmans, Green and Co.

32. R.M. Heron (1868) *The Irish Difficulty and its Solution by a System of Local Superintendence*. London: Hatchard and Co.

33. Quoted in R. English, *op. cit.*, p. 200.

34. Jeffrey Alexander says, 'The truth about the experience is perceived, but only unconsciously. In effect, truth goes underground, and accurate memory and responsible action are its victim. Traumatic feelings and perceptions, then, come not only from the originating event but from the anxiety of keeping it repressed. Trauma will be resolved, not only by setting things right in the world, but by setting things right in the self. The truth can be recovered, and psychological equanimity restored only, as the Holocaust historian Saul Friedlander once put it, "when memory comes".' J. Alexander, R. Eyreman, B. Giesen, N. Smelser, P. Sztomka (2004) *Cultural Trauma and Collective Identity*. Berkeley, CA: University of California Press.

35. J. Herman, *op. cit.*

36. E. Bass and L. Davis (1992) *The Courage to Heal*. New York: Harper Collins, p. 243.

37. V. Kenny (1985) 'The post-colonial personality', *Crane Bag* 9: 70–8, p. 73.

38. P. Ekeh (1975) 'Colonialism and the two publics in Africa: a theoretical statement', *Comparative Studies in Society and History* 17(1): 91–112, p. 92.

39. Ibid., pp. 106–7.

40. Ibid., p. 92.

41. R. Wraith and E. Simpkins (1963) *Corruption in Developing Countries*. London: George Allen and Unwin, p. 50.

42. J. Herman, *op. cit.*, p. 9.

43. F. Fanon (1967) *The Wretched of the Earth*. New York: Grove Wiedenfeld.

44. S. Connolly, UCC MultiText Project in Irish History: *Emancipation, Famine and Religion: Ireland Under the Union 1815–1870*, http://multi-text.ucc.ie/d/ Ireland_society_and_economy_1815ndash1870.

45. J.J. Lee (1989) *Ireland: Politics and Society*. Cambridge: Cambridge University Press, pp. 392–3.

46. C. Calhoun (1982) *The Question of Class Struggle: Social Foundations of Popular Radicalism during the Industrial Revolution*. Chicago: University of Chicago Press.

47. C. Arensberg and S. Kimball (1940) *Family and Community in Ireland*. Cambridge, MA: Harvard University Press, p. 60.

48. Quoted in L. Fogarty (ed.) *James Fintan Lalor: Patriot and Political Essayist (1807–1849)*. Dublin: Talbot Press, pp. 2–3.

49. G. Christianson (1972) 'Secret societies and agrarian violence in Ireland 1790–1840', *Agricultural History* 46(3): 369–84.

50. P. Feeley (1980) 'Early agrarian societies: Whiteboys and Ribbonmen', *Old Limerick Journal* 4: 23–7, p. 26.

51. C. Whitworth 'Statement of the Nature and Extent of the Disturbances which have Recently prevailed in Ireland and Measures Adopted in Consequence thereof', quoted in Christianson, *op. cit.*, p. 378.

52. P. Buckland (1998) 'Rural Unrest in Ireland Before the Famine', *Ireland in Schools: The Warrington Project*, BR6A.

53. P. Feeley, *op. cit.*, p. 26.

54. G. Christianson, *op. cit.*, p. 384.

55. R. English, *op. cit.*, p. 128.

56. Ibid., p. 133.

57. Ibid., pp. 208–9.

58. E. Larkin (1972) 'The devotional revolution in Ireland', *American Historical Review* 17(3): 625–52.

59. T. Garvin (1987) *Nationalist Revolutionaries in Ireland 1858–1928*. Oxford: Oxford University Press.

60. Quoted in K.T. Hoppen (1999) *Ireland Since 1800: Conflict and Conformity*. London: Pearson, p. 157.

61. Ibid., p. 160.

62. R. English, *op. cit.*, p. 214.

63. T. Garvin (2004) *Preventing the Future: Why was Ireland so Poor for so Long?* Dublin: Gill & Macmillan, p. 168.

64. D. Keenan (2005) *Ireland 1850–1920*. Available at www.Xlibris.com.

65. UCC MultiText Project in Irish History: *Ireland: Society and Economy 1870–1914*, http://multitext.ucc.ie.

66. P. Ekeh, *op. cit.*, p. 99.

67. C. Clear (2007) *Social Change and Everyday Life in Ireland 1850–1922.* Manchester: Manchester University Press, p. 37.

68. P. Ekeh, *op. cit.*, p. 99.

69. J.J. Lee, *op. cit.*, p. 84.

70. P. Ekeh, *op. cit.*, p. 102.

71. Quoted in T. Bartlett and K. Jeffrey (eds) (1996) *A Military History of Ireland.* Cambridge: Cambridge University Press.

72. J. McKenna (2011) *Guerrilla Warfare in the Irish War of Independence 1919–1921.* Jefferson, NC: McFarland.

Chapter 2

1. Quoted in T. De Vere White (1948) *Kevin O'Higgins.* London: Methuen, p. 49.

2. D. Lindsey (2010) 'The world from Berlin: Germany must make clear that its capacity to fund bailouts is limited', *Der Spiegel,* 23 October, www.derspiegel.de.

3. P. Ekeh (1975) 'Colonialism and the two publics in Africa: a theoretical statement', *Comparative Studies in Society and History* 17(1): 91–112.

4. E. Larkin (1972) 'The devotional revolution in Ireland', *American Historical Review* 17(3): 625–52.

5. D. Ferriter (2005) *The Transformation of Ireland 1900–2000.* London: Profile Books, p. 246.

6. L. McBride (1991) *The Greening of Dublin Castle: The Transformation of Bureaucratic and Judicial Personnel in Ireland.* New York: Catholic University Press of America.

7. J.J. Lee (1989) *Ireland, 1912–1985: Economy and Society.* Cambridge: Cambridge University Press.

8. Executive Council 11 April 1924, INA Department of the Taoiseach s.3435.

9. J.J. Lee describes the rural origins of many of the early generation of successful civil servants (*op. cit.*, p. 74).

10. E. Byrne (2012) *Political Corruption in Ireland 1922–2010: A Crooked Harp?* Manchester: Manchester University Press, pp. 28–9.

11. T. Garvin (2004) *Preventing the Future: Why was Ireland so Poor for so Long?* Dublin: Gill & Macmillan, p. 115.

12. D. Ferriter (2005) *The Transformation of Ireland 1900–2000.* London: Profile Books, p. 305.

13. S. Breathnach (1974) *The Irish Police: From Earliest Times to the Present Day.* University of Michigan: Anvil Academic.

14. J.J. Lee, *op. cit.*, p. 92

15. R. English (2006) *Irish Freedom*. London: Macmillan, p. 322.

16. S. L'Estrange (2007) 'A community of communities: Catholic communitarianism and societal crisis in Ireland 1890s–1950s', *Journal of Historical Sociology* 20(4): 555–78.

17. T. Brown (1981) *Ireland: A Social and Cultural History*. London: Fontana, p. 145.

18. Quoted in the *Irish Press*, 18 March 1943, p. 1.

19. Quoted in D. Ferriter, *op. cit.*, p. 306.

20. C. McCullagh (1991) 'A tie that binds: family and ideology in Ireland', *Economic and Social Review* 22(3): 199–213.

21. D. Meehan (1960) 'Views about the Irish', *The Furrow* 11(8), August, p. 506.

22. J.J. Lee, *op. cit.*, p. 360.

23. The production processes used in foreign direct investment (FDI) manufacturing were based on scientific principles and rule-based knowledge systems. Materials were standardised and the same production processes used in all branches of these global companies, wherever they were. In this world of standardised production, there was little room for intuitive knowledge, non-verbal communication and the general intimacy which had characterised Irish economic activity on family farms. See A. Bielenberg and R. Ryan (2013) *An Economic History of Ireland Since Independence*. London: Routledge.

24. Lemass, quoted in the *Irish Press*, January 1957.

25. J.J. Lee, *op. cit.*, p. 360.

26. E. Hazelkorn (1996) 'New technologies and changing work practices in the media industry: the case of Ireland', *Irish Communications Review* 6: 28–38.

27. T. Inglis (1998) *Moral Monopoly: The Rise and Fall of the Catholic Church in Modern Ireland*. Dublin: Gill & Macmillan, p. 93.

28. T. Garvin, *op. cit.*, p. 152.

29. F. Kennedy (2001) *Cottage to Crèche: Family Change in Ireland*. Dublin: IPA.

30. Ibid., p. 204.

31. H. Tovey and P. Share (2000) *A Sociology of Ireland*. Dublin: Gill & Macmillan, p. 206.

32. F. O'Toole (2013) 'What has the European Union ever done for us?' *Irish Times*, 10 January, p. 16.

33. B. Laffan and J. O'Mahony (2008) *Ireland and the European Union*. London: Palgrave.

34. A. Macken-Walsh (2009) *Barriers to Change: a Sociological Study of Rural Development in Ireland*. Athenry: Rural Economy Research Centre, Teagasc.

35. B. Tonra (2007) *From Global Citizen to European Republic: Irish Foreign Policy in Transition.* Manchester: Manchester University Press.

36. D. Ahern (2003) 'Macro Economic Policy in the Celtic Tiger: A Critical Assessment' in C. Coulter and S. Coleman (eds) *The End of Irish History: Critical Reflections on the Celtic Tiger.* Manchester: Manchester University Press; D. Donovan and A. Murphy (2013) The *Fall of the Celtic Tiger.* Oxford: Oxford University Press.

37. C. Arensberg and S. Kimball (1940) *Family and Community in Ireland.* Cambridge, MA: Harvard University Press.

38. P. Lunn and T. Fahey (2011) *Households and Family Structures in Ireland: A Detailed Statistical Analysis of Census 2006.* Dublin: Family Support Agency and Economic and Social Research Unit (ESRI).

39. For further discussion, see T. Brown (1981) *Ireland: A Social and Cultural History.* London: Fontana, p. 146.

40. K. Keohane and C. Kuhling (2005) *Collision Culture: Transformations of Everyday Life in Ireland.* Dublin: Liffey Press, pp. 108–9.

41. Ibid., p. 109.

42. T. Inglis, *op. cit.*

43. M. Testa (2012) *Family Sizes in Europe: Evidence from the 2011 Eurobarometer Survey.* European Demographic Research Papers,www.oeaw.ac.ct.

44. S. Tavernise (2011) 'Dip in birth rates reflects recession, report suggests', *New York Times,* 12 October.

45. M. Fine-Davis (2011) *Attitudes to Family Formation in Ireland: Findings from the Nationwide Study.* Dublin: Family Support Agency and Trinity College Dublin, p. 86.

46. Ibid., p. 63.

47. www.clubisfamily.ie.

48. www.austinstacks.ie, accessed Monday 21 October 2013.

49. Moran Hotel Group (2011) 'Our Family of Hotels: Our Hotels, a family story …'. Dublin: Moran Hotel Group

50. E. Byrne, *op. cit.*

51. J.P. O'Carroll (1985) 'Community programmes and the traditional view of community', *Social Studies,* 8(3/4): 137–48.

52. J.P. O'Carroll (1987) 'Strokes, cute hoors and sneaking regarders', *Irish Political Studies* 2(1): 77–92, p. 88.

53. S. L'Estrange (2007) 'A community of communities: Catholic communitarianism and societal crisis in Ireland 1890s–1950s', *Journal of Historical Sociology* 20(4): 555–78.

54. M. Cronin (1999) 'Ignoring post-colonialism: the Gaelic Athletic Association and the language of colony', *Jouvert: A Journal of Post-Colonial Studies* 4(1): 26–45.

55. M. Cronin, M. Duncan and P. Rouse (2009) *The GAA: A People's History*. Dublin: Collins Press.

56. M. Corcoran, J. Gray and M. Peillon (2010) *Suburban Affiliations: Social Relations in the Greater Dublin Area*. New York: Syracuse University Press, p. 101.

57. The 2006 Census indicated that 60.35 per cent of the population lived in urban areas, defined as settlements of 1,500 people or more. In particular, there was a clear pattern of high growth in the immediate hinterlands of all major cities and towns, with many villages located in the greater Dublin area becoming 'metropolised'. Ibid., p. 30.

58. P. Collier (2004) 'Ireland's rurban horizon: new identities from home development markets in rural Ireland', *Irish Journal of Sociology*, 13(1): 88–101.

59. Regus Ltd, 'Ireland's Seven Deadly Sins of Commuting', 28 February 2011, www.regus.presscentre.com.

60. R. Putnam (2000) *Bowling Alone: The Collapse and Renewal of American Community*. New York: Simon & Schuster.

61. M. Corcoran *et al., op. cit.*

62. M. Corcoran *et al., op. cit.*

63. T. Inglis, *Local Belonging, Identities and Sense of Place in Contemporary Ireland*. IBIS Discussion Paper No.4. Dublin: Institute for British Irish Studies, University College Dublin, p. 9.

64. www.Esso.ie/Ireland-english/.

65. www.enterprise-gov.ie.

66. www.canalcommunities.ie.

67. www.rte.ie/localheroes.

68. C. O'Sullivan (2014) '200 homes use placard protest over wind-farm', *Irish Examiner*, 1 January; E. Hade and P. Melia (2014) 'Windfarm and pylon protesters take message to corridors of power', *Irish Independent*, 16 April.

69. D. O'Flynn (2014) 'Ballyhea still says No to this gross injustice', *Irish Independent*, 26 February.

Chapter 3

1. N. Gaiman (2012) *The Sandman: The Kindly Ones*. London: Vertigo, p. 12.

2. Internet forums that discussed these issues include www.namawinelake. wordpress.com, www.politics.ie and www.irelandafterNAMA.wordpress. com. Fictional accounts of austerity include Tana French's *Broken Harbour* (Hodder) and Donal Ryan's *The Spinning Heart* (Doubleday). The new social movements that emerged between 2010 and 2011 and which also considered these issues include Democracy Now, the National Forum and the United Left Alliance.

3. Quoted in I. Honohan (2013) 'Citizenship Attribution in a New Country of Immigration' in M.P. Vink (ed.) *Migration and Citizenship Attribution: Politics and Policies in Western Europe.* London: Routledge.

4. Quoted in M. Daly (2001) 'Irish nationality and citizenship since 1922', *Irish Historical Studies* 33(127): 377–408.

5. Ibid.

6. I. Honohan, *op. cit.*

7. For further discussion see S. Mullally (2007) 'Children, Citizenship and Constitutional Change' in B. Fanning (ed.) *Immigration and Social Change in the Republic of Ireland.* Manchester: Manchester University Press.

8. Quoted in I. Honohan, *op. cit.*

9. www.issp.org.

10. B. Anderson (1991) *Imagined Communities: Reflections on the Origins and Spread of Nationalism.* London: Verso.

11. M. Herzfeld (1992) *The Social Production of Indifference: Exploring the Symbolic Roots of Western Bureaucracy.* Chicago: University of Chicago Press, p. 35.

12. B. Hanley (2010) *Inside the IRA: A Documentary History.* Dublin: Gill & Macmillan; P. Hanafin (2001) *Constituting Identity: Political Identity Formation and the Constitution of Identity in Post-independence Ireland.* Aldershot: Ashgate, pp. 83–96; www.32csm.net.

13. D. Ferriter (2012) *Ambiguous Republic: Ireland in the 1970s.* London: Profile.

14. J. Todd, O. Muldoon, K. Trew, L. Canas Bottos, N. Rougier and K. McLaughlin (2006) 'The moral boundaries of the nation: the constitution of national identity in the southeastern border counties of Ireland'. *Ethno-politics* 5 (4): 365–82.

15. Ibid.

16. M. Harte and K. Shannon (2003) *Kicking Down Heaven's Door: Diary of a Football Manager.* All-Star Books.

17. www.pga.com.

18. Quoted in K. Crouse (2013) 'McIlroy, a native son divides', *New York Times*, July.

19. Ibid.

20. Ibid.

21. www.thescore.ie/rory-mcilroy-olympics-decision-letter-591160-Sep2012/.

22. K. MacGinty and R. Riegel (2014) 'Rory McIlroy to play for Ireland at 2016 Olympics', *Irish Independent*, 18 June.

23. F. Xiaotong (1930) [1992] *From the Soil: The Foundations of Chinese Society.* University of California Press.

24. Between May 2004 and September 2005, 133,258 social insurance numbers were issued to immigrant workers from the new accession states in Ireland; in the same period 293,000 numbers were issued in the UK, whose population is 15 times that of Ireland. The newly arrived migrant population at this time also included 27,136 non-EU economic permit holders, those arriving on student visas, and workers from the 'old' EU countries. Immigration to Ireland for that period alone was around 160,000; the comparable figure for New Zealand, a country with a similar population size to Ireland, was 48,815. The speed and scale of immigration relative to the size of the population troubled some commentators. David Begg, General Secretary of the Irish Congress of Trade Unions, commented, 'the recent census showed our population to have increased by some 600,000 since 1996 (and this is, in all likelihood, an underestimate). This change has happened over a timescale of 2–3 years whereas it took countries like Germany and Britain over 40 years to make this kind of transition.'

25. J. Crosbie (2013) 'The growth of intolerance', *Irish Times*, 29 June.

26. F. McGinnity, E. Quinn, G. Kingston and P. O'Connell (2013) *Annual Monitoring Report on Integration 2012*. Dublin: ESRI and Integration Centre.

27. B. Uí Chonaill (2007) 'The impact of migrants on resources: a critical assessment of the views of people working/living in the Blanchardstown area', *Translocations* 2(1): 10.

28. E. Moriarty (2005) 'Telling identity stories: the routinization of racialisation of Irishness', *Sociological Research Online* 10(3).

29. G. Fitzgibbon (2013) 'Defiant Limerick councillor facing FF expulsion over migrant comments', *Limerick Leader*, 5 April 2013.

30. B.Fanning, K. Howard and N. O'Boyle (2010) 'Immigrant candidates and politics in the Republic of Ireland: racialization, ethnic nepotism or localism?' *Nationalism and Ethnic Politics*, 16: 420–42.

31. In her research on the experiences of 'blow-ins' in Connemara, Lisa Moran has highlighted that definitions of 'our own' can change over time, but this process can take a long time and often depends on how similar the newcomer is to established members of the community. L. Moran (2007) 'Negotiating boundaries or drawing the line? Transcending "insider/ outsider" distinctions in Connemara', *Irish Journal of Sociology* 16(2): 136–59.

32. Ibid.

33. Quoted in M. Corcoran (2003) 'Global cosmopolites: issues of self-identity and collective identity among the transnational Irish elite', *Études Irlandaises* 28(2): 2–15, p. 11.

34. Quoted in C. Ní Laoire (2008) 'Complicating host–newcomer dualisms: Irish return migrants as home-comers or newcomers?', *Translocations: Migration and Social Change* 4(1): 35–50.
35. Quoted in M. Corcoran, *op. cit.*, p. 8.
36. Ibid., p. 8.
37. Ibid., pp. 7–8.
38. Quoted in C. Ní Laoire, *op. cit.*, p. 42.
39. Ibid, p. 40.
40. Quoted in M. Corcoran, *op. cit.*, p. 12.
41. Quoted in C. Ní Laoire, *op. cit.*, p. 40.
42. Ibid., p. 12.

Chapter 4

1. Some of the circumstances of this incident have been changed to protect the anonymity of those involved in the tragedy.
2. F. Ó Cionnaith (2012) 'Miscarrying women told to "read between lines" and go to UK', *Irish Examiner*, 16 November.
3. Oxford English Dictionary (1989), OED Online, www.dictionary.oed.com.
4. Office of the Attorney General (1986) Courts (No. 3) Act: Issues of Summons in relation to Offences, Irish Statute Book. Available at www.irishstatutebook.ie.
5. Kasulis comments, 'We often say such people are "principled", that is, they believe in an external, often universal set of values and standards they apply to different situations. The principles, not the situation, dictate the behaviour. Even when a person of integrity undergoes a change, the change is in the principles to which this person feels a sense of duty. Principled people can change their behaviour but only by changing their principles.' T. Kasulis (2002) *Intimacy and Integrity: Philosophy and Cultural Difference.* Honolulu: University of Hawaii Press, p. 54.
6. Matthew 7:12. This concept appears in early Confucianism as well as many of the other major global religious traditions including Hinduism, Buddhism, Taoism and Zoroastrianism. Epstein argues that it is a concept that 'essentially no religion misses entirely'. G. Epstein (2010) *Good without God: What a Billion Non-Religious People do Believe.* New York: HarperCollins, p. 115.
7. Kant's categorical imperative states, 'Act only according to that maxim by which you can at the same time will that it should become a universal law.' R. Johnson (2013) 'Kant's Moral Philosophy' in E.N. Zalta (ed.) *The Stanford Encyclopaedia of Philosophy*, http://plato.stanford.edu/archives/win2013/entries/kant-moral.

8. The term 'fair' is defined as treating people without favouritism or discrimination. Oxford English Dictionary (1989), OED Online, www.dictionary.oed.com.

9. V. Sutton (2011) *The Good Samaritan Laws*. SARL: Amazon Media EU.

10. The name of the victim, her friends and the location of this event have been changed.

11. Kasulis concludes, 'in the integrity orientation, ethics is primarily a morality of principles; in the intimacy orientation, however, ethics is a morality of love.' *Op. cit.*, p. 120.

12. Mark 12:31; Tripitaka – Sutta Nipata 705.

13. For further details of HIQA's auditing procedures for a range of services in the Irish health care system, see www.hiqa.ie.

14. Oxford English Dictionary (1989), OED Online, www.dictionary.oed.com.

15. S. Tadelis (1999) 'What's in a name? Reputation as a tradable asset', *American Economic Review* 89(3): 548–63; L. Ma and J. McLean Parks (2012) 'Your good name: the relationship between perceived reputational risk and acceptability of negotiation tactics', *Journal of Business Ethics* 106(2): 161–75.

16. C. McCullagh (2011) 'Getting a Fix on Crime in Limerick' in N. Hourigan (ed.) *Understanding Limerick: Social Exclusion and Change*. Cork: Cork University Press, pp. 23–37.

17. J. Finch and J. Mason (1989) *Negotiating Family Responsibilities*. London: Routledge/Tavistock, p. 130.

18. Ibid., p. 149

Chapter 5

1. E. Byrne (2012) *Political Corruption in Ireland 1922–2010: A Crooked Harp?* Manchester: Manchester University Press, pp. 143–91.

2. D. Desmond (2011) 'If Ireland is to prevent itself sleepwalking into another crisis in twenty years' time we must radically reform the political system to a design that puts Ireland first', *Irish Times*, 12 February, p. 15.

3. www.unitedleftalliance.org.

4. F. O'Toole (2011) 'The decision that I made on contesting this general election', *Irish Times*, 29 January.

5. S. Farrell, C. Meehan, G. Murphy and K. Rafter (2011) 'Assessing the Irish general election of 2011', *New Hibernia Review* 15(3), Autumn: 41.

6. C. Volkery (2011), *Der Spiegel*, www.spiegel.de, 24 February.

7. The party lost 57 seats, falling from 77 to 20 TDs in Dáil Éireann.

8. S. Farrell *et al.*, *op. cit.*, pp. 36–53.

9. Ibid., p. 37.

10. M. Bax (1976) *Harpstrings and Confessions: Machine Style Politics in the Irish Republic.* Amsterdam: Van Gorum; P. Sacks (1976) *Donegal Mafia: An Irish Political Machine.* New Haven, CT: Yale University Press; R. Carty (1981) *Party and Parish Pump.* Ontario: Wilfred Laurier University Press.

11. S. Donnelly (2012) 'Here's what a week off for a TD actually looks like', www.thejournal.ie, 4 November 2012.

12. The PR-STV system of voting was originally designed to ensure that the Protestant minority would have political representation, something that would not have been delivered under the existing British 'first past the post' system. During the twentieth century, there were a number of attempts to revert to the British system, but as historian Diarmaid Ferriter notes, 'The Irish electorate were not for turning on the issue of proportional representation, which Fianna Fáil, having failed in 1959, again attempted to abolish in 1968, through a constitutional referendum. Vigorous opposition by the main opposition parties (indeed they briefly discussed a merger in the event of PR's abolition), coupled with a prediction unveiled by political scientists on RTÉ that Fianna Fáil could secure 100 of the 144 seats with just 40% of the vote, ensured its rejection by a margin of 60/40.' D. Ferriter (2005) *The Transformation of Ireland.* London: Profile Books, p. 562.

13. F. O'Toole (2010) *Enough is Enough: How to Build a New Republic.* London: Faber & Faber, pp. 40–60.

14. L. Komito (1985) *Politics and Clientelism in Urban Ireland: Information, Reputation and Brokerage.* Ann Arbor, MI: University Microfilms. Available at www.ucd.ie.

15. B. Chubb (1992) *The Government and Politics of Ireland* (3rd edn; first published 1970). Harlow, Essex: Longman, p. 14.

16. L. Komito, *op. cit.*

17. N. Whelan (2011) 'FF paid a high price for Ahern-era sidelining of Cumainn', *Irish Times,* 3 September.

18. M. Marsh (2004) 'None of the that post-modern stuff around here: grassroots campaigning in the 2002 Irish general election', *British Elections and Parties Review* 14: 245–67, p. 260.

19. B. Chubb, *op. cit.,* p. 19.

20. M. Marsh, *op. cit.*

21. Ibid.

22. L. Komito, *op. cit.*

23. A. Cohen (1981) *The Politics of Elite Culture: Explorations in the Dramaturgy of Power in a Modern African Society.* Berkeley, CA: University of California Press.

24. J. Fallon (2011) *Dynasties: Irish Political Families.* Dublin: New Island.

25. E. Byrne (2012) *Political Corruption in Ireland 1922–2010: A Crooked Harp?* Manchester: Manchester University Press, pp. 165–6.

Chapter 6

1. *Hibernia* magazine, 13 September 1974.
2. T. Garvin (2004) *Preventing the Future: Why was Ireland so Poor for so Long?* Dublin: Gill & Macmillan, p. 55.
3. J.J. Lee (1989) *Ireland 1912–1985: Economics and Society.* Cambridge: Cambridge University Press.
4. NLI, MS 18339, FG. Lemass memo, p. 4.
5. R. Crotty (1979) 'Capitalist Colonialism and Peripheralisation: The Irish Case' in D. Seers, B. Schaffer and M. Kiljunen (eds) *Underdeveloped Europe: Studies in Core–Periphery Relations.* Hassocks: Harvester Press; D. Fennell (1985) *Beyond Nationalism: The Struggle Against Provinciality in the Modern World.* Dublin: Swords; R. Kearney (1988) *Across the Frontiers: Ireland in the 1990s.* Dublin: Wolfhound Press.
6. D. McClelland (1961) *The Achieving Society.* New York: Martino Fine Books.
7. J.J. Lee, *op. cit.,* pp. 391–2.
8. E. Butler (2011) 'The secret millionaire Q and A', *Irish Times,* 17 September.
9. www.stira.com/stira-company-history.
10. W.B. Yeats (1913) 'September 1913', *Collected Poems.* Collectors Library/CRW.
11. H. O'Connell (2012) 'Peter Quinn: we can't bring assets back without Anglo help', www.thejournal.ie, 3 August.
12. F. O'Toole (2012) 'Support for shameless Quinn is misplaced', *Irish Times,* 31 July, p. 14.
13. Ibid.
14. Ibid.
15. Quoted in M. O'Keefe (2013) 'Why didn't they give him a chance?', *Irish Daily Mail,* 3 July 2013, pp. 1, 8–9.
16. Quoted in M. O'Keefe, ibid.
17. Taoiseach Enda Kenny.
18. A. Lucey, C. O'Brien and A. McMahon (2012) 'GAA support for Quinns defended', *Irish Times,* 30 July 2012.
19. C. Arensberg and S. Kimball (1940) *Family and Community in Ireland.* Cambridge: Harvard University Press.
20. J. McCarthy (2007) 'Ballygoforwards', *Sunday Tribune,* 20 May.
21. A. Lynch (2013) 'The battle for Ireland's moral high ground', *Sunday Business Post,* 14 April, p. 29.
22. D. O'Hearn (2003) 'Macroeconomic Policy in the Celtic Tiger Period: A Critical Reassessment' in C. Coulter and S. Coleman (eds) *The End of Irish*

History: Critical Reflections on the Celtic Tiger. Manchester: Manchester University Press.

23.   D. Ferriter (2007) *Judging Dev.* Dublin: Royal Irish Academy.

24.   T. Ryle Dwyer (2001) *Short Fellow: A Biography of Charles J. Haughey.* Dublin: Marine Books, p. 28.

25.   E. Byrne (2012) *Political Corruption in Ireland 1922–2010: A Crooked Harp?* Manchester: Manchester University Press, p. 88.

26.   T. Ryle Dwyer, *op. cit.*, p. 59.

27.   K. Boland (1982) *The Rise and Decline of Fianna Fáil.* Dublin and Cork: Mercier Press, p. 102.

28.   T. Ryle Dwyer, *op. cit.*, p. 146.

29.   E. Byrne, *op. cit.*, p. 84.

30.   World Bank (2000) *Anti-Corruption in Transition: Contribution to the Policy Debate.* World Bank Publications.

31.   E. Byrne, *op. cit.*, p. 107.

32.   Byrne argues that this tribunal 'sought to comprehensively redefine the traditional interpretation of legal corruption'. Ibid., p. 160.

33.   Ibid., p. 121.

34.   Mr Justice Liam Hamilton, *Report of the Tribunal of Inquiry into the Beef Processing Industry* (1994). Dublin: Dublin Stationery Office, pp. 23, 568.

35.   The rule involved changing a performance clause built into the Goodman International IDA development plan by the state.

36.   G. Taylor (2011) 'Risk and financial Armageddon in Ireland', *Political Quarterly*, 82(4): 596–607.

37.   M. Cooper (2010) *Who Really Runs Ireland?* Dublin: Penguin Ireland, p. 81.

38.   Ibid., p. 83.

39.   T. Lyons (2014) 'Issue of how much Brian Cowen knew never arose', *Irish Times*, 18 April.

40.   *The Herald* (2011) 'Taoiseach denies "secret agenda" after golf game with disgraced banker', 11 January.

41.   Ibid.

42.   For further discussion see D. Donovan and A. Murphy (2013) *The Fall of the Celtic Tiger.* Oxford: Oxford University Press.

43.   A. O'Hora (2014) 'Banking inquiry: five top questions that need to be answered', *Irish Independent*, 19 June.

44.   B. Chubb (1992) *The Government and Politics of Ireland* (3rd edn; first published 1970). Harlow, Essex: Longman.

45.   E. Byrne, *op. cit.*, p. 123.

46.   B. Dowling (2001) 'Row looms over £200,000 O'Brien donation to parties', *Irish Independent*, 23 January.

47. Quoted in T. Lyons and B. Carey (2011) *The FitzPatrick Tapes.* Dublin: Penguin Ireland, p. 115.

48. D.S.A. Carroll, quoted in I. Kenny (1984) *Government and Enterprise in Ireland.* Dublin: Gill & Macmillan, pp. 1–9.

49. Ibid.

50. Ibid.

51. The changes to the Asset Covered Securities Act concerned covered bonds. '[A] covered bond is a bond backed by assets such as public sector debt or mortgage loans. The bonds remain on the issuing of the banks' balance sheet. The Asset Covered Securities Act 2007 included a provision that allowed banks to issue covered bonds backed solely by commercial mortgages. Under the previous 2001 act, the bonds could be backed only by residential mortgages or public sector debt. Given that Anglo Irish Bank was not a residential mortgage lender, the move opened up a new source of funding for Anglo.' K. Barrington (2011) 'Bowing to the bankers', *Sunday Business Post*, 13 February.

52. Ibid.

53. Ibid.

54. D. Beekers and B. van Gool (2012) 'From patronage to neopatrimonialism: postcolonial governance in Sub-Sahara Africa and beyond', ASC Working Paper 101/2012. African Studies Centre, University of Leiden.

55. B. Ahern (2009) *Bertie Ahern: The Autobiography.* London: Random House, p. 352.

Chapter 7

1. M.J. Power, M. O'Flynn, A. Courtois and M. Kennedy (2013) *Neoliberal Capitalism and Education in Ireland.* University of Limerick Department of Sociology Working Paper Series WP2013-03, April.

2. W. Easterly (2003) 'IMF and World Bank Structural Adjustment Policies and Poverty' in M.P. Dooley and J.A. Frankel (eds) *Managing Currency Crises in Emerging Markets.* Chicago: University of Chicago Press.

3. Oxfam (2013) *A Cautionary Tale: The True Cost of Austerity and Inequality in Europe.* Oxfam Briefing Papers 174: www.oxfam.org.

4. T. Callan, B. Nolan, C. Keane, M. Savage and J.R. Walsh (2013) *Crisis, Response and Distributional Income: The Case of Ireland.* ESRI Working Paper No. 456.

5. Oxfam (2013) *Ireland Case Study – The True Cost of Austerity and Inequality.* Oxfam Case Study, September.

6. P. Gerlach-Kristen (2013) 'Younger and older households in the crisis', *Quarterly Economic Commentary*, Spring. Dublin: ESRI, p. 53.

7.   A. Barrett and V. O'Sullivan (2014) 'The wealth, health and well-being of Ireland's older people before and during the economic crisis', *Applied Economics Letters* 21(10): 675–8. ESRI Research Bulletin 2014/1/6.

8.   F. Reddan (2012) 'Irish austerity budgets shown to be progressive – except for the latest', *Irish Times*, 27 March.

9.   National Youth Council of Ireland (2011) *Budget 2012: Unfair and Austere. Post-Budget Analysis.* Dublin: NCYI.

10. W.J. Murphy (2014) Letter to the *Irish Times*, 16 May.

11. J. Hogan (2014) 'Dole queues and debt are scars which remain in post-austerity Ireland', *Irish Post*, 25 April.

12. RTÉ News (2013) 'Social Justice Ireland says austerity is not working', 24 June, www.rte.ie.

13. Society of St Vincent de Paul (2012) *The Human Face of Austerity as Witnessed by the Society of St Vincent de Paul.* Dublin: SVP, www.svp.ie

14. For instance, Professor Nouriel Roubini of New York University's Stern School of Business commented in October 2009, 'it is essential that bad assets are taken off the balance sheets of the financial institutions and that the Government separates the good assets from the bad assets to clean up the financial system.... But if it does it in such a way that implies it is buying these assets at overpriced prices that do not reflect the underlying value, then it is giving a subsidy to the bank shareholders and unsecured creditors.' D. Doyle (2009) 'Roubini says Irish Bad Bank is right approach', www.bloomberg.com, 21 October.

15. J. Ihle (2013) 'Life and debt', *Sunday Business Post*, 16 June, p. 12.

16. Even after the Act's introduction, concerns have been expressed about the extremely low take-up of these debt resolution options and potential legal problems with the legislation. RTÉ News (2014) 'Call for clarity on flaw in personal insolvency legislation', 21 July.

17. R. Quinlan (2013) 'Look at elite puts "NAMA for little people" into perspective', *Irish Independent*, 24 March.

18. T. Healy (2013) 'Wife of McFeely's former business partner wins living expenses of €9000 a month', *Irish Independent*, 13 November.

19. Insolvency Service of Ireland (2013) *Guidelines on a Reasonable Standard of Living and Reasonable Living Expenses.* Dublin: ISI, www.isi.gov.ie.

20. Ibid., p. 27.

21. M. Clifford (2013) 'Sadly the Celtic Tiger bubble is still bursting', *Irish Examiner*, 16 November.

22. NAMA Winelake (2013) Response by OMF to post 'Hypocrisy of contrasting treatment of NAMA developers and individuals under new Personal Insolvency Act', 22 January, https://namawinelake.wordpress.com.

23. B. Lucey (2013) 'Bloodboiling double standards in Ireland regarding bankruptcy', http://brianmlucey.wordpress.com, 13 November.

24. Name changed to protect the identity of the individual.

25. D. McDonald (2010) 'Not one white collar criminal ever jailed, admits watchdog', *Irish Independent*, 5 July.

26. D. McDonald (2011) 'Effort to prosecute the bankers is turning out to be a damp squib', *Irish Independent*, 3 June.

27. Quoted in C. Kelpie (2013) 'Elderfield says laws must be stronger on white collar crime', *Irish Independent*, 14 June.

28. E. Byrne (2013) *Ireland's White-Collar Crime Oversight Agencies: Fit for Purpose?*, http://elaine.ie, p. 4.

29. RTÉ News (2014) 'Sean FitzPatrick not guilty on all counts in Anglo trial', 16 April.

30. P. Doherty (2014) 'Irish public serving a jail sentence for Anglo bankers' crime', www.sinnfein.ie, 29 April.

31. *Irish Independent* (2012) 'Man jailed for six years over €1.6m garlic tax scam', 9 March, www.independent.ie.

32. RTÉ News (2013) 'Increase in people jailed over unpaid fines', 8 May.

33. C. O'Keefe (2014) '60% of Cork prison inmates are jailed for non-payment of court fines', *Irish Examiner*, 2 January.

34. *Irish Independent* (2011) 'You won't do time for white-collar crime – no laws seem to cover it', 9 June.

35. C. Ó Fátharta (2013) '93% believe that no banker will be jailed over crisis', *Irish Examiner*, 26 September.

36. C. O'Brien (2013) 'Reports of welfare fraud up 2500% since 2008', *Irish Times*, 31 December.

37. *Irish Examiner* (2013) 'Refreshing to hear of welfare savings', 9 March 2013.

38. H. O'Connell (2013) 'Welfare amnesty would allow people who defraud the State to escape scot-free', www.thejournal.ie, 19 January.

39. C. Browne (2012) 'Emphasis on social welfare fraud ignoring issue of tax evasion', *Irish Examiner*, 27 February.

40. In the blog Gombeen Nation, the author comments, 'Given that tax avoidance by the very wealthy is lauded by much of the general public, who rush to pay homage to the likes of Bono, J.P. McManus, Denis O'Brien and all the rest of them. "Ah sure he gives a lot to charity, isn't he great?" is the mindset of these ragged-trousered, knuckle-headed philanthropists. Evasion is only the next illegal step'. 'Social welfare fraud, public office fraud and tax evasion. The differing Irish attitudes towards each', www.gombeennation.ie, 10 August.

41. H. Browne (2013) *The Frontman: Bono (In the Name of Power)*. London: Verso, p. 43.

42. Garda Inspectorate (2014) *The Fixed Charge Processing System: A 21st-Century Strategy*. Dublin: Garda Inspectorate.

43. P. Counihan (2013) 'Deputy Ming Flanagan accused police of corruption but had penalty points quashed', www.irishcentral.com, 14 March; N. O'Connor (2013) 'Gardaí insisted I have penalty points revoked says Ming', *The Herald*, 11 March.

44. At the time of going to press, the Irish government was in the final stages of preparing new legislation to give stronger powers to the courts and the Director of Public Prosecutions to deal with corrupt public officials. These new measures draw on recommendations of the Mahon Tribunal. T. Brady 'Corrupt TDs to be banned from office for a decade', *Irish Independent*, 22 September.

Conclusion

1. N. Kitsantonis (2010) 'Anti-austerity protest in Greece turns violent', *New York Times*, 15 December.

2. E. O'Malley (2014) 'Why didn't we riot?', *Irish Politics Forum*, 3 January.

3. D. Donovan and A. Murphy (2013) *The Fall of the Celtic Tiger*. Oxford: Oxford University Press.

4. J. Mercille (2013) 'Why don't the Irish protest against austerity?', www.thejournal.ie, 26 November.

5. M. Brennan (2008) 'Pensioners jeer minister at 15,000 strong protest rally', *Irish Independent*, 23 October.

6. J. Smyth (2011) 'Students protest in Dublin over fees', *Financial Times*, 16 November, www.ft.com.

7. C. Bohan (2012) 'Three anti-household charge TDs unhappy with national rally', www.thejournal.ie, 24 May.

8. B. Roche (2014) 'Campaigners welcome removal of water meters from Cork estate', *Irish Times*, 14 May.

9. G. Titley (2012) 'Budget-jam! A communication intervention in the political economic crisis in Ireland', *Journalism* 14(2): 292–306.

10. S. Farrell, C. Meehan, G. Murphy and K. Rafter (2011) 'Assessing the Irish general election of 2011: a roundtable', *New Hibernia Review* 15(3): 36–53.

11. J. Corcoran, J. Drennan and D. McConnell (2014) 'Coalition feels the fury of the people at the ballot box', *Irish Independent*, 30 June, www.independent.ie.

12. *Irish Independent* (2014) 'Ireland was a shipwreck … we had to do things we did not want to do – Labour's Pat Rabbitte', 25 May.

13. K. Allen and B. O'Boyle (2013) *Austerity Ireland: The Failure of Irish Capitalism*. London: Pluto.

14. J. Sloam (2013) 'The outraged young: how young Europeans are reshaping the political landscape', *Political Insight* 4(11): 4–7.

15. *Irish Voice* (2013) 'Is Ireland sinking again? 87,000 emigrate and unemployment still 14.6 per cent', editorial, 30 January.

16. S. Moore (2010) letter to the editor, *Irish Times*, 19 February.

17. T. Healy (2010) letter to the editor, *Irish Times*, 23 February.

18. T.P. Coogan (2013) 'Are we helpless before the guilty?', www.timpatcoogan.ie, 3 February.

19. R. Hearne (2013) 'Politics and protest in Ireland: a brief history and a call to action', http://IrelandAfterNama.wordpress.com, 14 October.

20. R. McKiernan (2013) 'Protest and survive or injustice will thrive', *Irish Examiner*, 17 June.

21. V. Kenny (1985) 'The post-colonial personality', *The Crane Bag* 9:70–8.

22. F.C. Harris (2006) 'It takes a tragedy to arouse them: collective memory and collective action during the Civil Rights movement', *Social Movement Studies: Journal of Social, Cultural and Political Protest* 5(1): 19–43, p. 21.

23. RT News (2014) 'Troika governor of European colonies: lawmakers fed up with debt crisis tactics', 27 February, http://rt.com.

24. L. Armitstead (2013) 'Ireland: the poster child of recovery but not of austerity', *The Telegraph*, 29 August.

25. L. Alderman (2011) 'In Ireland, austerity is praised but painful', *New York Times*, 5 December.

26. D. Donovan and A. Murphy (2013) *The Fall of the Celtic Tiger*. Oxford: Oxford University Press.

27. J. Smyth (2013) 'Ireland unfairly treated over bondholders in bust banks', *Financial Times*, 19 December, http://ft.com.

28. B. van der Kolk (1989) 'The compulsion to repeat: re-enactment, re-victimization and masochism', *Psychiatric Clinics of North America* 12(2): 389–411, p. 399.

29. Ibid., p. 393.

30. In these cases, the abuse has been deliberately created by scientists.

31. B. van der Kolk, *op. cit.*, p. 395.

32. E.G. Vermilyea (2003) *Childhood Trauma and Adult Revictimization*. Sidran Institute, www.sidran.org.

33. Ibid.

34. Oxford English Dictionary (1989), OED Online, www.dictionary.oed.com.

35. Merriam-Webster Dictionary, www.merriam-webster.com.

36. T. Ryle-Dwyer (2001) *Short Fellow: A Biography of Charles J. Haughey*. Dublin: Marine Books, p. 174.

37. T. Kinsella (1968) *Nightwalker and Other Poems*. Dublin: Dolmen.

38. L. Collins (2008) 'Doors close at Haughey's Abbeyville for the last time', *Irish Independent*, 31 August.

39. B. Ahern (2005) 'Fianna Fáil will never take risks with the economy', *The Nation* II, Autumn, p. 24.

40. Ibid.

41. T. Roethke (1961) *The Collected Poems of Theodore Roethke*. New York: Doubleday.

42. F. O'Toole (2010) *Enough is Enough: How to Build a New Republic*. London: Faber & Faber, p. 204.

43. Ibid., p. 20.

44. G. Peters (1989) *The Politics of Bureaucracy* (3rd edn). New York: Longman.

45. M. Herzfeld (2005) *Cultural Intimacy: Social Poetics of the Nation-State*. New York: Routledge, p. 10.

46. K. Sheridan (2014) 'Moving on after crash is easier for well-heeled', *Irish Times*, 2 July, p. 14.

47. S. Bardon (2014) 'HSE finance shame', *Irish Daily Mirror*, 27 June, p. 6.

48. P. Cullen (2014) 'Hospital consultants among the best paid in world', *Irish Times*, 1 July.

49. M. Herzfeld (1992) *The Social Production of Indifference: Exploring the Symbolic Roots of Western Bureaucracy*. Chicago: University of Chicago Press.

50. It is important to note that the HSE still has consultative structures at regional level. However, there is no press attendance at these meetings and little compulsion on attending HSE executives to implement or process any of the feedback received at them.

51. S. McCarthaigh and F. O'Cionnaith (2010) 'Unadvertised HSE jobs filled by relatives of staff', *Irish Examiner*, 14 June.

52. D. Fleming (2014) 'We need to talk about Russia', *Sunday Independent*, 23 February.

53. D. Lloyd (2000) 'Colonial trauma/post-colonial recovery?', *Interventions* 2(2): 212–28, p. 227.

54. E. Bass and L. Davis (1992) *The Courage to Heal*. New York: Harper Collins.

55. C. McCarthy (2014) 'Responsibility for flawed design of eurozone rests with Germany', *Sunday Independent*, 6 July, p. 26.

56. Ibid.

57. Ibid.

INDEX